THE **LIFE** HISTORY OF THE UNITED STATES

Volume 12: From 1945

THE AGE OF CHANGE

TIME LIFE BOOKS ®

Other Publications:

WORLD WAR II

THE GREAT CITIES

HOME REPAIR AND IMPROVEMENT

THE WORLD'S WILD PLACES

THE TIME-LIFE LIBRARY OF BOATING

HUMAN BEHAVIOR

THE ART OF SEWING

THE OLD WEST

THE EMERGENCE OF MAN

THE AMERICAN WILDERNESS

THE TIME-LIFE ENCYCLOPEDIA OF GARDENING

LIFE LIBRARY OF PHOTOGRAPHY

THIS FABULOUS CENTURY

FOODS OF THE WORLD

TIME-LIFE LIBRARY OF AMERICA

TIME-LIFE LIBRARY OF ART

GREAT AGES OF MAN

LIFE SCIENCE LIBRARY

TIME READING PROGRAM

LIFE NATURE LIBRARY

LIFE WORLD LIBRARY

FAMILY LIBRARY:

    HOW THINGS WORK IN YOUR HOME

    THE TIME-LIFE BOOK OF THE FAMILY CAR

    THE TIME-LIFE FAMILY LEGAL GUIDE

    THE TIME-LIFE BOOK OF FAMILY FINANCE

THE **LIFE** HISTORY OF THE UNITED STATES

Consulting Editor, Henry F. Graff

Volume 12: From 1945

THE AGE OF CHANGE

by William E. Leuchtenburg

and the Editors of

TIME-LIFE BOOKS

TIME-LIFE BOOKS, ALEXANDRIA, VIRGINIA

Time-Life Books Inc.
is a wholly owned subsidiary of
TIME INCORPORATED

FOUNDER: Henry R. Luce 1898-1967

Editor-in-Chief: Hedley Donovan
Chairman of the Board: Andrew Heiskell
President: James R. Shepley
Vice Chairman: Roy E. Larsen
Corporate Editor: Ralph Graves

TIME-LIFE BOOKS INC.
MANAGING EDITOR: Jerry Korn
Executive Editor: David Maness
Assistant Managing Editors: Dale Brown,
Martin Mann
Art Director: Tom Suzuki
Chief of Research: David L. Harrison
Director of Photography: Melvin L. Scott
Senior Text Editors: William Frankel, Diana Hirsh
Assistant Art Director: Arnold C. Holeywell

CHAIRMAN: Joan D. Manley
President: John D. McSweeney
Executive Vice Presidents: Carl G. Jaeger,
David J. Walsh
Vice President and Secretary: Paul R. Stewart
Treasurer and General Manager: John Steven Maxwell
Business Manager: Peter B. Barnes
Mail Order Sales Director: John L. Canova
Public Relations Director: Nicholas Benton
Personnel Director: Beatrice T. Dobie

THE LIFE HISTORY OF THE UNITED STATES
Editorial Staff for Volume 12
SERIES EDITOR: Sam Welles
Designer: Frank Crump
Staff Writers: Gerald Simons, Timothy Carr,
Lucille Schulberg, Paul Trachtman, Peter Yerkes
Chief Researcher: Clara E. Nicolai
Researchers: Patricia Tolles, Ruth Silva,
Terry Drucker, Ellen Leiman,
Jacqueline Coates, Martha Brean, Theo Pascal,
Doris Kinney, Sondra Albert

EDITORIAL PRODUCTION
Production Editor: Douglas B. Graham
Operations Manager: Gennaro C. Esposito
Assistant Production Editor: Feliciano Madrid
Quality Director: Robert L. Young
Assistant Quality Director: James J. Cox
Associate: Serafino J. Cambareri
Copy Staff: Susan B. Galloway (chief),
Gail Weesner, Ruth Kelton,
Florence Keith, Celia Beattie
Picture Department: Dolores A. Littles,
Joan T. Lynch
Traffic: Barbara Buzan

THE AUTHOR of the first seven chapters of this volume, William E. Leuchtenburg, has concentrated on the study of the United States during the 20th Century. He holds the DeWitt Clinton Chair of History at Columbia University and has taught at Smith College, New York University and Harvard. During the summer of 1956, Dr. Leuchtenburg lectured at the Salzburg Seminar for American Studies in Austria, and in 1961 and 1962 he was a Fellow at the Center for Advanced Study in the Behavioral Sciences, Palo Alto, California. Dr. Leuchtenburg was Harmsworth Professor at Oxford in 1971 and 1972. He is the author of A Troubled Feast and The Perils of Prosperity, 1914-1932, and won the 1964 Bancroft Prize for Franklin D. Roosevelt and the New Deal, 1932-1940.

Chapter Eight of this volume was prepared by Harold C. Field and the staff of TIME-LIFE Books.

CORRESPONDENTS: Elisabeth Kraemer (Bonn); Margot Hapgood, Dorothy Bacon (London); Susan Jonas, Lucy T. Voulgaris (New York); Maria Vincenza Aloisi, Josephine du Brusle (Paris); Ann Natanson (Rome). Revisions Staff: Joan Chambers, Monica Horne.

CONTENTS

1. COLD WAR

ON a sunny Wednesday afternoon in late June 1945 the *Queen Mary*, carrying more than 14,500 veterans of the war in Europe, steamed into New York harbor. As word went out that the first large shipment of soldiers was arriving from the fighting fronts, harbor whistles screeched their greeting, and ferryboats, rust-caked old freighters, baby flattops—all the craft of the river —turned out to bid it welcome. The boys were on their way home. By late August, after the fall of Japan, they were beginning to arrive back from every part of the globe.

They returned to a world where much seemed the same. The country was whistling the same kind of songs, showing the same kind of movies. Nothing could have been more reassuring. The veterans wanted above all to put the strife of the world behind them and pick up the broken ends of their lives.

The war had been fought with few illusions, and there was little expectation that the postwar years would be utopian. Yet it did seem that a secure peace had been won and that a long era free from the demands of war now lay ahead. To be sure, there was already some uneasiness over Russian actions, but since it seemed certain that the U.S.S.R. would take years to recover from the devastation of the war, and since America held a monopoly on the atomic bomb which the Soviet Union was not likely to break for many years to come, there was little cause for alarm.

Besides, most Americans thought it would be simple to get on with the

A MONUMENT TO PEACE, the United Nations Building juts into the Manhattan dusk. Truman called the U.N. Charter an avowal of "faith that war is not inevitable."

Russians. As Franklin D. Roosevelt had put it during the war, the Russians might not be "housebroken," but they were nevertheless "a very good breed of dog." On his return from a trip to Moscow in late 1945, General Dwight D. Eisenhower concluded that "nothing guides Russian policy so much as a desire for friendship with the United States."

Few men in 1945 foresaw how swiftly these expectations would be shattered. When the *Queen Mary* was nudged into its berth in the North River, no one had yet heard the words "Cold War" or "Iron Curtain." In less than two years they would be on everyone's lips. In less than three years the two great wartime allies would be on the brink of war in Berlin. In little more than four years the White House would summon newsmen to announce that Soviet Russia had exploded an atomic device. Thereafter either power could trigger a world war that would devastate both countries and leave much, perhaps all, of the world uninhabitable.

Commemorating America's postwar aid to Greece under the Truman Doctrine, a huge statue of President Harry S. Truman is installed in a square in Athens. The figure was attacked as a work of art, and Truman himself doubted the wisdom of erecting a statue of a living person. "You never know," he said, "when you have to turn around and tear it down."

To guide the American people in this treacherous new world, fate had singled out a man who was, like the people themselves, untested. On April 12, 1945, Vice President Harry S. Truman, after a day of presiding over a dull Senate debate, was summoned to the White House. When he reached the executive mansion, Mrs. Roosevelt came forward, put her arm about his shoulder and said: "Harry, the President is dead." Stunned, Truman finally managed to blurt out: "Is there anything I can do for you?" She responded: "Is there anything *we* can do for *you*? For you are the one in trouble now."

Herbert Agar later wrote: "During the next few years this strange little man—lively and pert to the verge of bumptiousness; more widely read in history than any President since John Quincy Adams; more wilful than any President since James K. Polk; more incompetent in dividing the good from the bad among his own friends at home than any President since Warren Harding—would make and enforce a series of decisions upon which, for better or for worse, our world now rests, or shakes."

Truman greeted his elevation to the highest office in the land as if it were a cruel trick of the gods. "Boys, if you ever pray, pray for me now," he told reporters. "I don't know whether you fellows ever had a load of hay fall on you. But when they told me yesterday what had happened I felt like the moon, the stars and all the planets had fallen on me."

Shriner, Eagle, member of the Baptist Church, Harry Truman of Independence, Missouri, had a hard time realizing he was President of the United States of America. On his first full day in the office, he went up to Capitol Hill to have lunch with his friends in the Senate as he always had. He started to walk onto the Senate floor, but the Secretary of the Senate, Leslie Biffle, stopped him: "You can't go out there, Harry, you are the President now!" Truman turned unhappily away.

No presidential transition is ever easy, but this particular one could not have come at a worse time. The grand alliance between the U.S.S.R. and the West was beginning to disintegrate as Russian commissars, in violation of agreements, snuffed out the independence of Eastern European countries. Truman confessed that he was not particularly well informed on foreign policy. He had not been privy to the negotiations at Yalta or the details of vexing issues like the Polish boundaries. Night after night he sat up late poring over State Department documents in the effort to bring himself up to date.

To complicate matters, neither Secretary of State Edward Stettinius Jr. nor James F. Byrnes, who succeeded him in July 1945, had any special competence in foreign affairs. Winston Churchill later noted the "deadly hiatus which existed between the fading of President Roosevelt's strength and the growth of President Truman's grip of the vast world problems."

Truman's first steps were not reassuring. In his fourth week in office he signed, without even reading it, an order which precipitately halted the delivery of lend-lease goods. The abrupt termination of the program caused not only hardship but acute resentment among America's allies, especially Russia. Truman later wrote: "That experience brought home to me not only that I had to know exactly where I was going but also that I had to know that my basic policies were being carried out. If I had read the order, as I should have, the incident would not have occurred." Lend-lease was resumed, but the damage had been done. Some of the blame for breaking up the grand alliance had to be borne by the United States.

Truman also revealed in his first days in office that he had little patience with Soviet tergiversations. When Russian Foreign Minister V. M. Molotov attempted to explain away the U.S.S.R.'s failure to honor its pledges with respect to Poland, Truman gave him a dressing down. "I have never been talked to like that in my life," Molotov exclaimed. "Carry out your agreements," Truman snapped, "and you won't get talked to like that!"

YET Truman also had a profound faith in the possibilities of a world organization to preserve the peace. In the summer and fall of 1944 at the Dumbarton Oaks estate in Washington, D.C., the major powers had worked out a tentative sketch of a new international organization; this was to be presented to delegates at a conference scheduled for San Francisco in April 1945. Truman's first decision was that the San Francisco Conference was not to be postponed because of Roosevelt's death but would meet on schedule.

Foreign leaders had been delighted by America's willingness to sponsor the world conference, but during the planning period they still feared that Republican isolationists such as Senator Arthur Vandenberg of Michigan would block American commitment to an international organization, just as Henry Cabot Lodge and his supporters had in 1920. Vandenberg had voted against repeal of the arms embargo, against the Selective Service bill, against lend-lease. When the lend-lease bill was adopted in 1941, the Michigan senator had noted in his diary: "If America 'cracks up' you can put your finger on this precise moment as the time when the crime was committed."

But the war shook Vandenberg's confidence in America's ability to isolate itself from the rest of the world. On January 10, 1945, before an astonished and raptly attentive Senate, he abandoned isolationism. "I do not believe," he said, "that any nation hereafter can immunize itself by its own exclusive action." American newspapers hailed Vandenberg's "conversion." One writer noted: "In an old-fashioned revival meeting, the conversion of an ordinary citizen stirs only perfunctory hosannas. But when a notorious, grizzled old sinner hits the sawdust trail, the hallelujahs shake the tabernacle." Quick to take advantage of Vandenberg's change of heart, President Roosevelt invited him to be a delegate to the forthcoming San Francisco Conference.

On April 25, 1945, the day American and Soviet troops embraced on the Elbe, the conference opened in San Francisco's Opera House. For the next

Home from the war in Europe, two GIs aboard the "Queen Mary" celebrate as the ship docks in New York in July 1945. Those veterans returning with long combat records were sent to separation centers and quickly discharged. Many others, reassigned to finish the war against Japan, complained bitterly. But the fighting was over before many of them even arrived.

nine weeks, while the war in the Pacific was still being waged, 800 delegates debated the shape of the world that would emerge from the fighting.

The main design of the new organization had already been drawn by the big powers at Dumbarton Oaks. Each member nation would be represented in a General Assembly, but the real authority would reside in an 11-member Security Council in which the United States, Britain, Russia, France and China would have permanent seats. A permanent member could veto any move to impose sanctions against it. In time the veto would seem to be a Soviet invention: In the first 25 years the U.S.S.R. would have used it more than 100 times, the United States never. But in fact no nation insisted more strongly on the right to the veto than the United States.

In addition to the Security Council and the General Assembly and an International Court of Justice, there were to be subsidiary agencies: an Economic and Social Council, a Secretariat, a Trusteeship Council, among others. At the Bretton Woods Conference in 1944, the International Bank for Reconstruction and Development and the International Monetary Fund had been created to stimulate and stabilize the world's economies. In November 1943 the United Nations Relief and Rehabilitation Administration had been set up; most of UNRRA's campaign to bring relief to war-ravaged areas was financed by the United States, and two Americans, Herbert Lehman and Fiorello La Guardia, successively held the top administrative post in the agency.

While the Soviet Union came out of the San Francisco Conference with only minimal concessions, the United States won a charter that embodied all the major objectives it sought. In particular, it achieved the substance of its desire to preserve the Pan-American system and to handle the colonial question in a fashion that would not prejudice its future control of Japanese-mandated islands in the Pacific.

Soviet intransigence on one minor procedural question almost wrecked the conference. Molotov insisted that a permanent member should be empowered to use the veto even to prevent any discussion of a complaint directed against the member. As the conference foundered, Harry Hopkins, critically ill, pleaded with Stalin to reverse his envoy. When Stalin agreed to accept the American interpretation, the last roadblock was removed. At noon on June 26, 1945, the delegates filed in to the Veterans' Building in San Francisco to affix their names to the Charter of the United Nations.

The United States had played a major role in creating the new postwar organization. But the United States had played such a role before, and then, when the treaty had come before the Senate, it had been rejected. All through the months of negotiation, the world had wondered anxiously whether the unhappy experience of the League of Nations would be repeated. Such fears were groundless. A month after the signing of the charter, the Senate approved it 89-2. The United States was the first major power to ratify.

BUT devotion to world co-operation was hardly enough. The United States had to be willing to mobilize sufficient military force to discourage the Soviet Union from actions that would jeopardize the peace. Eventually America would learn this lesson so well that it would lay itself open to the criticism that it was relying almost wholly on military power. But in the immediate aftermath of the war, America had yet to learn the simplest lessons of power politics. The United States, indeed, extended a wide-open invitation to the

Patrician F.D.R.'s intimate friend and adviser was Harry Hopkins, son of an Iowa harness maker. When Roosevelt died and Truman took over, Hopkins went to Moscow and got Stalin to reverse a stand that threatened the U.N. talks at San Francisco. Truman said Hopkins saved the conference.

U.S. Senator, Supreme Court Justice and Secretary of State, James Byrnes was a tough-minded pragmatist. He was known above all else as a man who got things done. A cab driver, analyzing Byrnes's success, said, "That's his specialty—getting people to say yes to things that they want to say no to."

Russians to expand their sphere by pulling its own troops out of Europe and the Orient at breakneck speed. Of the eight million men in the Army on V-J Day, only 4.3 million were left at the end of the year.

Even this pell-mell demobilization was not fast enough for war-weary veterans. On January 4, 1946, the War Department announced that it would be necessary to slow up discharges and modify the discharge system in order to retain some essential men. GIs overseas touched off a series of angry protests. Riots started in Manila, where 2,500 soldiers marched on the headquarters of the commanding general, and quickly spread to Hawaii, Guam, Germany, Britain and other points. In Washington General Eisenhower was ambushed by irate women representing "Bring Back Daddy" clubs. The experience, Ike said, left him "emotionally upset." By the summer of 1946, the Army had been reduced to 1.5 million men; the Navy to 700,000.

Arthur Vandenberg, preparing for a meeting with European statesmen, decided to learn Russian. In listening to Foreign Minister Molotov talking to an interpreter, he asked what a phrase he had heard meant. "You don't need to know the phrase 'Ya soglasen,'" replied Molotov, ". . . it means 'I agree.'"

BY this time the West was beginning to learn some of the hard facts of military power. In the spring of 1945 Russian armies had overrun Eastern Europe, and the Kremlin, its military authority supreme, left no doubt that it would prevent the creation of autonomous, democratic governments there. At an Anglo-American-Russian meeting held in the summer of 1945 at Potsdam, Stalin had explained bluntly that in Eastern Europe any "freely elected government would be anti-Soviet and that we cannot allow." Powerless to reverse the Soviet policies, the Allies had to acquiesce in them.

The drafting of peace treaties with the minor Axis powers had been left to an Allied Council of Foreign Ministers. Its sessions, held from September 1945 to December 1946 in London, Paris and New York, made it clear that the wartime unity with the Soviet Union could not be maintained. The parleys were interminable and futile. Senator Tom Connally, who participated in these meetings, said, "All you do is sit all day going yah, yah, yah."

But that was just a sideshow; the fundamental test of unity among the big powers was Germany. Each of the four occupying powers—America, Britain, Russia and France—was to administer its own zone in the defeated nation, but all were to participate in an Allied Control Council responsible for Germany as a whole. Germany was a land neither side possessed, the testing ground of whether East and West could learn to live with one another.

When Harold Stassen joined the Navy, many thought him just another glory-seeking politician. But he became an object of veneration as a good luck omen. Even after the costly fighting at Bougainville and Manila, his ships were only slightly damaged. "They used to rub me for luck," Stassen recalled.

The United States, at the outset, was less troubled by possible disagreement with the U.S.S.R. than with making sure that Germany never again gave birth to a monstrous regime like that of Nazism. In the closing weeks of the war, American troops had discovered the full horror of Hitler's Germany—the concentration camps, the gas chambers, the instruments of death and torture which had been used to exterminate millions of Jews and other victims of the Nazis. The United States was determined to punish the perpetrators of these deeds. It joined with the Russians, British and French to create an International Military Tribunal before which 22 high German officials were tried between November 1945 and October 1946.

Into the courtroom on the opening day of the Nuremberg trials filed the prisoners: Reich Marshal Hermann Goering, fat and restless in his pearl-gray uniform; the blank-faced, listless Rudolf Hess, feigning amnesia; Hans Frank, the brutal governor of Poland; Holland's gauleiter Arthur Seyss-Inquart; the Jew-baiting Julius Streicher; military leaders including Field Marshal Wilhelm Keitel; civilian functionaries led by Hjalmar Schacht. On November

29, 1945, the courtroom darkened, and for 52 minutes films of the concentration camps were shown. Goering's face reddened, Keitel mopped his brow, Schacht refused to look at the screen ("No! I'll get sick," he cried).

On October 1, 1946, the court found 19 of the accused guilty; three, among them Schacht, were acquitted. Twelve—including Hitler's missing lieutenant Martin Bormann, tried *in absentia*—were sentenced to die. The unregenerate Goering escaped the noose by committing suicide on October 15. The following day the remaining 10 were hanged.

Some people were troubled by the doubtful legal basis for the trials, which, as Churchill stated, created the dangerous precedent that "the leaders of a nation defeated in war shall be put to death by the victors." Yet none of the critics advanced a proposal that met the widely felt need to punish those responsible for such terrible crimes. "Either the victors must judge the vanquished," said American prosecutor Robert Jackson as the trials started, "or we must leave the defeated to judge themselves."

To establish a fair priority system for demobilization, the Army devised the discharge-point method. To get his "ruptured duck" discharge button (below), a soldier had to have a certain number of points. The biggest point getters were dependent children. The happy father in the cartoon is saying, "Come to Daddy, ya wonderful little twelve-point rascal."

THE United States began its occupation of its zone of Germany with a tough policy. American troops were forbidden to "fraternize" with Germans. To erase Germany's war potential, steel and chemical production were curbed and cartels disbanded.

But as friction with Russia over occupation policies increased, the United States began to modify its attitude toward Germany. At Potsdam the powers had agreed that each country was to take reparations from its own zone; since the Russian zone was more agrarian, the Western powers would ship 15 per cent of the capital equipment in their zones to the U.S.S.R. in return for food, coal and other raw materials. However, the Russians were not only stripping their zone of factories but, contrary to the agreement, were taking goods from current production. Such a policy could lead only to chaos or, as the Russians drained more from Germany than the British and Americans were putting in, to saddling the West with the burden of relief for people who lived in an impoverished economy.

On May 3, 1946, less than a year after V-E Day, General Lucius Clay, the deputy American commander in Germany, suspended delivery of reparations to the Russians until the Soviets agreed to operate their zone as part of a united Germany. The U.S.S.R. had not only converted its zone into a Communist satellite but had rejected Byrnes's unprecedented offer of a 25-year alliance against German militarism. As the Americans and British despaired of reaching an agreement with the Russians, they eased their occupation policies and took steps to make the German economy self-sustaining.

Clay's decision indicated a new hardening of American policy toward the U.S.S.R. The United States was irritated not only by Soviet intransigence in Germany but by Russia's attempt to extend its influence into the Middle East by exerting pressure on Iran and Turkey. By January 1946 Truman was writing, "Unless Russia is faced with an iron fist and strong language another war is in the making. . . . I'm tired of babying the Soviets."

Truman's determination to pursue a "get tough" policy with the Russians led him in March 1946 to accompany Winston Churchill to Fulton, Missouri, where the former prime minister delivered a major address in the gymnasium of Westminster College. The British leader declared: "From Stettin in the Baltic to Trieste in the Adriatic, an iron curtain has descended across the

Continent. Behind that line lie all the capitals of the ancient states of central and eastern Europe." To curb the Kremlin's "expansive tendencies," Churchill urged an Anglo-American "fraternal association." There was nothing the Russians admired, he said, "so much as strength, and there is nothing for which they have less respect than for . . . military weakness."

America was not ready for such blunt talk. The Boston *Globe* rejected Churchill's invitation "to become heir to the evils of a collapsing colonialism." The Chicago *Sun* said: "To follow the standard raised by this great but blinded aristocrat would be to march to the world's most ghastly war."

It was the knowledge that the A-bomb might result in "the world's most ghastly war" that made some Americans hesitate to accept the fact that the world was divided into two political spheres or to approve appropriate military preparations. Instead, the country urged the President to continue to pursue ways to end the threat of the bomb. On June 14, 1946, the American delegate Bernard Baruch proposed to the first session of the United Nations Atomic Energy Commission the creation of an international atomic development authority, to which America would turn over its atomic secrets—provided that there be effective international control and inspection of bomb production. Under this plan, there would be no further manufacture of bombs, and existing stocks would be destroyed. "We are here," Baruch declared, "to make a choice between the quick and the dead." The Soviet Union quickly erased all hope for effective control by insisting that the United States demolish stockpiles *before* a system of inspection was set up, and by stipulating that the veto be retained in the international atomic agency.

T HE attempt to halt the atomic arms race had failed. The United States had already set up an atomic program, and in the absence of an international agreement, it pushed forward on its own with the secret development of nuclear energy under an Atomic Energy Commission. The McMahon Act established the principle that the government should have an absolute monopoly of fissionable materials, and that the program should be run by civilians.

In the summer of 1946 the United States conducted atomic tests at the Bikini atoll in the Pacific. The results were awesome. Dr. David Bradley, who was involved in the tests, wrote a book, *No Place to Hide*, which told what the scientists found after Bikini—the sides of ships so charged with radioactivity that only sandblasting would clean it away, rocks miles from the blast charged with deadly particles. "The question," Dr. Bradley wrote, "is not political so much as biological. It is not the security of a political system but the survival of the race that is at stake."

Many Americans were deeply troubled by the point to which the world had come in the summer of 1946. It was hard to remember now the happy expectations of only 12 months before. Most of the trouble had been precipitated by the Russians, but not a few Americans were worried by the bleak consequences which might follow from the Truman-Byrnes "get tough" approach. To many, America's new foreign policy—A-bombs, verbal threats, the contemplated *rapprochement* with the former enemy Germany against the wartime ally Russia—seemed destined to plunge the United States into a fearful war with the Soviet Union.

No one was more troubled than Secretary of Commerce Henry Wallace, who, as former Vice President under Franklin Roosevelt, personified the

Before Herbert Lehman became head of UNRRA, he served for 10 years as governor of New York. Concern over state finances led Lehman to call his new dog Budget. Later, Budget's puppies were dubbed Surplus and Deficit by newsmen eager to see which grew bigger. Surplus won—and Lehman changed a $107 million budget deficit to an $80 million surplus.

13

liberal tradition of the Roosevelt years. On July 23, 1946, Wallace wrote Truman that he was disturbed by the size of military appropriations; an arms race, he warned, would eventually lead to a situation where several nations had the bomb and the world would be prey to "a neurotic, fear-ridden, itching-trigger psychology." Instead of an extensive arms program, Wallace wished to develop trust in the U.S.S.R. by recognizing its power and allaying what he felt were its many reasonable suspicions.

Wallace's letter made small impression. On September 6, 1946, Byrnes made a speech in Stuttgart which indicated America's determination to rebuild Western Germany. Six days later Wallace addressed a Democratic rally at New York's Madison Square Garden. His speech was a blunt attack on Byrnes's policy. "We have no more business in the political affairs of Eastern Europe than Russia has in the political affairs of Latin America, Western Europe and the United States," Wallace said. Although the speech was not wholly one-sided, Wallace not only omitted two references in the prepared draft that were critical of the Communists, but interpolated: "I realize that the danger of war is much less from Communism than it is from imperialism." He said that he was "neither anti-British nor pro-British, neither anti-Russian nor pro-Russian," and added pointedly: "When President Truman read these words, he said that they represented the policy of his Administration."

Truman had, in fact, told reporters that he approved Wallace's speech, but in the ensuing uproar the President apparently had second thoughts. Secretary Byrnes, still in Europe, was incensed. He wired the President: "If it is not completely clear in your own mind that Mr. Wallace should be asked to refrain from criticizing the foreign policy of the United States while he is a member of your Cabinet, I must ask you to accept my resignation immediately." A little before 10 o'clock on the morning of September 20, Truman phoned Wallace: "Henry, I am sorry, but I have reached the conclusion that it will be best that I ask for your resignation." Truman proceeded to make an unhappy situation even worse by asking the country to accept the unlikely story that he had never approved the speech in the first place.

T RUMAN had supported Byrnes in his dispute with Wallace, but the President was far from happy with his Secretary of State. He resented Byrnes's cavalier manner of reporting to the White House; his subordinate appeared to feel that he had more right to be in the presidential office than Truman had. When, in January of 1947, Byrnes resigned because of ill health, Truman was delighted to name General George Catlett Marshall in his place.

On February 24, 1947, barely a month after he took office, Marshall was confronted with the greatest crisis in foreign affairs since the end of the war. On that day the British ambassador revealed that within six weeks financial troubles would compel Britain to cut off its aid to Greece and Turkey. Rarely in human events has there been so dramatic an occasion as this decision by one power to turn over the reins to another. From the Indian Ocean to the Mediterranean, British authority was dissolving. If the United States did not assume the burden, dire results could be foreseen. Greece would fall to the Communist bands that were sustained by Russian satellites on its borders; Turkish resistance would falter; Iran would be encircled; and no one knew if Europe could sustain the shock of seeing the Soviets break through to the Mediterranean and the Persian Gulf.

In the grotesque parade of criminals at the Nuremberg Trials was Hermann Goering. He testified with arrogant candor, announcing his own conception of totalitarianism: "The opposition of each individual person was not tolerated unless it was a matter of unimportance." Goering's final defiance was to cheat the hangman at the last minute by poisoning himself.

Truman, supported by Marshall and his aides, instantly recognized the nature of the crisis. But he faced formidable obstacles in persuading a country already suspicious of the "get tough" policy that the United States should take on the unpopular job of carrying on Britain's imperial policies in Greece. Senator Vandenberg, aware of the problem, advised: "Mr. President, if that's what you want, there's only one way to get it. That is to make a personal appearance before Congress and scare hell out of the country."

ON March 12, 1947, the President went before Congress to ask for $400 million for economic and military aid to Greece and Turkey. In presenting what quickly became known as the "Truman Doctrine," the President declared: "I believe that it must be the policy of the United States to support free peoples who are resisting attempted subjugation by armed minorities or by outside pressures."

Truman's tough address stirred up a storm of debate. Liberals, critical of Greek and Turkish leaders, objected that the Truman Doctrine proposed to fight totalitarianism by associating the United States with the defense of totalitarian regimes. Yet in the end most such critics swung to the support of the Truman Doctrine, however reluctantly. Although conservatives claimed that liberals were "soft on Communism," a majority of liberals in Congress voted in favor of foreign-policy measures to check the Russians.

Ironically, many of the most vigorous objections to the Truman Doctrine and similar proposals came from the other end of the political spectrum. Though many conservatives in Congress were vocally anti-Communist, they were unwilling to appropriate funds to contain the Soviets. They feared that unbalanced budgets would bankrupt the nation and lead to a Communist triumph. To avoid the expensive commitment required by the Truman Doctrine, Republican critics—not previously considered ardent admirers of the U.N.—argued that the President was "bypassing the U.N." But the adroit Senator Vandenberg marshaled enough Republican votes to win approval for the Greek-Turkish aid bill.

In its initial test, the Truman Doctrine proved singularly successful. An American mission, financed by Truman Doctrine funds, helped bolster the Greek economy and reorganize the army. Both nations ultimately were saved from Communist domination. Yet the critics of the Truman Doctrine objected that it was essentially a negative response which left the initiative in foreign affairs to the Russians and which encouraged a warlike posture toward the Soviet Union. In a speech in Columbia, South Carolina, Bernard Baruch used a new phrase to describe the deterioration of Soviet-U.S. relations: "Let us not be deceived—today we are in the midst of a cold war."

The Truman Doctrine had been an emergency response to an emergency situation in the "Cold War." Marshall had already taken steps to develop a more fruitful long-range policy. After he took over the State Department, a Policy Planning Staff was set up, and the world-wise George Kennan, a 20-year veteran of the diplomatic corps who was one of the State Department's few Russian experts, was named to head it.

Kennan took a hardheaded look at the nature of Soviet-American relations. In an article published soon afterward he said that United States policy should be one of "long-term, patient but firm and vigilant containment of Russian expansive tendencies"—by force if necessary, but always leaving the

"Don't mind me—just go right on talking."   FEB. '47

Long before Russia detonated a nuclear device, cartoonist Herbert Block felt it was impossible for the U.S. to maintain a permanent monopoly in atomic weapons, and here he warned of the worldwide menace of the bomb. The patently nonalignable Mr. Atom, cast as an undertaker, measures the earth for a coffin while he addresses a stubborn group of negotiators.

way open for the U.S.S.R. to submit without losing too much face. By Kennan's reckoning, a successful policy of containment would force the Kremlin to adopt a more circumspect policy and "promote tendencies which must eventually find their outlet in either the breakup or the gradual mellowing of Soviet power." With some modification, Kennan's views guided American policy toward Russia well into the 1960s.

Marshall also directed the Policy Planning Staff to study what could be done to save Western Europe from ruin; the only condition he laid down was "Avoid trivia." Some drastic solution was desperately needed. By 1947 Europe was on the verge of breakdown. The end of lend-lease had created an international economic crisis. Allied nations owed the United States $11.5 billion for goods they had acquired but could not pay for. To close this "dollar gap," the United States resorted to emergency measures—such as a $3.75 billion loan to Britain in 1946—but these brought only momentary relief. Although the United States by the middle of 1947 had given $10 billion to Europe, the European economy was collapsing and the people faced starvation. In March 1947 the situation became perilous when UNRRA drew toward its end at the very time that Europe was reeling from the blows of a vicious winter.

It was to this new crisis that Kennan and the Policy Planning Staff turned their attention. In May 1947 they sent Marshall their recommendation: an offer of massive American economic aid to Europe on condition that the Europeans take the initiative in working out the details of the program. The policy planners favored a program that was not set within a framework of anti-Communism, but of America's willingness to take the lead in stamping out hunger and poverty. They believed that military measures alone would not contain Communism, that it was crucial to deal with the economic dislocations and the "profound exhaustion of physical plant and of spiritual vigor," which the Communists could exploit.

Sarcastically captioned "Helpful Uncle Sam," these cartoons from the semiofficial Soviet magazine "Krokodil" accompanied an editorial which damned the Marshall Plan as cynical and selfish. In typical party-line distortions, Uncle Sam remarks above, "Why bother strengthening your currency—use mine," while below he says, "Don't sow wheat—I'll sell you corn."

IN a historic speech at Harvard University on June 5, Secretary Marshall spelled out the program. He offered economic aid to all nations which would co-operate, not excluding the Soviet Union. "Our policy," the Secretary declared, "is directed not against any country or doctrine, but against hunger, poverty, desperation and chaos." The plan proposed that the nations, instead of approaching the United States with separate shopping lists, should decide among themselves how resources were to be allocated. By placing the responsibility on Europe, the United States was ridding itself of the onus of bickering or delays and of the charge of American domination.

No one anticipated the swift European response to the Marshall Plan. In London Foreign Secretary Ernest Bevin stated: "This is the turning point." Within 22 days the British, French and Russians were meeting in Paris. But in the midst of discussions Molotov received word from Moscow that he was to pull out. Thereafter the Kremlin denounced the Marshall Plan as a capitalist plot; once again a wedge had been driven between East and West. The other European nations, 16 in all, presented the United States with a four-year plan of economic rehabilitation which would cost $22 billion (the Administration pared this estimate to $17 billion). At the end of four years these countries were to be economically self-supporting.

It was a breathtaking program, and many anticipated that Europe's hopes would be dashed by opposition in America to spending such an astronomic sum. Henry Wallace, more and more echoing the line of Communist advisers, denounced the proposal as a "Martial Plan," while Robert Taft spoke for Republican conservatives who complained that the plan would bankrupt the United States and that it ignored Asia.

Taft's opposition provided an acid test for Vandenberg's ability to hold the Republicans to a bipartisan foreign policy. (At one point ex-isolationist Vandenberg wrote to his wife regarding Republican opposition to the plan: "I get so damned sick of that little band of G.O.P. isolationists who are always in the way that I could scream.") But he made the kinds of concessions to the isolationists which conceded nothing in substance but which won the necessary votes. Even with Vandenberg's skill at compromise, the issue was long in doubt. The Russians inadvertently came to the plan's aid. On February 25, 1948, Communists seized control of the Republic of Czechoslovakia, which had been regarded as a bridgehead between East and West, and Jan Masaryk, son of the founder of the republic, died under mysterious circumstances. A new Soviet threat toward Finland, and fear that Italy would go Communist in its upcoming elections, also served to win support for the Marshall Plan. Yet the argument in support of the plan also altered; it came to be portrayed simply as an anti-Soviet stratagem. To beat the deadline of the Italian elections, the Senate met in night sessions. It finally passed the bill by the impressive majority of 69-17. The House quickly gave its approval, and on April 3, 1948, the Marshall Plan became law.

George F. Kennan proved his insight into Soviet affairs years before he outlined the policy of "containing" Communism. Well versed in Russia's language, history and psychology, he had warned against Stalin's duplicities as early as 1933. Accounting for his preoccupation with Russia, Kennan said he "must have lived before and been a Russian."

THE plan was a stunning success. It met and surpassed every production target. Its funds were put to work to build dikes in the Netherlands, drain malarial swamps in Sardinia, build railroads in Turkey and erect steel mills in France. By 1950 the dollar gap was down to a postwar low of two billion dollars. By 1952 production in Europe was 200 per cent higher than in 1938. Even though most of the benefits of the plan were siphoned off by the wealthier classes in such countries as France and Italy, an economic base was built upon which future reforms could be grounded. The plan cost almost five billion dollars less than had been anticipated. Opponents had claimed that foreign aid would bankrupt the country, but during this period the United States enjoyed unparalleled prosperity—while winning incalculable good will abroad. The London *Economist* said: "Marshall aid is the most straightforwardly generous thing that any country has ever done for others."

For a brief season it seemed that Marshall aid would show the world the way toward peace, but as the Cold War intensified, America's foreign-aid goals took on a new military focus. In 1948 Congress had stipulated that not one penny of Marshall Plan funds was to be used for military purposes. But in 1951 America informed Europe that every penny would be allotted to aid Western defenses. By 1952 about 80 per cent of United States aid was going for military weapons, the other 20 per cent for defense support.

The new military objectives of the Marshall Plan were a response to Soviet aggressiveness in Europe and the Far East. The Marshall Plan had frustrated Soviet hopes that Western Europe would disintegrate. Even more troublesome to Russia was the renascence of Germany under the aegis of Western capitalist powers. The American and British zones had been forged into a single region of rich industrial resources, and in June 1948 the Allies carried out a drastic currency reform. These moves helped set off a remarkable economic revival in Western Germany. At the same time, the Western powers encouraged the creation of a new, independent nation there. The Russians reacted by precipitating a quarrel that brought a real risk of war. The focus of the dispute was the old German capital of Berlin, which since 1945 had been occupied by all four powers as an enclave 110 miles behind the Iron Curtain. On June 24, after weeks of harassment of Western traffic into Berlin, the Soviets clamped a rail blockade on the Western sectors.

The Berlin blockade posed a thorny problem for Western leaders. Some wanted to ram an armored train through the Russian blockade. Others wanted to withdraw altogether to avoid the danger of war. But General Clay cabled: "IF WE MEAN . . . TO HOLD EUROPE AGAINST COMMUNISM, WE MUST NOT BUDGE . . . I BELIEVE THE FUTURE OF DEMOCRACY REQUIRES US TO STAY."

At the end of the first week of the blockade, Berlin had enough bread to last only 25 days; enough meat for 33 days. The air lanes seemed the only practical route to the city. Clay called General Curtis LeMay at U.S. Air Force headquarters in Wiesbaden: "Curt, can you transport coal by air?" After a startled pause, LeMay replied: "Excuse me, General, would you mind repeating that question?" Then LeMay rounded up all the planes in his command, including some old B-17 bombers. C-54 Skymasters were flown in from all over the world. By October 1948 the Berlin Airlift was carrying almost 5,000 tons into the city daily. Even those who had faith in the project were amazed by what they were accomplishing.

"But," wrote the *New Statesman and Nation* in London, "every expert knows that aircraft, despite their immense psychological effect, cannot be relied upon to provision Berlin in the winter months." Yet the remarkable ferry of planes continued through the Berlin winter. For months, Berliners lived with the incessant roar of the planes in their ears. So heavy was the traffic —one plane every three minutes—that a plane which could not land on the first attempt had to return all the way to its parent base.

B Y the spring of 1949, the achievements of the airlift erased any doubt that it would succeed. On one day, April 16, American and British flyers hit a record total of 12,941 tons, and it was clear they could keep it up forever.

On May 12, 1949, after 321 days, the Russians capitulated. Rail lines and highways to Berlin were reopened. At a meeting of the City Assembly, Mayor Ernst Reuter paid moving tribute to the 48 airmen who had been killed. The Assembly renamed the plaza in front of Tempelhof Airport "Platz der Luftbrücke" (Airlift Square) in commemoration.

The Soviet Union had sustained an unmitigated defeat. Instead of driving the West out of Europe, it had welded the United States and the Western European nations more closely together. And something even more significant had happened. The tactics of the Kremlin had dissolved the spirit of the old wartime alliance against Germany once and for all. Correspondent Theodore H. White noted a "curious change in phraseology" during the airlift. "When, at a bar in the Ruhr or Frankfurt, one heard Americans use the pronoun 'they,' 'they' almost invariably referred to the Germans, still the enemy to be watched and controlled. But at a bar or over dinner in Berlin when one heard 'they,' 'they' almost invariably referred to the Russians. The Germans were included in 'we.'"

By now events in Europe had convinced leaders of the need to organize

George C. Marshall, victorious general and Secretary of State, had the rare distinction of having graduated from the Virginia Military Institute without a demerit. To say that he never broke a rule would be incorrect: He risked being "busted" on many a moonless night when he slipped out of his barracks for rendezvous with a certain Lily Coles—his future wife.

According to a friend, soft-spoken General Lucius DuBignon Clay's great weakness was a tendency to forget that his mind worked four or five times faster than others'. Another general decided to see whether Clay's mental prowess equaled its reputation. He raced through a bulky report in half an hour and then handed it to Clay. Clay calmly read it in five minutes.

some kind of regional alliance to prepare against possible Russian aggression. In March 1948 Britain, France, Belgium, the Netherlands and Luxembourg had signed the Brussels Pact, pledging military aid to any member under attack. A year later, while the Berlin blockade was still in effect, the United States signed the North Atlantic Treaty with the five Brussels Pact nations, plus Canada, Italy, Norway, Portugal, Denmark and Iceland. (In 1952, Greece and Turkey joined; in 1955, West Germany.) Article 5 of the NATO treaty stipulated that "an armed attack against one or more of the signatories in Europe or North America shall be considered an attack against them all."

Not since the Convention of 1800, when the United States freed itself from the alliance with France, had the American government agreed in peacetime to a treaty of alliance outside the Western Hemisphere. Nothing indicated so clearly the end of isolationism in the United States.

Almost all of the foreign policy of the postwar years had been directed at stabilizing Western Europe. Now, with Western Europe reasonably secure, Washington could turn its attention to the uncommitted regions of Asia and Africa as well as Latin America. When President Truman delivered his inaugural address in 1949, the fourth point of his international recommendations was "a bold new program" to help the underdeveloped areas of the world free themselves of poverty and exploitation. The United States government would provide technical assistance and encourage investment abroad.

By 1952 America's "technical missionaries" were working in 33 nations. A former county agent from Tennessee helped increase wheat output in the Ganges plain; a Georgian bounced over the Iranian roads in a jeep, spreading the gospel of literacy; a team from Oklahoma A & M set up an agricultural secondary school in Ethiopia.

Despite these achievements, Point Four was longer on promise than on fulfillment. Private investment proved disappointingly small. Congress showed little interest in a costly foreign-aid program which might go on for years and which had no predictable relation to national security. Like Marshall aid, Point Four, too, was quickly transformed into a weapon of the Cold War.

Five years after the *Queen Mary* steamed into New York harbor with its burden of returning soldiers, the postwar world had taken a shape quite unanticipated on that sunny afternoon in 1945. The wartime alliance with Soviet Russia had been shattered and the two great powers were engaged in a Cold War that might, at any moment, erupt into a hot one. America's frontiers were now on the Elbe and the Bosporus. Leaders of both American parties had become committed to Kennan's doctrine of "containment"—of meeting Russian expansion with force or the threat of force.

The Cold War had divided the world into two armed camps. Every American move in foreign policy was now weighed for its military consequences. Yet despite this heavy reliance on military power, the United States was in a vulnerable position—particularly if the Soviet Union decided to start a war in a marginal area in which the United States would not wish to use an atomic bomb, a war which the United States would be ill equipped to fight. Such a war, particularly if it could not be fought through to final and decisive victory, might unleash all the angry, explosive feelings which the country harbored about the overwhelming experience of the postwar years—the years when the nation's bland confidence in its military security vanished forever.

The round-the-clock roar of the 11-month airlift gave to the people of Berlin a profound awareness that they "were not alone." When severe weather conditions or a mishap caused a momentary lull in air traffic, there was "a paralyzing silence . . . the silence of a corpse." When the roar could be heard again, "a hundred thousand sighs of relief" rose from the city.

The challenge of a troubled peace

As American and Russian soldiers, in a historic meeting at the Elbe River, sealed the defeat of Germany, a spirit of hope seized a war-torn world. On that same day, April 25, 1945, the United Nations was born at a conference in the San Francisco Opera House. In the White House, in Westminster and in the Kremlin, Allied leaders were preparing to meet for the last of the great war conclaves, at Potsdam, to chart the defeat of Japan and arrange the peace. However, the atomic bombing that brought Japan's surrender enveloped the peace in a poisonous mushroom cloud: With the splitting of the atom, confidence in the future seemed to have shattered. The grand alliance cracked and gave way to an era of cold war between the Soviet Union and the West.

At Potsdam President Truman took a tough stance toward Stalin. Senator Arthur Vandenburg soon jotted in his diary: "FDR's appeasement of Russia is over." Truman's attitude was summed up at an early Cabinet meeting: Russians could either join us or "go to hell." Stalin responded with equal intransigence, coldly tightening the Communists' grip on Eastern Europe, threatening the Middle East and Mediterranean as well. Winston Churchill warned that "an iron curtain" had fallen across Europe. After George Marshall, wartime Chief of Staff, became Secretary of State in January 1947, he gave the keynote for the coming decade as he warned Americans to think back to the fall of democratic Athens, its strength sapped in its struggle with the tyranny of Sparta. In the cold war, America now faced as crucial a test.

ON THE ELBE, astride a ruined bridge, GIs of the American First Army clasp hands with the Russians of the First Ukrainian Army. After their handshakes, they plied each other with K rations (which the Russians seemed to enjoy) and chocolate and later exchanged toasts over vodka and captured cognac. Germany, split in two by this linkup of the Allies, surrendered 13 days later, May 8, 1945.

AT POTSDAM in August 1945, Joseph Stalin sits with the new leaders of the West, President Truman and British Prime Minister Clement Attlee, accompanied by their principal advisers.

President Truman was "tremendously pepped up" by the first successful test of the atom bomb, information that bolstered his decision to take a firm line in negotiating with Stalin.

A new policy of containment and reconstruction

IN the spring of 1947 a man in Indianapolis observed, "Yes, spring is here, all right, but there's something wrong." Asked what was wrong, he said, "I don't know, just something." Millions of Americans shared the feeling as news of crisis came from Europe, Iran, Palestine and China. As President Truman prepared a $37.5 billion budget for fiscal 1948, he proudly noted that the budget would be balanced for the first time since 1930. It was also announced that America's contribution to winning World War II had come to $341 billion, or $7,333 apiece for every U.S. taxpayer. For relief from such grim figures, Americans went off to a new movie, *Duel in the Sun*, the costliest, most lushly technicolored, sexiest western yet made. But there was no escaping events.

Only five weeks after General George Marshall became Secretary of State in January 1947, Britain sent a note saying it could no longer support Greece and Turkey against Communist forces. On March 12 the President gave Congress a challenging program of aid to countries threatened by "armed minorities or by outside pressures." One irate Congressman asked why America should pull "Britain's fat out of the fire." But most agreed with the new Truman Doctrine: the threat was not to Britain's "fat" but to American security. With a down payment of $400 million in aid to Greece and Turkey, the United States set out to contain the Communist threat.

The President and his Secretary of State were not unaware that mere military containment was only half a policy. For many countries in Europe were on the verge of economic collapse as a result of wartime destruction and dislocation. There, the Communists were simply waiting to pick up the pieces. Massive aid to Europe might strain the American budget, but the collapse of Europe would ultimately be far more damaging to the U.S. economy. Thus, nearly three months after Truman spoke on Greece, Secretary Marshall proposed the massive program of aid that soon became known as the Marshall Plan. Sixteen European nations were to be rebuilt in four years, at a cost of many billion dollars. "It was," said Churchill, "the most unsordid act in history."

JEEPS FOR GREECE are lined up on the New York waterfront (above) as the American aid program is launched. Here a two-and-one-half-ton truck is hoisted on board a ship. At this time, it was reported that Communist guerrillas were entering Greece.

TURKISH TROOPS commanded by U.S.-trained officers patrol the country's rugged eastern frontier (left). U.S.S.R. forces camped across the border were supporting guerrillas trying to infiltrate the area. American-made tanks were soon backing up the Turks.

IN MOSCOW to talk over cold war issues, Secretary Marshall finds the weather appropriately chilly (right). Later he offered to include Russia in the Marshall Plan. Russians attended the first planning session in Paris, but then quickly turned down the offer.

SUPPLYING BERLIN, a C-54 transport brings relief from the Russian blockade of the city. The 15-month airlift, called "Operation Vittles," required a total of 277,000 missions (some pilots made up to 400 runs) and delivered some 4.7 billion pounds of supplies to Berlin from bases in Frankfurt and Hamburg. On one day alone, almost 13,000 tons were flown in.

Showdown over Berlin and a return to arms

T HE TRUMAN DOCTRINE and Marshall Plan aid would prove spectacularly successful, reviving Western Europe and securing the Mediterranean. But, stalled in the West, the Communists staged a coup in Czechoslovakia, smashing the last democratic regime in Eastern Europe—except for West Berlin.

Four months later, on June 24, 1948, the Russians blockaded West Berlin. They meant, as West German Chancellor Konrad Adenauer put it, "to starve Berlin into their own sphere." The United States, with fewer than 100 combat aircraft on hand in Germany, hastily assembled an awesome fleet of C-54 Skymasters and began an airlift to sustain West Berlin. The Soviets shrewdly offered to supply coal, but the West Berliners refused and began cutting down their stately chestnut and linden trees for fuel. It took the Russians 321 days to admit defeat and abandon the blockade.

The blockade made Western leaders view the primary Soviet threat as military. Their response was a new military alliance, called NATO. Some Americans opposed this close tie to Europe's fortunes. Texas' Senator Tom Connally protested: "We cannot be Sir Galahads, and every time we hear a gun fired, plunge into war." The Senate, however, voted decisively for NATO: 82-13.

THE CZECH TRAGEDY of Communist takeover is epitomized by the mysterious death (reportedly a suicide) of Foreign Minister Jan Masaryk, mourned here by President Beneš *(center)*.

NATO meeting in Paris' Palais de Chaillot assembles representatives of Allied nations for a conference regarding the defense of Europe.

Aiding India, an American agricultural expert (in background) looks in on a night literacy class financed by Point Four in Uttar Pradesh.

Setback in Asia with domestic reverberations

OUT of the Cold War in Europe came a sense that the United States could "wage the peace around the world." Waging the peace in Asia proved more difficult than holding the line in Europe. In China, Mao Tse-tung's Communists had been battling Chiang Kai-shek's Nationalists for decades. America had long supported Chiang but advised him to make peace with Mao. Chiang demanded more aid and less advice.

Preoccupied with the struggle for Europe, most Americans felt more confused than threatened by the civil war in China. Not until Chiang's government began to collapse did China's fate pre-empt American interest. Then, coupled with political charges that Communists had infiltrated the American government itself, the "betrayal of China" became a subject of bitter debate.

Despite attacks on "Communists in government," President Truman won re-election in 1948—and at once emphasized the needs of Asia. In his inaugural address, he offered "a bold new program" of economic aid to the world's underdeveloped areas. The very next day, however, a defeated Chiang Kai-shek resigned as President of China and by the end of the year retired to Taiwan accompanied by a small army of supporters.

In August 1949 a 1,054-page State Department white paper made it official: China was gone. "The Nationalist armies," Secretary Acheson wrote, "did not have to be defeated; they disintegrated." Some Americans remained unreconciled to the loss: "Apparently the Administration," one Congressman charged, "would rather lose a continent than lose a little face." Another called it an "Oriental Munich." But there was little the President or his critics could do to recoup the loss.

The bold new program (named "Point Four" after its place in Truman's inaugural) did begin an American commitment to Asia. But soon American attention shifted back to the conflict with Russia. In September Truman revealed that the Soviets had exploded their first atom bomb. A new kind of cold war confrontation had begun.

ENTERING PEKING, Red troops parade after the city's surrender. As Mao's soldiers poured in, they left their Russian trucks behind, displaying only captured American vehicles.

CHINESE YOUTHS celebrate the tenth anniversary of Mao's regime against a background (*below*) of model missiles and planes. Among the guests was Russia's Premier Nikita Khrushchev.

2. THE
FAIR DEAL

In the era of free security that had existed before World War II, America had generally been able to seal off foreign affairs in a watertight compartment. In the Cold War this was no longer possible. Central to the containment theory was the belief that the United States must convince the world of its vitality as a free nation. Thus an economic recession could no longer be viewed merely as a matter of domestic concern, for it would cast doubt on America's ability to defend its allies. The attitude of the United States toward blacks would be watched closely not only in American communities but in the capitals of the emerging Afro-Asian countries.

In the postwar years the United States rarely made a move in domestic affairs without looking into a mirror to see what kind of "image" it was presenting to the world. In the process the nation had to find the right answers to some hard questions. Could Americans master the new technology—involving everything from atomic energy to automation—or would they let it master them? Could they solve the vexing problem of relations between the races? Could they improve their standard of living and meanwhile extend the benefits of America's productivity to the rest of the world?

At the end of World War II, this last question troubled Americans most. Memories of the Great Depression were still fresh; many feared that when the United States "reconverted" to a peacetime economy, there would be a new army of up to 10 million unemployed. The first indications were not

MASONIC GRAND MASTER Harry Truman gazes from his favorite portrait, which only hints at the courage and determination that marked him as an effective President.

encouraging. Asked in 1943 about how to reconvert, aircraft manufacturer Donald Douglas responded: "You shut the damn shop up." Ten days after Japan accepted surrender terms, three million Americans had lost their jobs.

Well before the end of the war, Congress had turned its attention to easing the transition. It had, among other things, passed a "GI Bill of Rights"; between 1945 and 1952 the government spent $13.5 billion to school and retrain veterans under this measure. Other ex-servicemen were able to borrow money to set themselves up in business or farming.

Congressmen disagreed on the role government should play in relation to business. The Employment Act of 1946 charted a middle course. It did not specify that the federal government must be solely responsible for full employment, as some backers had urged, but it did establish a three-man Council of Economic Advisers to aid the President and issue an annual economic report. Congress thus left the main areas of economic decision to business but granted the government new responsibility for the health of the economy.

In a remarkably brief period this hybrid government-business operation brought the country through the dangers of reconversion and carried the economy to a new level of productivity. During the war, when Henry Wallace had called for a postwar economy of 60 million jobs, he was scoffed at for setting his sights so high. By July 1946, less than a year after V-J Day, 56.4 million Americans were at work; four years later the total was 62 million and national income had jumped to $242 billion from $181 billion in 1946.

The federal government underwrote the postwar expansion in a variety of ways: farm price supports; long-term, low-interest GI mortgages; minimum wages. Billions of dollars were extended in consumer credit, much of it based on government securities held by financial institutions. Government spending during the war for new plants provided a basis for the vast expansion. At the end of the war the government owned 50 per cent of the country's machine-tool capacity, 70 per cent of the aluminum capacity, 90 per cent of synthetic rubber and magnesium processing capacity. The corporations operating these plants were able to buy most of them on very favorable terms.

But the impressive postwar expansion cannot be explained solely by the intervention of the federal government. By 1948 private capital was being invested in an explosive fashion, at an average three times that of 1929. No less important was the pent-up demand for consumer goods at the end of the war: Americans had come out of the war with $44 billion in savings, and they were itching to spend it.

Indeed, inflation soon became more of a problem than the anticipated depression. A tremendous pressure developed to lift all controls—and quickly. The country was tired of going without gasoline, of carrying around ration books, of eating liver instead of steak. American businessmen, after nearly nine years of New Deal regulations, had had to accept four years more of wartime controls, and they wanted to get back to "normal."

T RUMAN faced an impossible task. He had to manage the transition from a war to a peace economy at the same time that the country was moving back toward a quasi-war economy because of developments abroad. Called on to get rid of controls and yet prevent inflation, he succeeded only in making a difficult situation worse. For weeks he permitted two of his subordinates to war over the issue without indicating what he wanted. Chester Bowles,

"You folks hear any talk about a housing shortage?"   AUG. '47

It took extreme optimism to ignore the nation's housing problem in 1947. Yet federal action was so slow, that Herblock's cartoon of a congressional investigator had a point. The government's figures revealed there were nearly six million families living doubled up, two million farm homes unfit to live in and another seven million city dwellings ripe for demolition.

director of the Office of Price Administration, opposed large price boosts, while John Snyder, a Missouri banker the President named director of the Office of War Mobilization and Reconversion, claimed that price rises would stimulate production. When Truman did act, he came down on the side of Snyder.

Truman was already under fire from conservatives for advancing a domestic program squarely in the New Deal tradition. Now his support of Snyder over Bowles threatened to cost him liberal support as well. From the outset the New Deal Democrats had compared the new President's every move with Roosevelt's. In particular they questioned Truman's appointments. "The Truman inner circle is not vicious," noted an editor; "it is plodding, unimaginative, easily impressed by men who have 'met a payroll,' and deeply suspicious of 'intellectuals'—meaning creators of ideas." The Roosevelt people felt increasingly out of place in the Truman Administration, and many who had been with Roosevelt from the beginning—among them Frances Perkins and Henry Morgenthau Jr.—soon left the government.

When Truman named Edwin Pauley, a California oilman, to the post of Under Secretary of the Navy, Secretary of the Interior Harold Ickes rebelled. Ickes told a Senate committee that Pauley had pressed him to halt a suit claiming federal title to tidelands oil because it would hamper Democratic party fund raising—the "rawest proposition" he had ever heard, Ickes said. Truman suggested Ickes might be "mistaken"—whereupon the irascible Secretary of the Interior resigned.

T HE conflict between the President and the New Dealers came to a head in a quarrel over the nettlesome problem of the rights of union labor. After the war labor leaders demanded increased wages to make up for the drop in take-home pay caused by the loss of overtime hours. The Administration agreed, suggesting that the economy could stand a 24 per cent wage rise without a rise in prices. But business objected to keeping the lid on prices, and labor was not satisfied with 24 per cent.

On November 21, 1945, one of America's largest unions, the United Automobile Workers of the CIO, launched a 113-day strike against one of the country's wealthiest corporations, General Motors, and got a 17.5 per cent wage-and-fringe-benefit rise amounting to 19.5 cents an hour. The next February 800,000 steelworkers won an 18.5 cent boost in another strike. But industry in turn was permitted to jack up steel prices five dollars per ton.

Wages and prices now seemed likely to chase each other out of sight. A 59-day coal strike in the spring of 1946 ended only after Truman ordered government seizure of the mines. Mine leader John L. Lewis won most of what he demanded during government operation, but at the cost of mounting anti-union sentiment in the nation.

In the midst of the coal crisis came an even more serious development: the threat of the first total strike on the railroads since 1894. To head off the walkout, Truman took over the railroads. But on May 23, 1946, in defiance of the President, union leaders called a national rail strike, and 25,000 loaded freight cars were halted. With perishable food sidetracked, prices shot up, and there were runs on groceries. More than 90,000 passengers were marooned— war brides on their way west, baseball clubs traveling between cities, the Philadelphia Symphony on its way to San Francisco. In Europe hundreds of thousands faced starvation as shipments of food to Eastern ports were delayed.

Chester Bowles made a fortune as a partner in the advertising firm of Benton & Bowles. Before retiring at 40, he had coached comic Fred Allen and created a radio landmark, the "Maxwell House Showboat." Turning to public service, he soon became director of the OPA, where he fought rising prices from 1943 to 1946—the "battle of the century," he called it.

Furious at rail union leaders, the President went before Congress on May 25 with a bombshell proposal: a request for authority to draft the workers into the armed forces. Halfway through his speech, Truman received a note announcing that the strike had been settled on his terms. But the President's proposal shocked Congress. It was denounced by senators running a spectrum from liberals like Claude Pepper ("I would give up my seat in the Senate before I would support this bill.") to conservatives like Robert Taft ("This proposal goes farther toward Hitlerism, Stalinism, totalitarianism than I have ever seen proposed in any strike.").

Grimy with coal dust, John L. Lewis, president of the United Mine Workers of America, emerges from an Illinois mine. The 1946 strike he led enraged many but won a multimillion-dollar welfare fund for his union, raised by a royalty on every ton of mined coal. A lover of rhetoric, Lewis spoke sweepingly of labor as "18 million stomachs clashing against backbones."

TRUMAN'S address appeared to have severed his last ties with liberals and labor. R. J. Thomas, national secretary of the CIO-PAC, took down the picture of the President and himself that hung on the wall over his desk and dropped it into a wastebasket. "Labor," he announced, "is through with Truman." Then, when Congress framed a milder labor bill, Truman antagonized conservatives by vetoing the measure as antilabor. Truman was now in trouble with all sides. Yet the President sensed correctly that if he did not curb wage rises, business demands for price concessions would seriously impair the effectiveness of the Office of Price Administration.

By the early summer of 1946, OPA was under heavy attack. Although rationing had been virtually abandoned and controls eased on over 4,000 items, foes of price control complained that OPA ceilings imposed hardships on farm and business interests. Price control was due for renewal July 1, 1946. Three days before the deadline Congress voted a new bill which ended many controls and provided for the rapid abandonment of others. Chester Bowles, now economic stabilization director, resigned in protest.

Truman vetoed the new bill—even though it meant that until Congress could be persuaded to pass a more satisfactory measure, there would be no price control at all. In the first 16 days of July, the prices of basic commodities jumped 25 per cent, about twice as much in two weeks as in the previous three years. Meat rose 20 cents a pound, corn 80 cents, rents 20 per cent in Chicago.

On July 25 Truman signed a new price-control bill, and in late August price ceilings were reimposed on selected items, including meat. Angry stockmen held back their cattle from market. The Armour meat company's main plant in Chicago, which normally handled 9,000 head of cattle a week, now received only 68. In New York City nine out of every 10 butcher shops closed down. By early October the country was swept by a frenzy of protest over the meat shortage. A *New York Times* headline read: "Queens Restaurateur, Worried Over Meat, Dives off Brooklyn Bridge." Charges were heard that American steaks were being sold on the European black market or had gone "into the larders of the Russians."

"The weird cry for 'meat,'" noted the astute newspaperman Tom Stokes, "seemed, as one heard it, to symbolize the desire for all things material." Although the shortage was the result of a strike of cattlemen, the country vented its anger not at them but at the government. Gallup polls showed that Truman's popularity had fallen from a peak of 87 to a lowly 32 per cent. The meat shortage coincided with the 1946 congressional and state election campaigns, and the Republicans made the most of it. Representative Charles Halleck, chairman of the Republican Congressional Campaign Committee, jeered that the Democratic election slogan should be "Let 'em Eat Horse

Meat." Alarmed Democratic leaders urged the President to lift controls.

On the night of October 14 Truman angrily announced in a radio address that since Congress had not given him adequate controls, and since the desire of cattlemen to "fatten their profits" had been fostered by conservatives, he now had no alternative but to end controls on meat. With decontrol, prices broke loose. When meat reappeared, steak cost one dollar a pound and up. Truman was now blamed for high meat prices.

The campaign of 1946 reflected widespread dissatisfaction in the nation. Labor resented Truman's handling of the rail strike; cattlemen and housewives, his meat policy. Conservatives disliked his reform proposals, liberals doubted that these proposals were meaningful. On the advice of party leaders, Truman dropped out of the campaign, and the Democratic party played transcriptions of F.D.R.'s old campaign speeches over the radio instead.

When the ballots were counted that November it was clear that the country had gone to the polls in an ugly mood. Even Republicans were staggered by the dimensions of their victory. For the first time since 1930, they won control of both houses of Congress. Moreover, although some moderate Republicans won election, the majority of the new lawmakers were conservative, nationalistic men from the Midwest and the Far West. "Bring on your New Deal, Communistic and subversive groups," Ohio's new Senator John Bricker had announced during the campaign. "If we can't lick them in Ohio, America is lost anyway." In Wisconsin the 40-year-old La Follette dynasty in the Senate was terminated by a little-known 37-year-old veteran, Joseph McCarthy. (Among the notable newcomers to the House were two young men from opposite ends of the country: 29-year-old John F. Kennedy of Massachusetts, one of the few Democratic winners from the North, and 33-year-old Richard M. Nixon, a California Republican.)

ONE possible interpretation of the elections was that the Roosevelt coalition was falling apart. The Democratic party seemed to have lost its vitality. The bright young men who had built the New Deal alignment were now weary middle-aged men. The city machines which for so long had been the party's mainstay were old and flabby; the Republicans picked up five House seats in New York City, four each in Chicago and Los Angeles.

Most important, the elections appeared to be a brutal repudiation of President Truman's leadership. On the day after the election, Democratic Senator William Fulbright of Arkansas urged Truman to name a Republican Secretary of State as his successor and resign from office, and the usually responsible Chicago *Sun* and Atlanta *Constitution* called upon the President to adopt Fulbright's suggestion. Any possibility of Truman's re-election in 1948 now seemed out of the question.

To most observers that year the elections seemed to mark a turning point in the history of American politics, the point at which the Republican party had established its dominance for the next generation after 14 years out of power. A poll after the elections showed that only 8 per cent of the respondents thought the next President would be a Democrat.

The ideological significance of the 1946 elections seemed even more clear-cut: The country was in a conservative mood. But the same poll that predicted a Republican President in 1948 came up with some striking additional data. It found that Democratic voters who switched to the G.O.P. had no

During the mine strike of 1946, 3,000 coal cars stand empty at Williamson, West Virginia. Many cities and industries felt the effect. In Detroit, Ford shut up shop. Chicago turned off store and theater lights. Steel mills banked their fires. Many trains stopped running, and Washington was readying a freight-shipment embargo as the strike was settled.

desire to undo the New Deal reforms. All groups, including traditional Republicans, favored an extension of social security. Thus, there was ample evidence that if the Republicans actually interpreted the vote as a mandate for reaction, they would seriously imperil their fine chances for victory in 1948.

This is precisely what the Republicans of the 80th Congress did. They set about their tasks like a royalist faction returned from years of exile. Committee chairmen seized the opportunity to join with conservative Southern Democrats (numbering 100 of the 180 Democrats left in the House) to launch what was called a counter-revolution to the New Deal.

THE most imposing figure in the new Congress was the 57-year-old Republican senator from Ohio, Robert A. Taft. Taft appeared to be the epitome of conservatism. Testy, stiff in manner, he seemed to make a point of tactlessness, as though tact were an indication of dishonesty. He was respected even by his enemies for his earnestness and his industry, and he was probably the best-informed man in Congress. But he had a parochial image of both America and the world. Taft, someone observed, had the best mind in Washington, until he made it up.

Yet Taft was not the hidebound reactionary he was often thought to be. He sensed that the 1946 elections offered his party an opportunity to prove it could govern, and that the chance would be thrown away if the G.O.P. pursued the reactionary line advocated by such House leaders as Speaker Joseph W. Martin or by senators like his fellow Ohioan, Bricker. Taft sponsored modest proposals for federal aid to medical care, education and housing. "You don't get decent housing from the free-enterprise system," he explained with characteristic bluntness. By 1947 Bricker was complaining: "I hear the Socialists have gotten to Bob Taft."

On most issues it was the Brickers who dominated the 80th Congress. They rejected not only Truman's recommendations to extend social-security and minimum-wage legislation, but even Taft's moderate proposals. They slashed funds for power and reclamation projects in the West, for rural electrification, and for soil conservation and crop storage. They wreaked posthumous vengeance on Franklin Roosevelt in 1947 by adopting the 22nd Amendment, limiting all Presidents after Truman to two terms; ratification of the amendment was completed by the states in February 1951.

The response of the 80th Congress to the displaced-persons crisis was especially unfortunate. World War II and its aftermath had uprooted great multitudes of Europeans from their homes. Driven into exile, sometimes herded into Allied detention camps, many hundreds of thousands pleaded for admission to the United States. When in June 1948 Congress finally adopted a Displaced Persons Act to admit a scant 205,000 refugees, Truman signed the bill only "with very great reluctance"; the measure, he said, was "flagrantly discriminatory," for by stipulating that a high percentage of those admitted should come from the Baltic territories and should be farmers, the act effectively limited the immigration of Jews and Catholics.

In the 1946 campaign Republicans had claimed that the end of price control would end the nation's economic difficulties. Four days after the election, Truman surrendered to the opponents of controls. He took ceilings off everything but rents and two items in short supply: sugar and rice. As a result, prices rose between 1946 and 1947 more than they had in all of World

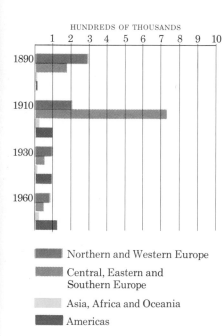

HUNDREDS OF THOUSANDS

■ Northern and Western Europe

■ Central, Eastern and
Southern Europe

■ Asia, Africa and Oceania

■ Americas

IMMIGRATION TRENDS
IN KEY YEARS FROM 1890

Because of earlier restrictions, the largest single group of immigrants by the 1960s came from the Western Hemisphere. In 1890 most had been from northwestern Europe. In 1910 the great bulk was from the rest of Europe. In the 1920s, as the wave seemed due to resume soon after World War I, Congress passed tight quotas favoring northwestern Europeans—the group least anxious to come. One unexpected by-product was that industrial areas, cut off from unskilled European labor, hired more and more blacks, thus speeding black migration from the South.

War II. In 1947 organized labor, its gains cut by inflation, demanded and won a second round of wage boosts, and in 1948 a third round. As the inflationary spiral mounted relentlessly, there were signs that people on fixed income and those in modest circumstances were losing faith in the Republican promise that laissez faire would solve the country's economic problems. A Gallup poll in August 1948 found that the country, by a surprisingly emphatic margin, favored the restoration of price controls and rationing.

Both Taft and the Bricker wing of the Republican party interpreted the 1946 election as a mandate to discipline labor unions. Much of the country, they believed, was exasperated with union abuses. After hearing out one labor delegation of 125 from his home state, Indiana's Senator William Jenner exploded: "You've come down here saying you want no legislation. . . . Well, by God, you're going to get some."

In April 1947 the House voted a tough labor bill, sponsored by Representative Fred A. Hartley Jr. of New Jersey. In the Senate liberal Democrats and Republicans forced Taft, chairman of the Labor Committee, to soften the measure. But the legislation approved in June was still stringent. The Taft-Hartley bill outlawed the closed shop (under which some employers had been required to hire only union members), curbed the union shop (under which new employees had to join the union) and encouraged states to adopt "right-to-work" laws which would forbid the union shop altogether. The measure forbade jurisdictional strikes and secondary boycotts, required union officials to file non-Communist affidavits, prohibited political contributions by unions to candidates for federal office, provided that unions register and report on their affairs, empowered the government to obtain injunctions against unions and stipulated a cooling-off period before walkouts.

Scottish-born Philip Murray, a coal miner at the age of 10 for 80 cents a day, became head of a United Mine Workers local and rose to be John L. Lewis' lieutenant in the UMW. Murray was later president of the United Steelworkers, then succeeded Lewis as head of the CIO after Lewis quit its presidency in a heated disagreement over national politics.

L ABOR mounted a monumental campaign to persuade President Truman to veto the bill. National advertisements denounced it as a slave-labor measure. In New York City milk drivers left a veto appeal with each bottle of milk. The National Catholic Welfare Conference and Protestant and Jewish leaders urged a veto. At the White House mail trucks unloaded 800,000 letters.

On June 20, 1947, the President sent a 5,500-word veto message to Congress. After the first page, Hartley stopped listening; another Republican leader studiously read the Washington *Post's* comics. When the reading ended, there were cries of "Vote! Vote!" The House quickly overrode the veto. In the Senate liberals conducted the longest-sustained filibuster since 1927 in an attempt to prevent a vote; the body met in continuous session for almost 31 hours. When the filibuster broke down, the Senate voted to override by six votes more than needed.

The Taft-Hartley law was by no means the "slave-labor act" unions claimed it to be, but neither was it a balanced attempt at improving relations between labor and management. It imposed severe—and, in some respects, unworkable—restrictions on labor; from the political point of view it was a blunder, for it drove union labor, which had been antagonized by Truman in 1946, back into the arms of the Democratic party.

Of all the missed opportunities of the 80th Congress, none was so glaring as in the field of civil rights for blacks. On this issue the Democrats, with their powerful Southern minority, were most vulnerable. But since the Republicans in the 80th Congress needed Southern Democratic support on conservative measures, and since many G.O.P. congressmen opposed federal intervention, no action was taken.

Where the Republicans feared to tread, President Truman, a descendant of Confederate sympathizers, stepped in. In December 1946 he set up a Presidential Committee on Civil Rights under the chairmanship of Charles E. Wilson, president of General Electric. After 10 months of study the committee issued a historic report. It recommended laws to protect individuals against police brutality, a federal antilynching statute, equal opportunity to vote, equal educational opportunity and federal action to end segregation. It advocated the creation of a permanent federal commission on civil rights and reorganization of the civil rights division of the Justice Department.

On February 2, 1948, President Truman sent a message to Congress which urged implementation of these recommendations. Southerners responded with a furious outburst of invective. Senator James Eastland of Mississippi declared: "The recommendations would destroy the last vestige of the South's social institutions and mongrelize her people."

At the White House in mid-March, Mrs. Lennard Thomas, Alabama Democratic National Committeewoman, told the President: "I want to take a message back to the South. Can I tell them you're not ramming miscegenation down our throats—and you're not for tearing up our social structure—that you're for all the people, not just the North?"

"Well, I've got the answer right here for you," the President said, and pulling a copy of the Constitution from his coat pocket, he proceeded to read her the Bill of Rights.

In the next few months Truman indicated that he favored modest advances in civil rights. But many of the Southern Democrats were adamant in their refusal to accept change. They launched a campaign to deny the presidential nomination to Truman; failing that, they made plans to bolt their party.

That summer the Democratic National Convention, after a stiff fight, voted to adopt a strong civil-rights plank. The stony-faced Mississippi delegation and 13 of the Alabama delegates marched out of the convention in protest, waving the Confederate flag. Five days later the bolters, widely known as Dixiecrats, met in Birmingham to form the States Rights party. Speakers warned that civil-rights legislation would result in the races "mingling in the beauty shops and the swimming pools." For presidential candidate, the convention named Governor J. Strom Thurmond of South Carolina; for Vice President, Governor Fielding Wright of Mississippi.

W HILE at one extreme the Dixiecrats were undercutting Truman's following in the South, at the other, critics of his foreign policy were threatening to deny him liberal support. When Truman forced him out of office, Henry Wallace announced: "I shall continue to fight for peace." Over the next year, as editor of the *New Republic*, Wallace assaulted Truman's foreign and domestic policies. On December 29, 1947, the former Vice President announced that he would run as an independent candidate for President. Seven months later Wallace's supporters founded the Progressive party. The Progressives denounced both major parties as warmongers and demanded the scrapping of the Truman Doctrine and the Marshall Plan. "The choice," announced the keynoter at the Progressive convention, "is Wallace or war."

Most liberal groups rejected the Wallace party, in part because Truman

The news story above and the Jim Crow sign below summed up the fanatical racist views of Mississippi Governor Fielding Wright, Dixiecrat candidate for Vice President in 1948. Wright opposed all attempts to end segregation, and said he was engaged in a fight for the "return to the States of powers illegally snatched from them . . . by a Washington bureaucracy."

showed a new commitment to liberal measures in 1948, but even more because they disapproved the pivotal role played by the Communists within the Progressive party. Under the guidance of men like Representative Vito Marcantonio of New York, the new party had adopted a program which consistently followed the Communist line. Wallace himself, while clearly no Communist, openly welcomed their support.

With the Democratic coalition disintegrating, the Republicans contemplated the 1948 campaign with even higher expectations than they had had after the rout of the Democrats in 1946. The center of Republican power lay in the rural, conservative hinterland, so it seemed that 1948 would be the year for Bob Taft to come into his own. But since 1936 the G.O.P., however conservative and isolationist its congressional delegation, had unfailingly turned to a man of moderately internationalist and liberal views for its presidential candidate. In 1948 it returned again to Thomas E. Dewey, who had been re-elected Governor of New York by a huge 680,000-vote margin in 1946. California's liberal Governor Earl Warren was picked as his running mate.

Jackie Robinson, the first black player formally admitted to major league baseball since the 1880s, signs a contract with the Brooklyn Dodgers, cued by Branch Rickey, then Dodger president. Although a few light-skinned Negroes played in the early 1900s billed as Cubans, Indians or Mexicans, the color line was not openly broken until Robinson was signed in 1945. After one season with Montreal, a Dodger minor league "farm" team, Robinson became a regular on the Brooklyn team in the spring of 1947.

CERTAIN of victory, Dewey and his advisers treated the 1948 campaign as an ordeal that had to be undergone only because it was an American custom, not because it could affect the results. Dewey's cautious approach served to accentuate his colorlessness. Instead of making clear what he hoped to accomplish in office, he delivered speeches which abounded in platitudes: "Our future lies before us," or "We need a rudder to our ship of state. . . ." Dewey pursued the presidency, it was noted, with the "humorless calculation of a Certified Public Accountant in pursuit of the Holy Grail."

There was at least one man in the United States who believed Harry Truman could win, and that man was Harry Truman. On June 3, a month before the convention, Truman's train had departed Washington on a 9,500-mile "nonpolitical" swing around the country. Before leaving, the President told reporters: "If I felt any better I couldn't stand it." At first crowds were small, but after 10 days, people began to warm to him. Reporters noted a new campaign personality, "a blend of Will Rogers and a fighting cock." Truman was coming to find a winning appeal in assaults on the Republican 80th Congress. Stung by his rebukes, one G.O.P. congressman denounced the President as a "nasty little gamin." Truman was hitting with telling effect.

Most of the delegates in Philadelphia had not yet seen the "new Truman" in action. The President's acceptance speech electrified the convention. Truman aimed his main thrusts at the divergence between the promises in the G.O.P. platform and the performances of the Republican 80th Congress: "The Republican platform urges extending and increasing social security benefits. Think of that—and yet when they had the opportunity, they took 750,000 people off our social security rolls. I wonder if they think they can fool the people with such poppycock as that." Delighted with the new Truman, the crowd yelled, "Pour it on 'em, Harry!"

Truman had another surprise in store. In the same speech he announced to the startled but gleeful delegates that on July 26, the day turnips are planted in Missouri, he was going to summon the 80th Congress back into special session. "I'm going to call Congress back and I'm going to ask them to pass laws halting rising prices and to meet the housing crisis which they say they're for in their platform. At the same time I shall ask them to act on . . .

aid to education, which they say they're for; a national health program; civil rights legislation, which they say they're for . . . an increase in the minimum wage, which I doubt very much they're for . . . an adequate and decent law for displaced persons in place of the anti-Semitic, anti-Catholic law which this 80th Congress passed." He added: "They can do this job in 15 days if they want to do it." The convention was bedlam.

Not since 1856 had a President called back Congress in an election year. Critics denounced the President's move as blatantly political. "This petulant Ajax from the Ozarks," Republican Senator Styles Bridges of New Hampshire fumed, would find the "maddest Congress you ever saw." Bridges was right. "The Turnip Congress" passed nothing of consequence. But Truman had scored his point. He had switched the issue from Dewey's record to the hard-rock conservatism of the Republican Congress.

On September 17 when the President left Union Station, his running mate, Senator Alben Barkley of Kentucky, urged: "Mow 'em down, Harry." Truman responded: "I'm going to give them hell." In the next six weeks he traveled 22,000 miles and made 275 speeches. He jeered at Dewey's attempt to wage a campaign above issues ("He's been following me up and down this country making speeches about home and mother and unity and efficiency"). But he saved his most telling blows for the "do-nothing, good-for-nothing" 80th Congress and for the Republican party as the party of reaction.

In September both candidates were invited to address the National Plowing Contest at Dexter, Iowa. On the advice of his managers, Dewey declined. After all, Iowa had gone Democratic only three times since 1856, and polls showed him with 55 per cent of the vote in Iowa to Truman's 39 per cent. Truman accepted, and made the most of his opportunity. To a crowd of some 100,000 gathered at the Widow Agg's farm, the President declared that Congress had "stuck a pitchfork in the farmer's back."

Still almost no one thought Truman had a chance. Two months before Election Day, Elmo Roper stopped taking polls, noting that the heavy Dewey margin bore "an almost morbid resemblance to the Roosevelt-Landon figures as of about this time in 1936." Bookies quoted 1-15 odds that Dewey would win; in 1936, F.D.R. had been only a 1-3 favorite. Democratic leaders in Washington put their homes up for sale. *The New York Times* estimated that Dewey would receive 305 electoral votes, Truman 105, Thurmond 38, with 43 doubtful. There was one contrary note. When the Staley Milling Company of Kansas City offered its chicken feed for sale in bags marked with either a donkey or an elephant, 54 per cent chose the donkey sacks. The company thereupon discontinued its "pullet poll" because it did not believe its findings.

The Chicago "Tribune's" headline announcing Dewey's "victory" delighted a triumphant Harry Truman. In expectation of a G.O.P. landslide, a number of publications, including LIFE, were published before the election with articles written as though Dewey had won. Pollster George Gallup, equally red-faced, announced a survey to determine "just what happened."

On election night people settled down before their radios anticipating an early bedtime, since Dewey's victory statement could be expected not long after the polls closed. At 9 p.m. Truman was ahead, but commentators explained that that was to be expected; the Democrats always took a lead in the cities—Truman would be snowed under when the rural areas began to report. At 10 p.m. farm regions were coming in; they were not so Republican as had been predicted, but still the cognoscenti were unperturbed. In Chicago newsboys hawked a *Tribune* extra with the headline: DEWEY DEFEATS TRUMAN.

At midnight the cities were continuing to pile up Truman majorities, and the countryside was still misbehaving, but the 70-year-old H. V. Kaltenborn, who ever since Munich had been the voice of authority on the airwaves, advised his listeners to keep waiting for those rural returns. Early in the morning announcers began to wonder: Would Dewey have enough votes for victory in the Electoral College or would the election be close enough to be thrown into the House? A while later their voices held a note of incredulity. Was it possible? Did Harry have a chance? At Republican headquarters at the Roosevelt Hotel in New York, Associated Press columnist Hal Boyle noted, the mood of the "victory" celebrants changed from confidence to surprise, "from surprise to doubt, from doubt to disbelief, and then on to stunned fear and panic." At 4:46 a.m. *Newsweek*, which was preparing an election extra on Dewey's victory, flashed a hold-everything order to its Dayton printing plant.

By dawn no one doubted that Truman had a chance; any of three large states would push him over. Some people, bleary-eyed and disbelieving, tried to catch a few winks. At breakfast they switched the radio on once more; Ohio was teetering back and forth. At 9:40 on a brilliant sunny morning, Democratic headquarters received a call from Columbus: Truman had only a paper-thin lead, but the districts still out were from Democratic Cuyahoga County. Ohio was safe. Yes, it was true; Truman had done it.

THOMAS E. DEWEY
REPUBLICAN

R EPUBLICANS were stunned, Democrats delirious. The country as a whole was immensely pleased with itself. In an age of conformity, it had bucked the tide and showed a defiant independence of the bandwagon psychology created by the national media. Taft might fume: "I don't care how the thing is explained. It defies all common sense for the country to send that roughneck ward politician back to the White House." A Buick dealer in Dewey's home town of Owosso, Michigan, might grumble: "There are just more damned fools in this country than there are intelligent people." But most Americans, quite apart from partisan beliefs, seemed to be delighted. The bumptious Mr. Truman had fooled them all: the smug retinue around Dewey, the wiseacre reporters, the intellectuals who thought they knew the country's heart and mind. The pollsters were crestfallen. George Gallup confessed: "I just don't know what happened. I have no alibi."

For the first time since 1916, a presidential candidate won with less than a majority of the popular votes. Truman received 24.1 million votes to his opponents' 24.2 million, but he scored a 303-189 advantage over Dewey in the Electoral College. The rebellion of the two extreme wings of the Democratic party may have helped Truman more than they hurt him. To be sure, Wallace's 1.2 million ballots (much fewer than anticipated, with no electoral votes) threw New York, Maryland and Michigan to the G.O.P., but the Wallaceite defection also made the Democrats less vulnerable to the charge that they were dominated by leftists. The States Rights movement cost the Democrats four Southern states (Thurmond, too, polled 1.2 million votes—and 39 electoral votes), but together with the strong civil-rights plank, it added to Truman's appeal to black voters and to friends of civil rights. One black editor commented on the Dixiecrat walkout: "Negroes felt if they didn't support Truman after that, no other politician would ever take such a stand." The black vote was crucial in several key states.

The big surprise of the election was the "green uprising" in the farm belt. Dewey carried only seven states between the Alleghenies and the Pacific. "Safely Republican" Iowa, which F.D.R. had lost to Dewey by 47,000 votes

HENRY A. WALLACE
PROGRESSIVE

J. STROM THURMOND
DIXIECRAT

Truman's chances for election appeared dim against the competition of this determined trio: Dewey, labeled a "limber trimmer" by H. L. Mencken; Wallace, who was leading a new "Gideon's army" to victory in the "century of the common man"; and Thurmond, who solemnly declared that the other three candidates hoped to give the country that "new Russian look."

in 1944, swung to Truman by a 28,000 margin. The Democrats won back both houses of Congress: the Senate by a margin of 12, the House by 92. Truman's assault on the 80th Congress had struck home. The Republican conservative bloc in the Senate was almost obliterated.

The Democratic party, which had appeared so moribund in 1946, suddenly came to life with the election of new men in the New Deal tradition. Illinois sent to the State House a 48-year-old newcomer to politics, Adlai Stevenson, and elected to the U.S. Senate Paul Douglas, a University of Chicago economics professor. The 37-year-old mayor of Minneapolis, Hubert Humphrey, was elected to the U.S. Senate in a campaign directed by 30-year-old Orville Freeman. The 37-year-old G. Mennen Williams, who one day would inherit a shaving-cream fortune, was elected governor of Michigan. Chester Bowles was chosen governor of Connecticut. Tennessee elevated Estes Kefauver from the House to the Senate; Texas did likewise for Lyndon Johnson.

On January 20, 1949, Harry Truman was inaugurated President in his own right. Washington celebrated the biggest, noisiest inauguration in history. Confident of a G.O.P. victory, the Republicans of the 80th Congress had appropriated a record $100,000 for the forthcoming inauguration; the Democrats were delighted to spend it. The presidential car drove down Pennsylvania Avenue flanked by an honor guard from Truman's World War I artillery unit, Battery D, and trailed by a calliope tooting, "I'm Just Wild About Harry." For the first time, units representing organized labor marched in the inaugural parade with their own floats. On orders from the White

HOW TRUMAN DEFEATED
DEWEY IN 1948

In the election of 1948 Truman received 24.1 million votes—less than half the total popular vote but enough to win 28 states (below) having a total of 303 electoral votes. Dewey received 21.9 million votes, carrying 16 states with 189 electoral votes. The Dixiecrat party, which amassed 1.2 million votes, won four Southern states with 38 electoral votes (plus one ballot from a Tennessee elector who violated his Truman pledge) and also did well in Arkansas and Georgia. The Progressive party won no electoral votes; of its 1.2 million popular votes, New York cast 509,559.

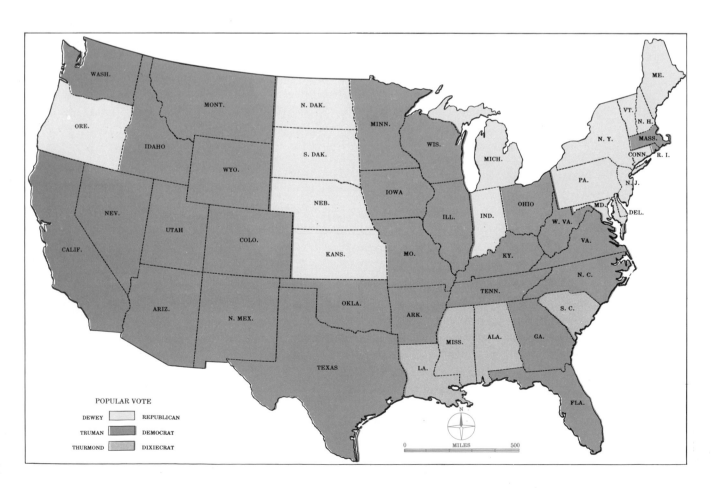

POPULAR VOTE

DEWEY		REPUBLICAN
TRUMAN		DEMOCRAT
THURMOND		DIXIECRAT

House, Negroes attended the inaugural gala and danced at the inaugural ball.

A British magazine entitled its postelection commentary: "Roosevelt's Fifth Term." Truman's State of the Union message indicated that the title was appropriate. As part of his "Fair Deal" program he called for the extension of old Roosevelt measures, such as social security, and added such new proposals as a national plan for compulsory health insurance.

Congress in 1949 expanded public power, soil conservation, flood control and rural electrification programs, and granted the President powers to cope with inflation. It provided for the construction of low-income housing units, and made grants for slum clearance and rural housing. It also voted a new and somewhat liberalized Displaced Persons Act. But Congress refused to heed Truman's requests on most of the major issues of the day: It turned down fair-employment-practices legislation, Secretary of Agriculture Charles Brannan's new plan for farm subsidies, and the President's proposal for a national health program. Federal aid to education lost out when controversy developed over extending such aid to parochial schools.

On some issues, Truman found that he had to oppose action by the Democratic Congress. He courageously vetoed a bill which would have raised the price of natural gas, even though the measure was supported by powerful elements in his own party.

By 1951 Truman and Congress had reached a stalemate. The President did not have enough support to win passage for his recommendations, and the conservatives were not strong enough to undo what had already been done. This was the same kind of stalemate that had characterized much of the country's legislative history since 1938, a politics of dead center.

But the country had been led through the difficult postwar transition—and by a man who, as one writer noted, was "not so much the average man as he is the national character in office." Under Truman America had forged a coalition of free nations in the Atlantic community, had made a start toward a development program for the Asian and African nations, had turned back the tide of Communism threatening Western Europe, had broken new ground in the relations of white and black Americans, and had made the difficult shift from a wartime to a peacetime economy without a serious depression.

A figure familiar to troops overseas, Francis Cardinal Spellman, archbishop of New York and Roman Catholic Military Vicar of the Armed Forces, visited units all over the world. At home, he often took stands on public issues. He urged, for example, that U.S. immigration restrictions be relaxed to admit the "starving, suffering peoples" who were displaced by war.

NONE of these advances had come easily. One analyst wrote: "Mr. Truman had to make many choices in situations in which there was no right way, but only an assortment of wrong ones. . . . It takes uncommon steadiness of mind to commit a nation to a choice between evils and having made the choice, neither to misrepresent it nor to wallow in regrets and unnerving doubts. If any one thing seems more nearly certain than another about Harry Truman as President, it is that he never shrank from a necessary choice."

Despite his extensive reading in history, Truman retained a simple, straightforward view of the world derived from a Missouri boyhood. "A man brought up in this tradition," Jonathan Daniels noted, "does not get bogged down in a political campaign or a cold war because of inner uncertainties or ideological complications. A Bolshevik is as simple as a bushwhacker." Sometimes this led the President to superficial judgments based on overly simple, unreflective views of complex subjects. But it freed him to make bold decisions, and he never flinched from those decisions. Perhaps the best clue to his actions was a sign on his White House desk: "The buck stops here."

ANTICOMMUNISTS in Leslie, Michigan (population 1,400), line up with a scroll bearing over 900 signatures. The document endorsed Judge Harold Medina's conduct of the 1949 trial in which 11 Communists were convicted of promoting subversive ideas.

Bitter years of fear and distrust

AMERICANS found little respite in the victory that crowned World War II. In place of the old enemy, Nazism, there was a new one, Communism; and it suddenly seemed to have planted itself everywhere. In a dark kaleidoscope of espionage and subversion, frightening disclosures were made by former Communists Elizabeth Bentley, Louis Budenz and Whittaker Chambers. Among those indicted were ex-government official Alger Hiss and a couple named Julius and Ethel Rosenberg, who passed defense secrets to Russia.

The first major loyalty trial, held in 1949, set a hectic pattern of sensational charges and countercharges. Eleven Communist leaders were convicted, not of committing subversive acts, but of advocating the forcible overthrow of the government. Before the defendants went to prison, their attorneys had angered Americans (above) with their violent abuse of the presiding judge. The next year saw the rise to power of Senator Joseph R. McCarthy, whose name became symbolic of the excesses of the whole period. But McCarthy himself finally alienated the public with his reckless attacks. The 1954 Army-McCarthy hearings (opposite) signaled the end of the senator's sway—and the end of enervating public suspicions and private anxieties. Eventually, there proved to be far less Communist infiltration than many believed, and the investigations did far less damage to civil liberties than many feared. But the wounds that were opened in those few years would be slow to heal.

THE CLIMAX OF McCARTHYISM is reached under glaring TV lights at the Army-McCarthy hearings in the Senate Caucus Room in 1954. Backs to the camera, Senators Mundt *(right)* and McClellan face Army Secretary Robert T. Stevens *(center)*. Stevens is flanked by his counsel, Joseph N. Welch *(right)*, and the departmental counselor of the Army, John G. Adams.

THE ACCUSER, Richard M. Nixon, takes notes at a Hiss hearing. The most tenacious of the committee members, Nixon insisted upon the personal confrontation of Hiss and Chambers.

Hiss vs. Chambers:
"A generation on trial"

MORE than the guilt or innocence of Alger Hiss was at stake when this former government official stood accused—in 1948 House hearings and later in court—of passing secret documents to Russia via ex-Communist courier Whittaker Chambers. Experts swore that these papers could have let Russia break State Department codes. The Hiss case, and treason charges against other trusted men at home and abroad, added up, said journalist Alistair Cooke, to "a generation on trial."

Chambers produced not only the documents, which had apparently been copied on Hiss's old Woodstock typewriter, but also summaries of secret papers in Hiss's handwriting. Other testimony produced at the trial linked Hiss to members of the Communist underground. He was found guilty of perjury and sentenced to prison.

THE ACCUSED, Alger Hiss, takes his oath before the House Un-American Activities Committee. He testified that in substance Chambers' charges against him were "complete fabrications."

THE WITNESS, Whittaker Chambers, takes the stand at a committee hearing. "I had myself served in the underground," he said quietly; "a member of this group . . . was Alger Hiss."

COMMITTEE MEMBERS ponder the conflicting stories of Hiss and Chambers. They are, from left, Karl Mundt of South Dakota, Chairman J. Parnell Thomas of New Jersey, F. Edward Hébert of Louisiana, Richard B. Vail of Illinois. Before Hiss was convicted, Thomas was imprisoned—for padding his payroll.

45

A wave of hearings that engulfed a nation

Few Americans were wholly unaffected by the wave of security investigations. Public-opinion polls, widespread suspicions and fears for civil liberties reflected the strain under which the country was laboring.

Among the countless citizens whose loyalty was impugned were the four below. Annie Lee Moss, a Pentagon clerk, was denounced in 1954 before the McCarthy committee; a year later the Army gave her back a job. Owen Lattimore, a minor Far Eastern policy adviser, was called by McCarthy the "top Russian espionage agent" in America; none of the charges against him ever came to trial. Screen writer Dalton Trumbo did go to jail in 1950 as one of the "Hollywood Ten" who refused to answer the questions of congressmen. In 1953 Methodist bishop G. Bromley Oxnam asked to testify, and for 10 hours he refuted unsubstantiated slurs against him. In the end he was given a clean bill of health.

Clerk Annie Lee Moss

Professor Owen Lattimore

Bishop G. Bromley Oxnam

Writer Dalton Trumbo

A FRIENDLY WITNESS, the late Robert Taylor, leaves a House hearing in October, 1947. Taylor and other actors indicated that Communists were at work in Hollywood.

FOUR UNDER FIRE in the hearings are shown opposite. Although many government employees were investigated as "security risks," not one was formally charged with sedition.

UNFRIENDLY DEMONSTRATORS march in Detroit in 1952. People of all shades of political conviction protested the investigations as a clear infringement on the Bill of Rights.

Joe McCarthy's downfall: "What did I do wrong?"

ARLY in 1954 Senator Joe McCarthy was riding high. To be sure, his no-holds-barred tactics had made powerful enemies. But few dared to challenge him.

Having cowed the State Department, McCarthy took on the Army in the spring of 1954. For 36 days the Army-McCarthy hearings kept Americans close to their TV sets. The Army's chief counsel was a Massachusetts lawyer, Joseph N. Welch *(below)*, who at first seemed too mild to cope with McCarthy's slashing forays. But when the senator attacked Welch's young assistant, Welch made a moving defense—and the hearing room burst into applause. In retrospect, many observers have dated McCarthy's decline from that dramatic moment.

"What did I do wrong?" asked McCarthy afterward. He never recovered. His Senate colleagues voted to "condemn" him. Worse, the newspapers ceased giving him headlines. His friends saw him deteriorate physically. When he died in 1957, Dean Acheson was asked to make a comment. McCarthy's archenemy coldly quoted in Latin the maxim, "Speak nothing but good of the dead."

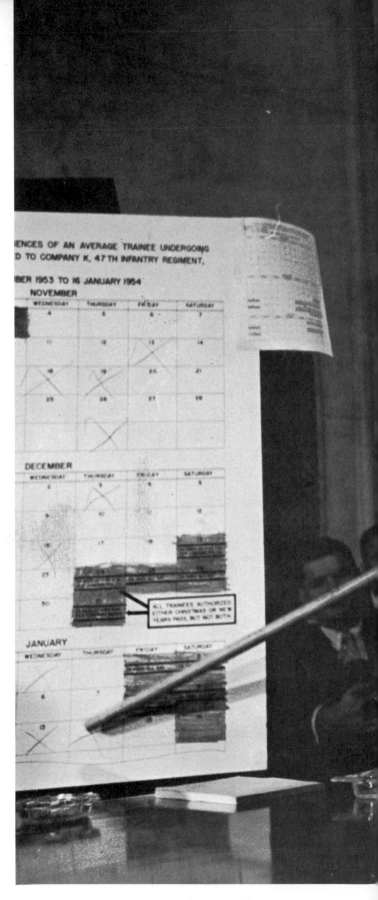

DEFENDING THE ARMY, Joseph Welch speaks up at the 1954 Army-McCarthy hearings. He later said America was protected from demagogues by "immense reservoirs of common sense."

ATTACKING THE ARMY, Joe McCarthy wields a pointer as Roy M. Cohn, McCarthy's subcommittee counsel, looks on. The charts were intended to show that the Army was unfair

in its treatment of Private G. David Schine, formerly an unsalaried investigator for the subcommittee. The Army charged that McCarthy and Cohn sought preferential treatment for Schine; McCarthy charged that the Army held Schine "hostage" to force him to call off his investigations. A few months after this hearing, McCarthy and McCarthyism were on the wane.

3. AN ERA
OF BAD
FEELING

IN the years after World War II, America's deep involvement in foreign affairs confounded the nation's critics and astonished its admirers. Yet this change from prewar isolationism was by no means so complete as it sometimes appeared. Many of the die-hard isolationists maintained an outlook based on some of the old assumptions: America's great strength freed it to act unilaterally in foreign affairs; America had a unique moral mission; Europe was not to be trusted. This group found much that was objectionable in United States foreign policy. They were particularly exasperated by a strategy of containment premised on the belief that the United States had to live with the danger of world Communism indefinitely.

Those Republicans who clung to isolationism found the postwar world especially vexing. Sincerely convinced that their way was best for the country, they were stunned by Harry S. Truman's 1948 victory. But even as the Democrats celebrated their triumph, the country was witnessing the first of a series of events which would persuade millions of Americans that subversive influences were to blame for upsetting the comfortable old order and for jeopardizing the nation's security. These developments—the Hiss trial, the fall of China, the advent of McCarthyism and warfare in Korea—would detonate an explosion of ill feeling that would shatter the Democratic coalition and bring the Republicans to power for the first time in 20 years.

Three months before the election of 1948, a stocky, carelessly dressed

AT WAR IN KOREA, American troops keep a deadly vigil in 1951, bearing the brunt of the United Nations' three-year struggle to restore peace to that ravaged peninsula.

magazine editor named Whittaker Chambers came before the House Committee on Un-American Activities. Chambers, an admitted former Communist, said that Alger Hiss, a former State Department official and now head of the Carnegie Endowment for International Peace, had been a longtime member of the Communist party. Hiss sued Chambers for libel. Chambers rested on his word, and Truman dismissed the affair as a "red herring" designed by the committee to distract attention from the failures of the 80th Congress.

Then on a December night in 1948, Chambers led two investigators to a pumpkin patch on his farm. He reached into one pumpkin and pulled out microfilm of classified State Department documents, which he swore had been passed on to him by a spy ring of which Hiss was a member. Now it was no longer a question of party membership; Chambers was accusing Hiss of having been a spy. On December 15, 1948, a grand jury indicted Hiss for perjury. The statute of limitations barred the indictment of Hiss for espionage, but everyone understood that treason was the real issue.

The Hiss case captured the attention of the nation. At first, Chambers seemed to have the worst of it. A confessed former spy was not a man whose word necessarily commanded belief. But when he was asked why he testified against Hiss, Chambers responded: "I do not hate Mr. Hiss. We were close friends, but we are caught in a tragedy of history. Mr. Hiss represents the concealed enemy against which we are all fighting, and I am fighting. I have testified against him with remorse and pity, but in a moment of history in which this Nation now stands, so help me God, I could not do otherwise."

The verdict in Hiss's first trial reflected the country's uncertainty: The hung jury voted 8 to 4 for conviction. In November 1949 Hiss stood trial a second time. As the months went by, even some Hiss partisans began to sense that the weight of evidence suggested he was not telling the truth. In January 1950 the jury found Hiss guilty, and he was sentenced to five years in jail.

"McCarthyism" became a household word shortly after it was coined in this 1950 Herblock cartoon. McCarthy's tactics as chief inquisitor of alleged Communists and subversives intimidated many officials. When Senator Margaret Chase Smith of Maine challenged McCarthy with her "Declaration of Conscience," only six Republican colleagues dared to support her.

FOR frustrated Republicans seeking an issue to return them to power, Hiss was a godsend. The charge had been raised that the country's lost security was the result of subversion. A sensational spy trial in Canada in 1946 had uncovered at least 14 government employees who had turned over secrets to foreign agents; several of the spy rings had operated in the United States. But the Hiss case had special aspects which made it almost as important for American history as the Dreyfus affair was for France at the turn of the century.

Hiss seemed a perfect symbol of the Roosevelt-Truman foreign policy. He had been director of the Office of Special Political Affairs in the State Department; he had served as executive secretary at the San Francisco Conference; he had been present—in an insignificant role—at Yalta. He represented all that the Midwestern Republicans distrusted: Harvard, the Atlantic Seaboard, the New Deal—all the forces of internationalism and social change that had been altering the familiar contours of the nation.

If the symbol of Hiss was lacking in any respect, it was in its irrelevance to the foreign policy of President Truman and his Secretary of State, Dean Acheson. The Chambers revelations dealt with events of the '30s, and Hiss had resigned from the State Department two years before Acheson became Secretary. It was the Secretary himself—natty, stiff-backed, with a bristling British-style mustache—who made the symbol complete. Senator Hugh Butler of Nebraska expostulated: "I look at that fellow, I watch his smart-aleck manner and his British clothes and that New Dealism, everlasting New Dealism in everything he says and does, and I want to shout, Get out, Get out. You stand for everything that has been wrong with the United States for years."

Four days after Hiss was convicted, Acheson, who had known Hiss for years, said in a press conference: "I do not intend to turn my back on Alger Hiss." Many felt that Acheson's statement did him credit as a man; nevertheless it was politically maladroit. Once again the Truman Administration was accused of indifference to treason. The accusation was unwarranted. Truman had initiated a program to oust subversives from government. By 1951 some 212 employees had been fired and 2,000 had resigned. Many people objected that the program was far too rigorous, and Truman himself came to share these opinions.

In the field of foreign policy the main grievance of many Administration critics seemed to be that the United States was much too closely involved with Europe and that too little attention was being paid to Asian affairs. Moreover, they recognized that it was in the Orient that the Democratic performance in foreign affairs was most vulnerable.

The United States had long regarded itself as a special friend of China. But during and after World War II, China was torn by internal strife between Communists led by Mao Tse-tung and the Kuomintang government of Chiang Kai-shek. During the war Ambassador Patrick J. Hurley had pressed Chiang to form a coalition government with the Communists, but Chiang refused. In December 1945 President Truman sent General George Marshall to China to try, if possible, to create just such a coalition. In January 1947 he returned, unable to effect this unrealistic agreement, and critical of both sides.

The smoldering civil war then erupted, and the Communists demonstrated their military superiority. Supporters of Chiang urged Truman to speed aid to him. The President was willing to give limited assistance—more than three billion dollars in grants and credits and one billion dollars in war materials sold at bargain-basement prices—but he would not make a massive commitment in China of the sort he was making in Europe, largely because he and his advisers doubted that Chiang could be saved unless troops were sent.

On August 5, 1949, the State Department announced the jolting news that China had fallen to the Reds. "The government and the Kuomintang," Acheson declared, ". . . had sunk into corruption . . . and into reliance on the United States to win the war for them." For the United States to have saved Chiang, he argued, would have required "full-scale intervention in behalf of a government which had lost the confidence of its own troops and its own people."

Critics of the Democrats' foreign policy insisted that China had been lost not because of Chiang's weakness but largely because of vacillation or subversion in the government. The conservative columnist George Sokolsky claimed: "The errors which brought on his defeat were not Chiang's; they were Marshall's. They were not China's; they were America's."

THERE is no question that the Roosevelt-Truman policy in China was open to criticism. The Chinese Communists had persistently been described as benign agrarian reformers. (Some conservatives, too, had underestimated the despotic character of the Reds. General Hurley, who had been ambassador to China, had once compared them to "Oklahoma Republicans," though he later changed his mind.) Critics also pointed out that the new State Department position on Chiang was in direct contradiction to the previous position

As China fell to the Communists, America's fear of Marxism reached a hysterical pitch. The scapegoat was Secretary of State Dean Acheson (above). The New York "News" predicted that Acheson would "enter the oblivion which he has so well and truly earned." Even Walter Lippmann advised Acheson's retirement. But Truman said tersely, "I refuse to dismiss Acheson."

Georgi Malenkov, secretary of the Soviet Central Committee, is pictured here as "Stalin's Stooge." Once described as "sinister" and "repulsive," Malenkov had a keen sense of political balance. He survived many purges and in 1946 preached a bold new idea that later became gospel: Marx just might not have foreseen every problem; experience might supply answers.

that he was a powerful ally who led one of the world's four great powers. The Administration, they claimed, had never given Chiang aid commensurate with that status. Nor had it prepared the United States for the China disaster.

However it seems unlikely that any action short of massive military intervention could have defeated the Chinese Reds—and responsible officials were convinced that Americans would never have tolerated any such move. In any event, Administration supporters insisted, the view that a half billion Asians had been sold out by a few American functionaries betrayed an unjustifiable belief in the omnipotence of the United States. Dean Acheson insisted that "Nothing that [America] did or could have done within the reasonable limits of its capabilities could have changed that result."

IN September 1949, only a few weeks after Chiang's collapse, reporters were called to the White House to hear more bad news. "Close the doors," ordered the President's press secretary. "Nobody is leaving here until everybody has this statement." The first reporter who read the terse announcement on the press handout let out a startled whistle. It read: "We have evidence that within recent weeks an atomic explosion occurred in the U.S.S.R."

Russia had The Bomb, at least three years ahead of the schedule American scientists had predicted. No doubt the United States had underestimated Soviet technical ability. But to some Americans another explanation suggested itself. "It now appears," said G.O.P. Senator Karl Mundt of South Dakota, "that earlier and prevailing laxity in safeguarding this country against Communist espionage has permitted what were once the secrets of our atomic bomb to fall into the hands of America's only potential enemy."

The threat of nuclear devastation now seemed immensely greater. "There is only one thing worse than one nation having the atomic bomb," said Nobel Prize winner Harold Urey, "—that's two nations having it." When in January 1950 Truman announced that America was working on the even deadlier hydrogen bomb, Albert Einstein warned: "General annihilation beckons."

Some of the mystery surrounding Russian acquisition of the A-bomb was ended in February 1950 when the British announced they had arrested Klaus Fuchs, an atomic scientist who had worked at Los Alamos. Fuchs confessed that from mid-1942 to early in 1949 he had turned over valuable scientific secrets to Soviet agents—enough, it was estimated, to speed up Soviet production of the A-bomb "at least a year." (Fuchs's confession was later to lead to the trial, conviction and ultimate execution for espionage of Americans Julius and Ethel Rosenberg, who were named as major accomplices.)

"How much more are we going to have to take?" fumed Republican Senator Homer Capehart on the Senate floor. "Fuchs and Acheson and Hiss and hydrogen bombs threatening outside and New Dealism eating away the vitals of the nation. In the name of Heaven, is this the best America can do?"

One man with a sense of the historic moment had a ready answer for Capehart's question. Still unknown to most of the country, he was in a few weeks' time to give his name to a brief, brutal era of American history. He was the junior senator from Wisconsin, Joseph R. McCarthy.

On February 9, 1950, two weeks after Hiss was sentenced to jail, McCarthy addressed a Republican meeting in Wheeling, West Virginia. The speech seemed of so little importance at the time that there is no authenticated transcript of McCarthy's remarks, but newsmen recalled his saying: "I have here in my hand a list of 205—a list of names that were known to the Secretary of State as being members of the Communist party and who nevertheless are still working and shaping the policy in the State Department." Most of the national press overlooked the Wheeling speech. The next day in Salt Lake City McCarthy made similar charges, and the following day he hit the same theme in Reno. By now the accusations were beginning to make headlines.

In a long address on March 30, McCarthy shifted his attack to focus on the Orient. He stigmatized Professor Owen Lattimore, a longtime student of Far Eastern affairs, as "the top Russian espionage agent." The fact is that however unsound Lattimore's judgment may have been, no substantial evidence was ever submitted that the Johns Hopkins professor was a spy; furthermore the State Department under Truman had rarely consulted Lattimore and had not followed his advice when it did.

McCarthy did not pause to answer refutations; he moved from sensation to sensation, ruining one career after another with unsupported accusations. Senators in both parties were troubled by his rashness. An investigating committee headed by Democratic Senator Millard Tydings of Maryland issued a majority report which ridiculed the substance of the Wisconsin senator's charges and denounced his methods. Unhappily, this report failed to make a judicious appraisal of the charges and thus added fuel to McCarthy's fire.

More impressive was a manifesto issued by seven G.O.P. senators—Margaret Chase Smith of Maine, Irving Ives of New York, Charles Tobey of New Hampshire, George Aiken of Vermont, Wayne Morse of Oregon, Edward Thye of Minnesota and Robert Hendrickson of New Jersey. In their "Declaration of Conscience," they dissociated themselves from "Certain elements of the Republican Party [who] have materially added to this confusion in the hopes of riding the Republican Party to victory through the selfish political exploitation of fear, bigotry, ignorance, and intolerance."

But a much larger number of G.O.P. senators—as well as many Southern Democrats—believed that McCarthy was right. Robert Taft was heard to remark: "McCarthy should keep talking, and if one case doesn't work out he should proceed with another." Taft said he had meant merely that McCarthy should not be muzzled; others interpreted the statement as a hunting license.

By September 1950, little more than six months after McCarthy's Wheeling speech, concern over subversion appeared to have conquered good sense. Monogram Pictures canceled plans for a movie on Longfellow because Hiawatha had tried to bring peace to the Indians, and the film might be construed as support for a Soviet "peace offensive." That same month the Senate, overriding Truman's veto, adopted the Internal Security Act, which placed stringent restrictions on Communist activities, provided for the detention of dangerous subversives in time of emergency and set up a Subversive Activities Control Board. Although the bill jeopardized civil liberties by curtailing freedom of speech, some distinguished liberals in the Senate voted for it; one senator confessed privately that he had done so out of fear of McCarthyism.

In linking anxiety over subversion to Truman's Far Eastern policy, McCarthy had struck gold. He pushed his assault further beyond the bounds of reason. "It was Moscow," he charged, ". . . which decreed that the United States should execute its loyal friend, the Republic of China. The executioners were that well-defined group headed by Acheson and George Catlett Marshall."

A FAKE PICTURE GETS
READ INTO THE RECORD

Public dread of anything linked to Communism was a powerful weapon in the hands of unscrupulous politicians. One noted victim was Senator Millard Tydings of Maryland. His opponent, John Marshall Butler, used the top picture above (of Tydings listening to election returns in 1938) and the reversed middle picture (American Communist leader Earl Browder in 1950) and published the composite (bottom) in a circular. Although the caption mentioned that it was a composite, the defeated Tydings sadly noted that "one picture is worth a thousand words."

55

"Like animal trainers . . . ready to show off a monster," the Atomic Energy Commission in 1952 held its first open-to-the-press atomic blast. Some guests, like Senators Margaret Chase Smith, Leverett Saltonstall and Lyndon Johnson (above), chose to watch it on television, but 200 notables were 10 miles from Ground Zero. Happily the bombardier's aim was perfect.

The State Department viewed criticism of its Far Eastern policy with no little complacency. It took pride in the fact that America's occupation policy, directed by General Douglas MacArthur, had converted its former totalitarian enemy, Japan, into a valuable democratic ally. And Japan, the planners were convinced, was the key to power in the Orient. "I am sure," George Kennan commented, "that the Russians would gladly exchange our control of Japan for their control of China." But when the State Department came to grief in the Orient, it was not over China or Japan—at least directly—but over a country to which few Americans had ever given any thought.

In the closing days of World War II, the United States had hastily proposed to accept the surrender of Japanese troops in Korea south of the 38th Parallel; the forces of the U.S.S.R. would have similar authority north of the parallel. This accommodation turned out to be temporarily advantageous for the United States because Russian troops had raced down the peninsula before the Americans landed. When the Americans arrived, the Soviets obligingly gave up the capital of Seoul and retired north of the parallel.

Within a brief period, however, the United States and Soviet Russia were deeply divided over the future of Korea. North of the 38th Parallel the Soviet Union fostered a Communist government. To the south, Dr. Syngman Rhee formed a Western-oriented republic under U.N. sponsorship and, for the moment, under the military protection of the United States.

For America, Korea posed a thorny political and military problem. Among others, General Charles G. Helmick, former Deputy Military Governor of Korea, had warned that the peninsula was indefensible. Truman favored a sharp cutback in military spending, and Republicans in Congress opposed sending aid. Although Lieutenant General John R. Hodge, commanding United States forces in Korea, warned that if the Americans pulled out, the Communists would take over, Washington proposed a withdrawal of both Soviet and American troops. In January 1949 the U.S.S.R. pulled out its forces; six months later the United States followed suit. However the Russians left the North Koreans heavily armed. The United States, on the other hand, in part out of fear that Rhee might mount an invasion northward, gave the Republic of Korea only modest military training and equipment.

On January 12, 1950, Secretary Acheson outlined a "defensive perimeter" which defined the limits of the area the United States believed vital to its national security. Both Korea and Formosa lay outside this perimeter. Acheson's statement did not preclude the possibility that the United States would fight if the Republic of Korea were attacked, but it suggested that Korea was by no means viewed as vital to America's national interest.

ON June 25, 1950, only five months after Acheson's address, North Korean forces invaded the Republic of Korea. The next day the United States took the question to the U.N. Security Council. The Council—in the absence of the U.S.S.R., which was boycotting sessions in an effort to oust Nationalist China—ordered the North Koreans to withdraw and then called upon U.N. members to come to the aid of the Republic of Korea.

That day Truman flew to Washington from Independence, Missouri, where he had been visiting his family. During the trip he "recalled some earlier instances: Manchuria, Ethiopia, Austria . . . how each time that the democracies failed to act it had encouraged the aggressors to keep going ahead. . . .

If this was allowed to go unchallenged, it would mean a third world war."

When General MacArthur reported that the collapse of South Korea was imminent, Truman ordered American air and naval power to the aid of the republic. Later, on MacArthur's advice, the President authorized the use of American ground troops. Truman stipulated that the intervention in Korea would be limited and that in no respect was it to be conceived as a war either with the U.S.S.R. or with Red China. He was equally intent on avoiding the spread of the conflict to the mainland. He sent the Seventh Fleet to serve as a barrier between Formosa and the Chinese mainland, an action which, in effect, contained the war. In the United States this action drew criticism from those who wanted to encourage Chiang to invade the continent.

THE intervention in Korea received the backing of most Americans; Henry Wallace approved, and so did Senator Kenneth Wherry of Nebraska, one of the most powerful of the isolationists. The U.N. swiftly endorsed America's actions and authorized the United States to assume command of U.N. troops in Korea. For the first time in the history of man, a world organization had mobilized force to halt aggression. But since the United States provided a disproportionate share of the troops, the U.N. intervention seemed to most Americans to be simply a United States engagement. (In the end, the United States supplied roughly 33 per cent of the U.N. forces; the Republic of Korea, 61 per cent; other nations, less than 6 per cent.)

In terms of immediately available troops, the Korean War caught America ill prepared. General MacArthur, named to command the U.N. forces, could for the moment draw on only four undertrained, poorly equipped occupation divisions in Japan; in reserve in the States he had only one Army division and part of a Marine division. He had no choice save to throw his green troops into the battle in the hope that their sacrifice would permit him to stabilize a defense line. The Republic of Korea forces were in full flight and might be driven into the sea. To prevent a disaster, soldiers of the 24th Division headed by Major General William Dean were hurried to Korea from Japan.

The GIs disembarked at the southeastern port of Pusan to a welcome with bands and banners. One soldier, perhaps boasting to cover the insecurity so many troopers felt, said, "Just wait till the gooks see an American uniform— they'll turn around and run like hell!" It took only one engagement to make a mockery of these words. The North Koreans, equipped with heavy Russian-made T-34 tanks, rolled through the American lines. In this first encounter the Americans had not a single tank, nor antitank mine, nor armor-penetrating bazooka. On July 8 General Dean informed MacArthur: "I am convinced that the North Korean Army ... [has been] underestimated."

The summer of 1950 was a bitter season. Not since the Civil War had the percentage of casualties among high-ranking officers of a U.S. army been so great. Outfought and outnumbered, the American soldiers sloshed through the steaming rice paddies in a disorderly retreat. General Dean was captured. American GIs were found lying in ditches with their hands bound behind their backs and bullet holes in their heads. The U.N. forces were driven all the way back to a small perimeter around Pusan. In six weeks the Americans had suffered 6,000 casualties, the South Korean forces 70,000.

But at the Pusan perimeter the Americans held. By September the North Koreans had been repulsed by fresh troops from the United States.

Japan's Emperor Hirohito was once considered a descendant of the gods upon whom no ordinary mortal might gaze. But a month after the occupation of Japan began, he made a precedent-shattering call on Supreme Commander MacArthur at the American embassy. This picture of their meeting was convincing proof to the Japanese that the old order had passed.

"Those are the flags of various gangster mobs and millionaires. Now shut up."   AUG. '50

Early in the Korean War, Warren Austin, U.S. ambassador to the U.N., said Russia was "assisting . . . the invaders"—and a top Soviet official admitted the North Koreans were using Soviet army equipment. In this Herblock cartoon a Russian officer scolds a North Korean soldier gazing apprehensively at the banners of the U.N. forces gathering against him.

Now that the enemy had been halted, the U.N. forces were ready to take the initiative. MacArthur decided on a bold tactic: to launch an amphibious assault far behind the North Korean lines at Inchon. "We shall land at Inchon," the general insisted, "and I shall crush them." And so he did. To carry out his brilliant scheme, MacArthur created the X Corps out of Army and Marine units. Early in the morning of September 15, Marines landed on Wolmi, the island which protected Inchon harbor. Taken completely by surprise, the North Koreans offered little resistance to the capture of Inchon. After some nasty fighting, Seoul, too, fell to the X Corps in late September.

In the southeast the Eighth Army stormed out of the Pusan perimeter and raced north, sometimes covering 30 miles a day. By the end of September the North Korean army had been shattered. Very few of those who had headed south across the parallel in June lived to recross it that fall. The triumph at Inchon had brought U.N. forces to the 38th Parallel by early October.

THE rapid change of fortunes confronted the United States and the U.N. with a crucial decision. Exponents of containment argued that since the North Korean invasion had been repulsed, the U.N. had achieved its objective; it should consolidate its lines on the 38th Parallel and negotiate a settlement. But MacArthur was eager to pursue the remnants of the North Korean army northward with the aim of preventing the enemy from regrouping; his larger purpose was to unite the peninsula.

Despite the grave risk that China might intervene, the Administration decided to abandon the containment policy in this instance. The Joint Chiefs ordered MacArthur to achieve "the destruction of the North Korean Armed Forces" and authorized him to cross the parallel. On October 7, 1950, the United Nations General Assembly endorsed the plan. A week later President Truman conferred with General MacArthur on Wake Island. Accounts of what took place vary widely, but on the basis of what MacArthur told him, Truman approved an advance to within a few miles of the Chinese border. Enemy resistance, MacArthur predicted, would be ended by Thanksgiving.

For several weeks it seemed that MacArthur's optimism was justified. The U.N. advance into North Korea gained steadily. On October 19 the North Korean capital of Pyongyang fell, and parachutists landing about 30 miles beyond trapped half of the North Korean army.

But on October 26 came a disquieting event: the capture of a Chinese Communist soldier. On November 1 Chinese troops badly cut up the 8th Regiment of the U.S. 1st Cavalry; it was, a spokesman reported, "a massacre like the one which hit Custer." Although the fact was still undetected by American intelligence, this isolated incident showed that the Chinese were ready to fight in full force; the gamble that China would not intervene had been lost.

The Chinese assault on the U.S. 1st Cavalry took place in the final week of political campaigning in America's midterm elections of 1950. After the Inchon victory, Democrats hoped to ride the crest of national pride in a triumphant war. But the Korean conflict was never a popular war, and the country was dismayed by its cost. By November 3, Election Day, casualties had reached 28,235, and these did not include dead, wounded and missing in the Chinese offensive. When the nation went to the polls, the newspapers were black with the unnerving news of the assault by Mao's troops.

In the election the Republicans picked up 28 seats in the House and five in the Senate. The gains were modest (the smallest in the House in an off-year election since 1934), and they left the Democrats still nominally in control, although by a narrow margin, in both houses. But the setback to Truman was more decisive than the figures indicated. A number of Administration supporters were ousted, including Senate Majority Leader Scott Lucas of Illinois and Majority Whip Francis Myers of Pennsylvania. A widely remarked feature of the elections was the power of what was now generally referred to as "McCarthyism." The Wisconsin senator received more invitations from G.O.P. candidates to speak in their states than all other senators combined, and he was credited with playing a part in the defeat of a number of Democrats. In Utah, Senator Elbert Thomas was ousted after 18 years in the Senate, in a campaign in which he was charged with being soft on Communism.

In California Congressman Richard M. Nixon exploited the McCarthyite issues to win a Senate seat from his Democratic opponent, Congresswoman Helen Gahagan Douglas. Nixon, who had first captured attention through his dogged pursuit of Alger Hiss in the House Un-American Activities Committee, linked Mrs. Douglas, as a former actress and the wife of Hollywood star Melvyn Douglas, to suspicions of Communist infiltration of the movie capital.

The main consequence of the 1950 elections was to fortify the opponents of Administration foreign policy. Shortly after the elections, heartened by their gains and no longer restrained by the ailing Senator Vandenberg, these critics began a "great debate" in the Senate on foreign affairs. Led by Senator Taft, they called for a re-examination of America's military and foreign policies and questioned whether the defense of Western Europe was vital to America's security.

Above all, Taft feared that obligations abroad might bankrupt America and lead to the destruction of the American system. "We cannot assume a financial burden in our foreign policy so great that it threatens liberty at home," Taft insisted. He found a strong supporter in Herbert Hoover, who argued that until Europe manned its own defenses, the United States should retreat to its own side of the Atlantic. "The foundation of our national policies," Hoover stated, "must be to preserve for the world this Western Hemisphere Gibraltar of Western civilization." In mid-February 1951 a majority of House Republicans endorsed Hoover's proposals. Not until April 4, 1951, did the Senate approve the sending of four additional divisions to Europe to fulfill American NATO commitments, and even then it advised the President to send no more troops to Western Europe without congressional authorization.

While Administration adversaries opposed a strong policy in Europe, they continued to favor a bold policy in Asia. They had no patience with the conception of "limited war," which they felt implied that America could not defeat its enemies. Much of the country shared this impatience, for history had not prepared Americans for the impasse in Korea.

I N late November 1950 Americans in Korea were optimistic about an early triumph. No Chinese had been seen for nearly three weeks. American commanders were convinced that there were only a few "volunteers" in Korea trying to bluff U.N. forces away from the Yalu River line. Actually, Mao's men, moving by night, were streaming across the Yalu. By mid-November 180,000 Chinese lay in the path of the Eighth Army, while 120,000 more were hidden in the mountains surrounding the Changjin Reservoir on the flank of the X Corps.

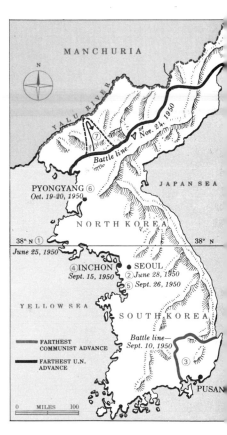

THE KOREAN WAR:

JUNE-NOVEMBER 1950

As shown above, both sides made their deepest penetration early in the Korean War. After crossing the 38th Parallel (1), the North Koreans quickly took Seoul (2), South Korea's capital. United Nations troops were driven south as far as the defense line shown around Pusan (3). Then the U.N.'s amphibious attack at Inchon (4) turned the tide. U.N. units recaptured Seoul (5) and seized Pyongyang (6), capital of North Korea. Patrols reached the Yalu River (7) as the U.N. advance neared high tide. But the U.N. forces had blundered into a trap (map, page 61).

Chairman of the Joint Chiefs of Staff Omar Bradley was a whipping boy for America's shocking unpreparedness in the Korean War. But Bradley was quickly exonerated: The $18 billion budget request for arms had been cut to $14.3 billion by economy-minded officials. Most importantly, ground troops had been neglected in favor of the nation's nuclear strike forces.

On November 24 MacArthur launched an "end the war" offensive. He promised his troops that they would be home for Christmas dinner. The next night the Chinese Communists struck in force. In a few days the outnumbered U.N. forces were reeling back. In sub-zero cold, through the icy month of December, they retreated steadily. The Marine survivors of the battle at the Changjin Reservoir beat a painful retreat in weather so bad that it took as many American fighting men as did the enemy. Ultimately the men of the X Corps made their way to the sea, where they were evacuated. The Chinese pushed the U.N. forces out of all the territory they had won in North Korea, again penetrated south of the 38th Parallel and recaptured Seoul.

MACARTHUR, who in September had been the hero of the Inchon maneuver, found himself in December the object of sharp criticism in the American press. He was censured for minimizing the strength of the Chinese and for deploying his troops so ineptly that they could be overwhelmed by lightly equipped Chinese infantry. Under assault, MacArthur issued public and private statements which hinted that blame for the discouraging situation in Korea lay on Washington.

As early as August 1950, the general had sent a message to the Veterans of Foreign Wars which by implication characterized the President's policy in the Far East as one of "timidity or vacillation." MacArthur believed the purpose of the war was not merely to repel the North Koreans but to eradicate Communist influence in the entire Korean peninsula. He pressed for authorization to pursue enemy planes over the Chinese border, to employ Nationalist troops from Chiang Kai-shek in the fighting, and to blockade and bomb Communist China's "privileged sanctuary" beyond the Yalu.

Many Americans shared MacArthur's impatience. In December 1950 a Montana draft board refused to induct men until MacArthur had been given a free hand to use the atomic bomb in China, although another Hiroshima might have damaged America's reputation in Asia beyond repair. House Republican leader Joseph Martin protested: "If we are not in Korea to win, then this Administration should be indicted for the murder of thousands of American boys."

But the Truman Administration, chastened by its unhappy experience with a liberation policy, now embraced the old policy of containment more fervently than ever. It refused to permit actions which might lead to all-out war with Red China. Though the Joint Chiefs of Staff briefly entertained the thought of supporting MacArthur, they changed their minds when two of their members, investigating the Korean crisis personally, found the situation not nearly so desperate as MacArthur had represented it to be. The Eighth Army was holding its own under its new leader, Lieutenant General Matthew B. Ridgway, and plans were under way for a limited counterattack.

In late January Ridgway ordered the U.N. forces to move north. By March U.N. troops recaptured Seoul and once again crossed the 38th Parallel. With South Korea liberated, Truman and the U.N. representatives believed the time was ripe for negotiation. MacArthur was informed of these plans, yet on March 24 he issued a statement, clearly in conflict with American and U.N. diplomatic efforts, which threatened Red China with the possibility of an attack on its "coastal areas and interior bases." Truman later asserted that MacArthur's statement killed any hope for an early truce.

MacArthur had been repeatedly cautioned not to make statements which conflicted with U.N. policy. His last manifesto had reached a point of disobedience which no longer could be indulged. "By this act," Truman afterward reflected, "MacArthur left me no choice—I could no longer tolerate his insubordination." Still Truman did not act. But five days before his March 24 statement MacArthur had sealed his fate. He had written Republican leader Martin: "There is no substitute for victory." He claimed "that here we fight Europe's war with arms while the diplomats there still fight it with words." On April 5 Martin read this letter on the floor of the House.

Six days later Truman dismissed MacArthur on the ground that the general was "unable to give his wholehearted support to the policies of the United States Government." Stunned by the news, the country rallied to MacArthur. Telegrams and letters to the White House ran 20-1 against the President. Flags flew at half-mast. When Truman appeared at Griffith Stadium for the opening of the baseball season, he was booed by the crowd. A Gallup poll revealed that only 29 per cent of Americans interviewed supported him. G.O.P. leaders agreed that the general should be invited to address Congress and that there should be a probe of the Administration's policy. "In addition," Martin told newsmen bluntly, "the question of impeachments was discussed."

In a dramatic address to a joint meeting of Congress on April 19, 1951, MacArthur defended his opposition to limited war: "Why, my soldiers asked of me, surrender military advantages to an enemy in the field?" After a dramatic pause he went on: "I could not answer." He concluded his talk with a reference to a barracks-room ballad of his youth "which proclaimed most proudly that 'old soldiers never die; they just fade away.' And like the old soldier of that ballad, I now close my military career and just fade away, an old soldier who tried to do his duty as God gave him the light to see that duty. Good-by."

In his 34-minute address MacArthur was interrupted by fervent applause 30 times. Congressman Dewey Short of Missouri (who had been educated at Harvard, Oxford and Heidelberg) cried out that he had seen "God in the flesh, the voice of God." Herbert Hoover saw the general as "a reincarnation of St. Paul into a great General of the Army who came out of the East."

But the MacArthur frenzy failed to survive a congressional investigation that spring. From May 3 to June 25 the country learned that, contrary to MacArthur's claim, the Joint Chiefs of Staff supported the President against the general. Critics of MacArthur protested that his attack on the concept of limited war rested on the assumption that small losses in limited conflicts were unjustifiable while colossal losses in all-out war were acceptable. MacArthur's approach, General Omar Bradley, Chairman of the Joint Chiefs of Staff, observed, "would involve us in the wrong war, at the wrong place, at the wrong time, and with the wrong enemy."

B UT the ending of the MacArthur episode did not stop the controversy over the Korean War and America's foreign policy. A week after the general's dismissal, Senator Vandenberg died. With his moderating influence gone, the conservatives led by Senator Taft made a bold bid to win control of the Republican party and, in the 1952 elections, of the government. Before long Taft, who had once supported American participation in the Korea conflict, was calling it an "unnecessary war," and "a Truman war."

In his campaign for the Republican presidential nomination Taft was supported by a majority of the G.O.P. delegation in Congress. But internationalist

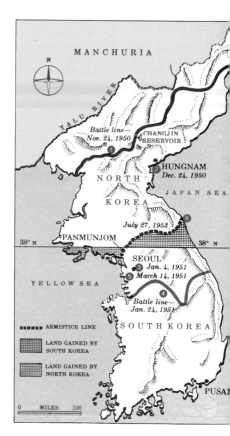

THE KOREAN WAR:

CHANGJIN TO PANMUNJOM

The war was five months old when United Nations forces, renewing the offensive along the battle line (1), were sent reeling backward by Chinese Communist attacks. One group, cut off at Changjin Reservoir, had to fight through to Hungnam (2) to be evacuated. In retreat, the U.N. forces again gave up Seoul (3) before they formed an effective defense line (4). Then a new U.N. offensive retook Seoul (5). For two years, during truce talks at Panmunjom, the fighting seesawed along the 38th Parallel. A dotted line (6) marks the front at the signing of the armistice.

61

This photograph of Adlai Stevenson's campaign-worn shoe (above) provided a light moment in the hard-fought 1952 presidential campaign. Later, when a riot erupted in an Illinois prison, Governor Stevenson sped home and halted it (below). Republican Richard M. Nixon was quick to assert that Stevenson was more interested in a local riot than in the Korean war.

party members disapproved of Taft's record of isolationism and doubted that he could win. They hoped to draft a man who was a national hero and who had never sought political office: General of the Army Dwight D. Eisenhower, then serving as Supreme Commander of NATO forces in Europe, having taken a leave of absence from his duties as president of Columbia University. There was, however, doubt that "Ike," as he was affectionately known, would be willing to run—and even some question that he was a Republican.

On January 6, 1952, after flying to Paris to confer with the general, Senator Henry Cabot Lodge told a crowded press conference in Washington that Eisenhower was in the race "to the finish." In France the NATO commander confirmed that he was a Republican and that he would not interfere with Lodge's move to enter him in the New Hampshire primary that spring. Despite Ike's absence in Europe while Taft stumped New Hampshire, the general defeated the senator in the primary by 10,000 votes.

Yet Taft showed strength too. He edged out Eisenhower at the North Carolina state convention and on one day won primaries in Wisconsin and Nebraska. If the general were to wage an effective campaign, he would have to return to America. Accordingly Eisenhower asked to be relieved as NATO commander.

E ISENHOWER'S first campaign speech—at his home town of Abilene, Kansas, on June 4—proved disappointing. It was clear that he needed an issue to bolster his claim that he was the candidate of "the people" running against the organization politician, Taft. He found one in the swiftly developing battle for control of the 38 convention votes of Texas.

Some weeks earlier Eisenhower's supporters in Texas, finding the Taft forces in control of the Republican state convention, had organized a rump convention and elected a rival slate of delegates. The general's backers claimed the Taft people were trying to steal the delegation; Ike denounced the Taft backers as "rustlers" who had purloined "the Texas birthright." The case against Taft was a weak one; many of Eisenhower's supporters in Texas were Democrats who had voted in the Republican primaries, and Taft's organization denounced this invasion. But by convention time Eisenhower's backers had created the image of the general as the spokesman for clean government, while portraying Taft as a sordid manipulator.

When the credentials committee held its sessions in Chicago under the naked lights of the TV cameras, Taft's delegates appeared to bad advantage. Amid great uproar, the Eisenhower delegates were seated. When the voting on candidates began, the general won the nomination on the first ballot. For its vice presidential nominee, the convention chose 39-year-old Senator Richard M. Nixon of California, a decision which recognized both the importance of the Pacific Coast and the vote-getting potential of the Communist issue.

Eisenhower's enormous popularity would have made him a hard man to beat under the best of circumstances, and his chances were heightened by evidences of corruption in the Truman Administration. Assistant Attorney General T. Lamar Caudle was implicated in the acceptance of costly gifts from "fixers" and from persons accused of tax frauds. A Senate investigation had turned up a group of "five percenters," who peddled their influence in government for a commission. Very damaging was testimony that a company which wanted help in Washington had given the President's military aide, Harry Vaughan, a freezer and through Vaughan distributed other units to officials. Even more notoriety resulted from an investigation of the Reconstruction Finance Corporation by Senator Fulbright. Among other things, it was disclosed that the wife of a former RFC loan examiner had been aided in acquiring a $9,540 mink coat by an attorney for a firm which had applied for an RFC loan. Together with "deep-freeze" and "five percenter," "mink coat" became a symbol for immorality in the federal government.

With the Truman Administration tarred by the responsibility for scandal in Washington, the country looked for a new political figure to lead it once more onto the paths of righteousness. Some Democrats thought they might have such a leader in the lanky senator from Tennessee, Estes Kefauver. While the RFC probe was at its height, Kefauver was winning national attention by summoning gangsters before his special crime investigation committee. Little was actually achieved by the hearings, but the senator whipped up the country's indignation at the effrontery of gang leaders and the venality of local governments. Thousands stayed away from work to gaze at the televised hearings. Women ignored their children and their housework. In Philadelphia a man intently watched the hearings while fire swept his house.

In 1952 Kefauver, now a national figure, made a strong bid for the Democratic presidential nomination. A coonskin cap on his head, he turned up on street corners to shake hands with voters. He made a good showing in primaries, but he never had a chance. His liberal record had alienated fellow Southerners, and many liberals thought him an intellectual lightweight. More important, Democratic chieftains held him responsible for the defeat of party candidates in cities where graft was an issue, and he had antagonized party leaders by announcing his candidacy before Truman had bowed out of the race.

Truman himself set out to win the nomination for a man little known to the American people: Adlai E. Stevenson. A graduate of Princeton whose grandfather had been Vice President in Cleveland's second term, Stevenson was the articulate and witty governor of Illinois, and he had a varied career of government service behind him. But with typical reticence and self-doubt, Stevenson refused to run. By the eve of the Chicago convention a draft-Stevenson movement had built up tremendous momentum. As Democratic governor of the host state, Stevenson welcomed the delegates with an eloquent speech that ruined whatever hope he might still have held of avoiding the nomination. He was nominated on the third ballot.

I N his acceptance speech, Stevenson set the tone of his campaign: "The ordeal of the Twentieth Century—the bloodiest, most turbulent era of the Christian age—is far from over. Sacrifice, patience, understanding and implacable purpose may be our lot for years to come. Let's face it. Let's talk sense to the American people. Let's tell them the truth, that there are no gains without pains, that we are now on the eve of great decisions. . . ."

In the remarkable campaign that followed, Stevenson told voters some hard truths. He warned the American Legion that a veteran was someone who owed America more than the nation owed him. He told a Labor Day rally in Detroit that he did not think the Taft-Hartley Act was a slave-labor law. In Richmond, Virginia, the governor announced his support of a program of civil rights for blacks. Stevenson captivated intellectuals with his incisive wit, his eloquence, and his troubled recognition of the problems the world faced and the need for intelligence and fortitude to meet them. But everyone knew

In the tradition of Davy Crockett, Estes Kefauver wore a coonskin cap as his trademark in his bid for the 1952 Democratic presidential nomination. Kefauver was strong in his native Tennessee, but he had almost no national organization. He did most of his campaigning on his own, inspiring Daniel Fitzpatrick to caption the above cartoon "The Lone Ranger."

that support by the intellectuals—or, in a word born during the campaign, the "eggheads"—did not add up to many votes on Election Day.

At the outset, the inexperienced Eisenhower proved a poor campaigner, but gradually he began to find himself. He was assisted by a large-scale advertising campaign, and major cities were inundated with spot television commercials aimed at "selling" the candidate to the voters. But Eisenhower needed no selling. The popular response to the general was tremendous and spontaneous. People who shouted "I like Ike" meant it. Americans warmed to his radiant grin, were cheered by his salute with both hands raised above his head, and were heartened by the man's fundamental decency and humility.

Satirizing Eisenhower's ineffectual resistance to McCarthyism, this Herblock cartoon has Ike brandishing a feather as a warning to the senator to "Have a care, sir." While the President often defended his Administration against Joe McCarthy's attacks, Eisenhower never replied in kind because, as he privately said, "I will not get in the gutter with that guy."

THE only serious problem the general faced was the division in the party caused by the failure of Taft to win the nomination. Taft himself gave Eisenhower a formal endorsement, but left the impression that he might choose to sit out the campaign. To win Taft to his cause, Eisenhower invited the Ohioan to the house in New York's Morningside Heights that he had occupied as president of Columbia University. Taft emerged with the announcement that he had won Ike's acceptance of a manifesto he had drafted which embodied the conservative viewpoint on domestic affairs. Eisenhower, the senator declared, was in accord with Taft's view that the main threat to the country's liberty came from the "constant growth of big government" and that the main issue of the campaign was liberty against "creeping socialization." Taft conceded that he and Eisenhower were not wholly in accord on foreign policy, but the senator thought the differences were only "differences of degree." The Morningside Heights conference healed the rupture in the party. Taft began to campaign actively. Democratic critics charged that Eisenhower had "surrendered," but the pact suggested less that the candidate had capitulated to Taft than that his views were unexpectedly close to Taft's.

Eisenhower's critics also took issue with his attitude toward McCarthyism. McCarthy and his followers posed a special problem for Eisenhower: They were party colleagues, but they had engaged in vicious criticism of Ike's old chief and patron, General Marshall. McCarthy had accused Marshall of being part of "a conspiracy so immense, an infamy so black, as to dwarf any previous such venture in the history of man." Nonetheless Eisenhower permitted McCarthy to ride on his campaign train in Wisconsin, and when the general spoke in Milwaukee, he deleted a paragraph praising Marshall. Eisenhower also repeated the charge that the Democrats were soft on Communism. ("We have seen this sort of thing go on and on until my running mate, Dick Nixon, grabbed a police whistle and stopped it.") Nixon, for his part, called Stevenson "Adlai the appeaser . . . who got a Ph.D. from Dean Acheson's College of Cowardly Communist Containment."

Young, vigorous, a hard fighter, Nixon delighted the Republican regulars. But on September 18 the New York *Post* revealed that Nixon, as senator, had been subsidized by California millionaires through a secret fund which, it subsequently developed, totaled $18,000 in a year and a half. Nixon's conservative voting record left him open to the charge that by his votes on taxation and housing he was repaying the men who had financed him.

For a party crusading against Democratic immorality, nothing could have been more embarrassing. Eisenhower insisted that if Nixon was to stay on the ticket he would have to demonstrate that he was "as clean as a hound's tooth." But before deciding whether to ditch Nixon, Ike agreed to wait until the senator had made a public defense on radio and TV.

An estimated 55 million Americans turned their dials to Nixon that night as he told the Horatio Alger story of his life: his rise from poor circumstances (as a boy he had worked in a grocery store); his war record in the South Pacific ("I guess I'm entitled to a couple of stars . . . but I was just there when the bombs were falling"); and his wife Pat who did not have a mink coat but did have "a respectable Republican cloth coat." Nixon related that a supporter had sent his little girls a dog that his daughter had named Checkers. "And you know the kids, like all kids, love the dog, and I just want to say this right now, that regardless of what they say about it, we're going to keep it."

Nixon's critics called it a slick soap-opera performance, but the Republicans were deluged with messages approving Nixon. When Nixon flew to Wheeling, West Virginia, Eisenhower, with tears in his eyes, extended his hand and said: "Dick, you're my boy." With the ticket reunited and Nixon far more popular than he had been, the Republicans were stronger than ever.

The formula for the Republican campaign was, in Senator Karl Mundt's words, K_1C_2—Korea, corruption and Communism. Of this trinity of issues, Korea was much the most potent. After U.N. forces turned back three Chinese offensives in the spring of 1951 with heavy losses, the Communists had agreed to armistice negotiations. Month after month, the truce parley dragged on. Meanwhile, to bring pressure on the negotiators, the Americans launched periodic limited offensives. In the summer and fall of 1951, thousands died to take insignificant knobs on Bloody Ridge or Heartbreak Ridge. Although there were no large engagements, casualties continued to mount, and it seemed as though this war might go on forever, hopelessly, pointlessly.

One consequence of the Korean War appeared, on the surface, to benefit Democrats. The war detonated a skyrocketing economic boom in the United States which brought the country unparalleled prosperity. But even this was turned against the Democrats, for the war boom was steeped in guilt. Prosperity seemed to have been paid for in blood. Moreover, along with the boom came higher prices—and, inevitably, the hated controls.

ON October 24 in Detroit, Eisenhower delivered the master stroke of the campaign. The general pledged to bring the war in Korea to "an early and honorable end." To achieve this, he promised, "I shall go to Korea."

On Election Day, Eisenhower won a landslide victory: 442 electoral votes to Stevenson's 89. Eisenhower was the first Republican candidate since 1928 to break the Democratic hold on the "Solid South," taking Virginia, Tennessee, Florida and Texas. But the triumph was a personal one for Ike rather than for his party. The G.O.P. had a House majority of only eight and an even split in the Senate; Vice President Nixon's vote, however, gave them a margin of one in case of a tie.

For Eisenhower the greatest challenges still lay ahead. He faced fearful tasks: to terminate the fighting in Korea without loss of honor or prestige; to accommodate to the revolution of rising expectations in the colonial world; to curb McCarthy, now nearing the apex of his power, and bring the era of bad feeling to a close. To these tasks, Eisenhower brought the advantage of enormous prestige. As 20 years of Democratic rule came to an end, the most crucial issue of all was what the new President would do with his great power.

Some political sages had predicted a long struggle for the 1952 Republican presidential nomination. But the delegates selected General Eisenhower on the first ballot, leaving "Mr. Republican," Robert Taft, as a political wallflower for the third time. It proved a wise choice; no matter what language it was said in, the voters—55.14 per cent of them—really liked Ike.

A FATEFUL VOTE, to commit U.N. forces in Korea, is taken by the Security Council in what has been called "the gravest decision in U.N. history." The resolution was approved on June 27, 1950. Just eight days later Americans were in combat in Korea.

A savage war for world security

THE Korean War began at 4 a.m. on June 25, 1950, when the People's Democratic Republic of Korea (North Korea), performing on strings pulled by Moscow, executed a carefully planned attack on the Republic of Korea (South Korea) across the 38th Parallel, which had divided the country since the end of World War II. On July 27, 1953, the conflict drew to an uneasy close along the same boundary, almost exactly where it had started. An armistice was signed at Panmunjom by an American general representing the United Nations and a Russian-born Korean general representing the North Korean People's Army and the Chinese Communist forces.

During the more than three years of fierce fighting, the tide of battle raged back and forth across the jumbled mountains and rough valleys of that inhospitable peninsula *(map, page 63)*. Seoul, the capital of South Korea, changed hands four times. Some two million servicemen from 18 countries were killed or wounded fighting for tracts of primitive wilderness. But issues of transcendent importance were at stake in Korea. The original invasion had been a Communist challenge—a blatant defiance of the United Nations. For the first time in history, a world community of nations had voted *(above)* to take arms "to repel . . . armed attack and to restore international peace and security." And the United States, in assuming the main burden of the U.N.'s commitment, had made it inescapably clear to the Communist powers that Americans were willing to fight and to die to resist aggression in faraway lands.

A RIPPLE OF ROCKETS rises over the central Korean front, as American Marines help to repel a Communist offensive in 1951. The rockets' blast revealed the position of the battery, and moments after the photograph was taken, the Marines had to pull out to escape return fire. The rockets, and most of the weapons used in Korea, were of World War II vintage.

GRIMACING WITH PAIN, a wounded Marine is carried to the rear by South Koreans during the U.N.'s fierce fight to hold the Pusan perimeter.

HURLING A GRENADE, a Marine rushes up to defend the crest of a hill against North Korean troops attacking from the next hill. This rain-drenched clash was part of U.N. efforts to expand the Pusan perimeter in September 1950.

Utter devastation is caught in an aerial photograph of the 1.5-million-barrel-a-year oil refinery at Wonsan inside North Korea. Despite

Mastery of the air—and
a hectic, scrambling retreat

CROSSING A RICE PADDY, American Marines dodge bursts of fire from enemy machine guns on the crests of nearby hills. Lying in their path is the body of a North Korean soldier.

IN JUNE 1950, when the North Koreans drove south across the 38th Parallel, they expected to triumph in one swift stroke. Top American generals believed that such aggression "could be neutralized by air action."

On both sides the appraisals proved to be wrong. By July 10 the United Nations had destroyed North Korea's air force and had landed troops to slow the invasion. But the first U.N. units, Americans fresh from soft billets in Japan, were in poor shape for long, hard combat. Even worse, their training had conditioned them to fighting in a continuous battle line; they often panicked when separated by the enemy's deep thrusts. General Douglas MacArthur realized that the U.N.'s air supremacy meant little without enough infantry to hold the ground.

Through the terrible weeks of July the Americans alternately fought and fled, struggling to buy time for the U.N. buildup. Early in August they managed to set up a thin defense perimeter around the port of Pusan at the bottom of the peninsula. General Walton Walker told them: "There will be no more retreating, withdrawal, or . . . anything else you want to call it." The U.N. troops finally had their continuous battle line, and they held.

overwhelming air superiority, which made it possible to inflict such heavy bomb damage, U.N. forces were almost driven into the sea.

U.N. vehicles and civilians flee across the flats from Seoul as the victorious Chinese occupy the South Korean capital in January of 1951.

In North Korea, a swift advance, a shattering defeat

Elated by the success of the Inchon break-out, General MacArthur mustered fresh troops to chase enemy remnants north across the 38th Parallel. On November 24, 1950, he confidently announced an attack that he believed would win the victory. But just four days later he reported: "This command . . . is now faced with conditions beyond its control and strength."

Two U.N. forces, rushing pell-mell toward the Manchurian border, had run into a trap. Their scattered units were hit hard by some 300,000 Chinese. Blowing bugles, the tough Chinese charged in waves, disregarding their own losses of life.

The U.N. troops resisted fiercely. In the freezing mountain passes around Changjin Reservoir, some 19,000 Marines and GIs held back up to 100,000 Chinese for several days. In the end these troops had to fight a cruel retreat *(below and opposite)*, and all the U.N. units were driven south over ground they had paid dearly to take. Again, Americans had suffered a smashing defeat.

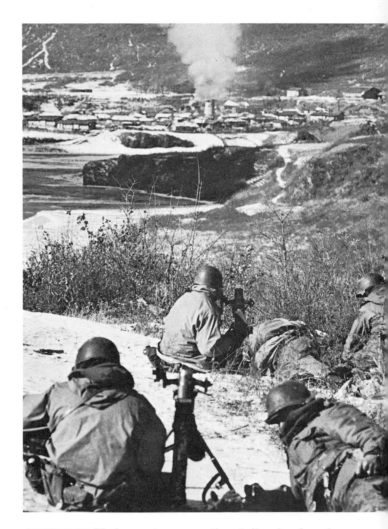

Only the wounded ride as U.S. Marines retreat in sub-zero cold.

AT THE YALU, GIs fire mortars across the winding river boundary—and over Chinese territory—to hit Korean targets. They were repulsed in the Chinese onslaught of November 1950.

DOWN FROM THE MOUNTAINS, Marines retreat along the road known as "Nightmare Alley." Their group suffered 7,500 casualties before reaching Hungnam to be evacuated.

A COMMUNIST GENERAL is given a hearing by weary American negotiators in the Peace Pagoda at Panmunjom. Both sides agreed not to start any major offensive during the truce talks.

Deadlock on the front and at the conference table

THE Chinese armies, swollen to a half-million men, renewed their onslaught on January 1, 1951, and cleared the U.N. troops out of North Korea. By January 25 the battle line spanned the peninsula well south of Seoul. But on that day the U.N. forces launched a counteroffensive, and in April they drove most of the Chinese back into North Korea. On June 23, with the front more

or less stabilized just north of the 38th Parallel, the Russian delegate to the United Nations proposed cease-fire talks between the warring parties.

The armistice conference convened for the first time at Kaesong on July 10. Here, and later at Panmunjom, the talks ran from propaganda speeches to bitter wrangling and brief breakdowns. The war of words would last two years; meanwhile the shooting war seesawed in minor but unremitting action. Russian-built jet fighter planes made raids, then fled to safety in their Manchurian sanctuary beyond the Yalu River. Thousands of Marines and GIs died fighting savagely for shell-torn hills named Bloody, Pork Chop, Arrowhead and Heartbreak.

AN AIRLIFT by helicopter lands a Marine unit on Heartbreak Ridge six men at a time. In mountainous Korea, this novel ferrying service saved vital hours of arduous travel by truck.

A NIGHT FIGHT flares up as Marines meet an assault by waves of screaming Chinese. Amid streaking tracer bullets appear the large explosions of heavy mortar shells.

73

VISITING THE FRONT, President-elect Eisenhower joins GIs at lunch in December 1952. In his campaign he promised, "I shall go to Korea," but stressed that he had no "trick solution."

In truce without victory, a legacy of bitterness

IN the spring of 1953, truce negotiators at Panmunjom agreed on a system for exchanging prisoners of war. With this main issue settled, the armistice was signed on July 27, and the guns finally fell silent along the front.

Some 3,700 American prisoners of war returned, many of them wounded or suffering from shock. They shuffled into reception centers to tell gruesome prison stories of executions, brutality and the destructive psychological techniques of "brainwashing." More than a few cried as the truth dawned on them that they were actually free. And the U.S. command realized with horror that more than 6,000 Americans had perished as captives.

In the first year of fighting a GI said, "It's the war we can't win, we can't lose, we can't quit." His bitterness was shared by most Americans in the grim aftermath of this "limited," victoryless conflict. Yet the United Nations had achieved all its objectives in Korea, and to many this gave renewed hope that Communist aggression could be contained without an atomic holocaust.

A BEWILDERED SOLDIER weeps with joy after being set free in a prisoner exchange at Panmunjom. "It's too good to be true," he kept repeating. "You're all so good to me."

4. THE
MIDDLE OF
THE ROAD

THE 33,936,000 Americans who voted Dwight D. Eisenhower into the presidency in 1952 did so for a variety of reasons. Some believed that he, as a nonpolitical figure of great stature, could restore national unity. Some anticipated that he would use his immense prestige to move the nation in new directions. Many Republicans who had never been reconciled to the changes wrought by Roosevelt and Truman hoped that he would do away with these innovations. But some seem to have backed him primarily because they hoped he would liberate them from the oppressive burdens of politics.

The country was to discover that it was not easy to turn away from public affairs. The United States was a mighty power in a world threatened by Communist tyranny and the disaster of thermonuclear war. To achieve national unity, it might for the moment postpone facing up to critical problems, but the problems would not go away.

The path to America's future, Eisenhower once stated, was "down the middle." To achieve the middle way, Ike sought to achieve a "revolution" in the national government, "trying to make it smaller rather than bigger and finding things it can stop doing instead of seeking new things for it to do." Eisenhower, more conservative than most supposed, would often find the middle of the road in domestic affairs, but only after veering well to the right.

The President's Cabinet was an index to his political orientation. Eisenhower named Charles E. Wilson, president of General Motors, as Secretary of

A POPULAR LEADER, Dwight D. Eisenhower is seen amid mementos of his military career. His appeal prompted a multitude of Democrats to vote for him as President.

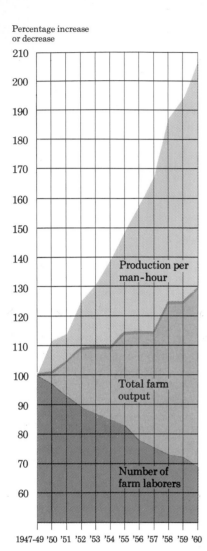

Percentage increase
or decrease

Production per
man-hour

Total farm
output

Number of
farm laborers

1947-49 '50 '51 '52 '53 '54 '55 '56 '57 '58 '59 '60

A FARM TREND: FEWER
MEN, GREATER YIELD

America's swift advances in agricultural automation and technology during the 1950s created major political and sociological problems. From 1949 to 1960 production rose almost one third (center of chart) while the number of farm workers (bottom of chart) fell off by about the same amount. Total productivity per man-hour (at top of chart) more than doubled. Pushing buttons, a single farmer in 10 minutes could feed 400 cows and 500 pigs. A few years before, it would have taken five men half a day. The result: an emptying countryside and a vast glut of many farm products. This trend continued in the 1960s. Displaced farm workers flocked to cities where they added to the problems urban areas were facing.

Defense; George Humphrey, president of M. A. Hanna Company, to be Secretary of the Treasury; two wealthy former General Motors dealers, Douglas McKay and Arthur Summerfield, to the posts of Secretary of the Interior and Postmaster General; and a New England industrialist, Sinclair Weeks, as Secretary of Commerce. Secretary of State John Foster Dulles had been a wealthy corporation lawyer. Other appointees were generally of a conservative stamp: Secretary of Agriculture Ezra Benson; Attorney General Herbert Brownell Jr.; and as head of the newly formed department of Health, Education and Welfare, Mrs. Oveta Culp Hobby, wife of a wealthy Texas publisher. The one marked exception was Secretary of Labor Martin Durkin, a Stevenson man who had been president of the international plumbers' union. The Cabinet, suggested one writer, consisted of "eight millionaires and a plumber." By September 1953 Durkin had resigned.

Many were dismayed that Eisenhower, who was regarded as the spokesman for the national interest, had chosen a Cabinet that appeared to represent only a single interest. Even before the Administration took office, Wilson added fuel to the fire. In the midst of hearings on his appointment (which aroused concern over a possible conflict of interest, since General Motors was the largest single contractor to the Defense Department), Wilson announced: "I thought what was good for our country was good for General Motors, and vice versa." Circulated in a twisted form ("What is good for General Motors is good for the country"), the remark reinforced the impression in some quarters that big business had captured the government. The impression was not diminished when Douglas McKay remarked, "We're here in the saddle as an administration representing business and industry."

The most influential Cabinet member was Secretary of the Treasury Humphrey, a man whom the President admired and trusted. "In Cabinet meetings," Eisenhower said, "I always wait for George Humphrey to speak. . . . I know that when he speaks he will say just what I am thinking."

Humphrey and Eisenhower shared a common fear of inflation and a distaste for deficits. Their determination to maintain a stable dollar was to set the guidelines for the Administration's policy in both foreign and domestic affairs. Under Humphrey's aegis the Administration immediately sought to cut back federal spending, meanwhile raising interest rates. Government bonds slumped, and by May *Business Week* was grumbling: "We are glad to know the brakes work, but we don't want to go through the windshield." Within a few weeks, Humphrey was softening his tight-money approach.

MEANWHILE, as part of the major change in government he hoped to achieve, Eisenhower advanced the "partnership" theory for the development of the nation's resources. Instead of relying so largely on the federal government, as Roosevelt and Truman had, he proposed to encourage development by local governments and by private interests. Federal dam projects were shelved, regulatory agencies were staffed with men sympathetic to the utilities, and the offshore oil lands were turned over to the adjacent states.

Six months after he took office, Eisenhower explained that he was trying to roll back the "creeping socialism" of the past 20 years, and he cited expansion of the Tennessee Valley Authority. The attempt to circumvent TVA led the President into the major embarrassment of his first term.

Instead of permitting TVA to build a steam plant to provide power for the

Memphis area, the Administration authorized the Atomic Energy Commission to contract with the Dixon-Yates utility combine to produce the power. Democrats protested that the deal not only amounted to a giveaway to the utilities, but that it had been negotiated under suspicious circumstances. In February 1955 a Senate committee revealed that one Adolphe Wenzell had served as a consultant to the Budget Bureau while he was financially connected with the Dixon-Yates combine. The following July the President canceled the contract. When Dixon-Yates sued to recoup its losses, the Department of Justice responded that the contract, in which the Administration had taken such pride, had been illegal and "contrary to the public interest" from the very beginning. Fought up to the Supreme Court, the case was finally decided against the utility.

Joseph W. Martin became Speaker of the House when the Republicans roared back into the congressional majority in 1946. The title of Speaker was ironic for Martin. As a boy he had stuttered so badly that he often wept with embarrassment. But he would "cry and fight like hell all at the same time."

AMONG the most intractable of all the problems that Eisenhower confronted was the farm question. Even in boom times, the farmer had been in serious trouble. Although the farm population decreased by nearly seven million in the 1950s, output grew so remarkably that production vastly outstripped demand. Each year fewer farmers raised a greater yield; each year the surpluses mounted. To bolster rural income, the Truman Administration had maintained high, rigid price supports.

Benson's program of flexible and lower price supports on certain commodities, which replaced the previous schedule of fixed supports, was a costly failure. In addition he restricted credit and curtailed the rural electrification program. Market prices continued to drop, and from 1952 to 1956 the farmer's share of the national income fell from 6.4 per cent to scarcely 4.1 per cent. In sections of the Midwest Benson's name was anathema. A Missouri tenant farmer complained: "We've been plagued by one year of flood, three years of drought and two years of Benson." The Administration was compelled to compromise on various new forms of subsidies. By 1959 the government was spending six times as much on agriculture as in 1952.

When Sam Rayburn was a young boy he knew exactly what job he wanted: Speaker of the House of Representatives. Elected to Congress in 1912, he was later Speaker for an unprecedented 17 years. "Mr. Sam" spent nearly half a century in the House and said of it: "I love the House of Representatives."

Benson's experience was typical. There was often a wide gap between the Eisenhower Administration's generally conservative doctrine and its practice. When a cut in government spending triggered a moderate recession in 1953-1954, Humphrey borrowed New Deal techniques, including a tax cut, an increase in social security payments and extension of unemployment compensation, to help bring the country through the downturn by late 1954. After Eisenhower's eight years in office, the federal government was intervening in the economy in much the same fashion as when he entered the White House. Moreover, despite his belief in fiscal responsibility, his two Administrations accumulated a deficit of $21.9 billion; the $12.4 billion deficit of 1959 set a peacetime record. The Eisenhower budgets ran higher than all but one of the Truman budgets.

Yet Eisenhower's concept of the presidency was attuned to the mood of moderation. Convinced that Roosevelt and Truman had overstepped the bounds of proper executive action with regard to Congress, Eisenhower sought to "restore" the balance between the executive and legislative branches. He limited his own role to one of suggesting policies and then leaving congressmen free to "vote their own consciences." Nor did Eisenhower believe in imposing his will on his own Administration. He organized his staff on military lines, with Sherman Adams, former governor of New Hampshire, charged with regulating the flow of information to the President. Critics objected that this military staff arrangement limited the President to policies that had been screened and approved by his subordinates, and that he was extraordinarily isolated from information that did not flow through channels.

Eisenhower's reluctance to use his authority either with respect to Congress or in the councils of his party left him at the mercy of right-wing Republicans who seemed determined to assert their supremacy over the Executive. The President had fair success in his relations with Taft, but after the Ohioan died of cancer on July 31, 1953, G.O.P. conservatives became more rambunctious. They killed or delayed action on a series of domestic proposals. And they came within an ace of tying the President's hands in foreign affairs through the proposed "Bricker Amendment" that would have curbed the negotiation of executive agreements and limited the legal effect of treaties. By December 1953 Eisenhower was so vexed with Republicans in Congress that he contemplated forming a new third party.

Only the aid of the Democrats in both houses saved Ike from an almost total rout. In 1953 he was successful on 74 issues; Democratic votes accounted for 58 of his victories. The elections of 1954, in which the Democrats won a majority of one in the Senate and of 29 in the House, proved a blessing in disguise. Although during the campaign Eisenhower had warned that a Democratic victory could bring "a cold war of partisan politics," the Democratic Congress backed him on nearly 50 per cent of the issues it voted upon.

E ISENHOWER'S concept of his office also affected his relations with Senator McCarthy. McCarthy quickly took advantage of Eisenhower's belief in the limited powers of the President to run roughshod over the executive branch. Some of Eisenhower's advisers, and much of the country, urged the President to do battle with McCarthy, but he refused. When McCarthy rampaged through the Administration's foreign affairs agencies, neither Eisenhower nor Dulles attempted to stop him. Indeed, Dulles named a McCarthyite as the State Department's security officer, refrained from making diplomatic appointments that might offend McCarthy and sacrificed State Department career officers who had aroused the animosity of right-wingers.

Alarmed by the fearful drop in morale in the Foreign Service, five highly respected retired career diplomats warned in a public letter that the effectiveness of the service was being destroyed; men of integrity had been dismissed, and those still serving were afraid to report the truth from abroad.

Dulles' acts won him no special treatment from McCarthy. The senator sent two youthful aides, Roy Cohn and G. David Schine, on an 18-day tour of Europe to unearth evidence of subversion in the overseas information program. By the time Cohn and Schine had concluded their whirlwind junket, they had made a laughingstock of themselves and of the United States government. Nonetheless, the State Department bowed to McCarthy's demands for the dismissal of men who had met the disfavor of his two aides.

By early 1954, McCarthy was after bigger game. When he directed his attention to the Army, Secretary Robert Stevens pursued a course similar to Dulles', and with as little benefit. When McCarthy insisted that there were "earmarks of dangerous espionage" in the Signal Corps at Fort Monmouth, New Jersey, Stevens obligingly suspended those the senator had accused, despite protests that the suspensions disrupted valuable work.

Ezra Taft Benson seemed the perfect choice for Secretary of Agriculture: He was born on a farm, studied agricultural economics and had worked as a county agricultural agent. But his steps toward a free market in agriculture enraged the farm population. In 1959 a group of Iowa farmers, with the approval of their Democratic governor, hanged Benson in effigy.

But McCarthy persisted. In January 1954 he focused on the inconsequential case of Major Irving Peress, a New York dental officer, who had received a routine promotion and an honorable discharge although he had refused to sign the Army loyalty certificate. The senator summoned Army officials, including Brigadier General Ralph Zwicker, to a subcommittee hearing. When Zwicker refused to reveal certain privileged information, McCarthy stormed: "You are a disgrace to the uniform. You're shielding Communist conspirators. . . . You're not fit to be an officer. You're ignorant."

At this point, furious at such treatment of an esteemed general, Stevens ordered two other officers not to go before the subcommittee. McCarthy called Stevens an "awful dupe" and ordered the Secretary himself to appear before him. Stevens went, determined to read a strong statement. Instead he consented to a "Memorandum of Agreement," which was an unmistakable triumph for McCarthy. The Army had been humiliated.

Now the Administration, at long last, decided to take a stand. On March 11, 1954, the Army charged that McCarthy and his staff had sought to gain preferential treatment for Private G. David Schine, who had been drafted soon after the Cohn-Schine tour. McCarthy retorted that the Army was using Schine as a "hostage" to halt the probe of Fort Monmouth. Four days later the subcommittee voted to investigate the Army before television cameras.

The television tribunal proved the undoing of McCarthy. The senator met his match in his subcommittee opponent, Senator John McClellan, and even more in the Army's counsel, Joseph Welch, a scholarly, soft-spoken Boston attorney. The televised hearings enabled many people to see McCarthy in operation for the first time: to watch him bully witnesses, make baseless insinuations and indulge in self-serving interruptions in his sarcastic voice.

There was one special moment when, with startling suddenness, the character of the senator was exposed. On June 9, 1954, McCarthy broke into Welch's questioning with a gratuitous and irrelevant assault on a young member of Welch's law firm who, he charged, had once belonged to the National Lawyers Guild, which was alleged to have Communist ties. For the first time, Welch himself seemed to understand the full infamy of McCarthy's methods. His face taut with anger, the lawyer turned to McCarthy and cried: "Until this moment, Senator, I think I never really gauged your cruelty or your recklessness. . . . I like to think I am a gentle man, but your forgiveness will have to come from someone other than me. . . . Have you no sense of decency, sir, at long last? Have you left no sense of decency?"

As Welch finished, there was a hush; then, in violation of all the rules of decorum in the Senate Caucus Room, the audience burst into applause. Press photographers laid down their cameras to join in the clapping. In the Senate Caucus Room, shunned by reporters and spectators, McCarthy spread out his hands in genuine bewilderment and asked what he had done wrong.

THROUGHOUT the McCarthy years, the Senate, with a few notable exceptions, had played an inglorious role. Now that McCarthy's fortunes were declining, the senators belatedly began to act. They voted to form a select committee to consider a motion by Senator Flanders of Vermont to censure McCarthy for his actions. After a bitter debate, the Senate softened the terms of the resolution and voted 67-22 to condemn rather than censure the senator's methods.

George Humphrey, head of the Treasury Department in Eisenhower's Cabinet, was a brilliant businessman. This Midwestern conservative (his mother spelled Roosevelt with a small r) became a top executive with the M. A. Hanna Company. "He would fire his own grandmother if she wasn't doing a good job," an associate said, "but he'd put her on a pension."

81

The vote ignored the real issues—McCarthy was castigated not for reckless accusations or for assaults on men's rights but for offenses against the decorum of the Senate—but it marked the end of McCarthyism.

When the 1954 elections gave the Democrats a majority of one in the Senate, McCarthy lost his chairmanship of the Permanent Investigations Subcommittee. By 1956 he had fallen so far out of sight that he did not attend his party's national convention. On May 2, 1957, he died of "acute hepatitic failure," his force largely spent, his name a symbol for an episode in American history remembered with guilt. In his entire anti-Communist crusade he had not been responsible for rooting a single Communist out of any sensitive agency or for a single constructive piece of legislation.

The effects of McCarthyism survived McCarthy, particularly in the field of foreign policy. In this area the Eisenhower Administration was in a difficult position from the outset, caught between its desire to pursue a middle course and its promise to develop a dynamic new program. Secretary of State Dulles brought an internationalist outlook to his post. Yet he was concerned over the size of the nation's burgeoning military establishment and over the heavy burden of taxation requested to support foreign commitments.

Impatient with containment—"treadmill policies which, at best, might perhaps keep us in the same place until we drop exhausted"—Dulles wanted to seize the initiative. First of all he proposed giving official support to the "liberation" of the captive peoples behind the Iron Curtain. The satellites were to be liberated not by force but "by intelligent care" and by the intensity of human indignation. Those who minimized the power of moral pressure and propaganda, he claimed, "just do not know what they are talking about."

Americans remitted their record-smashing 1951 taxes with a helpless shrug. The boss of a strip-tease joint complained that his girls were being taxed "as if they could strip forever." One cynic wrote: "One score and 19 years ago, our fathers brought forth upon this nation a new tax, conceived in desperation and dedicated to the proposition that all men are fair game."

DULLES placed no faith in the concept of limited war. On January 12, 1954, he announced that henceforth America would depend less on local defense and more on "the deterrent of massive retaliatory power." Dulles' speech, noted Merlo Pusey, a historian friendly to the Administration, marked "the zenith of the cold war." The flaw in the massive-retaliation doctrine, protested political scientist Henry Kissinger, was that it turned every dispute into an occasion for a war of nuclear annihilation.

In keeping with the policy of massive retaliation, the Eisenhower Administration had taken what was called a "New Look" at defense spending. Twice it slashed the budget recommended by the Joint Chiefs of Staff. The idea was to reduce costly ground forces and rely instead on nuclear weapons and a large Air Force to deliver them. Despite the cutbacks, the Administration claimed the United States was getting greater security—in the expression of the period, "a bigger bang for a buck."

All of these Eisenhower programs—liberation, massive retaliation, the New Look—appeared to spell out a bold departure from the policy of containment and moderation. In practice they were much more modest, in part because some of the very people who disliked containment also wanted him to bring peace and even a withdrawal from international obligations. Eisenhower's election had owed less to his proposals for new initiatives in world affairs than to dismay over the fighting and casualties in Korea.

Even before taking office, Eisenhower fulfilled his pledge to go to Korea. After his inspection he conceded: "We have no panaceas." He rejected the MacArthur policy of risking total war to achieve total victory and determined instead on carrying out the Truman policy of negotiation and containment. On March 5, 1953, Stalin died, raising the possibility of a thaw in the Cold War. Three weeks later the Communists in Korea suddenly eased their demands, and on July 27 a cease-fire agreement was signed at Panmunjom. The agreement was, in fact, an armed truce with the peninsula divided along the battle line which roughly approximated the 38th Parallel. The U.N. returned more than 75,000 North Korean and Red Chinese prisoners, but it held to the principle that had long held up the negotiations—that no prisoner was to be forcibly repatriated. In all, the U.N. got back 3,746 Americans, together with some 9,000 prisoners of other nationalities, most of them South Koreans. Some 22,000 North Koreans and Chinese captured by U.N. forces refused repatriation; 21 Americans and 326 others chose to remain with the Communists.

IN securing a cease-fire in Korea, the President had set the pattern for the rest of his years in office: Warlike rhetoric would give way to deeds of peace. Such was the case in Indochina. Since 1946 the French rulers of that colony had been fighting the Communist leader Ho Chi Minh. Since the war was extremely unpopular in France, the United States had met much of the expense. In the spring of 1954 the French position became critical. Red forces besieged a French and Indochinese army at the vital fortress of Dien Bien Phu. Dulles feared that if Indochina went under, the United States defense perimeter might be forced back as far south as Australia; Richard Nixon asserted: "It is impossible to lay down arms until victory is completely won." Nevertheless, Dien Bien Phu fell without armed intervention by America. In July at Geneva, Indochina was divided, with the northern sector going to the Communists.

In an attempt to salvage something from the Indochina disaster, Dulles put together a Southeast Asia Treaty Organization in September 1954 to contain Communist expansion. But SEATO was a fragile reed. The terms of peace denied the new Indochinese nations the right to participate, and several important Asian states, including India and Indonesia, refused to join. The only nations in or near Asia to join SEATO, other than Pakistan and Thailand, were countries with which the United States already had security pacts: Australia, New Zealand and the Philippines, an independent republic since 1946.

That same month, a new crisis was developing that would demonstrate the precariousness of America's Far Eastern policy. In 1950, to help keep the Korean War from spreading beyond the peninsula, the Truman Administration had sent the U.S. Seventh Fleet into the Formosa Strait to act as a barrier between Red China and the Nationalist island of Formosa (Taiwan). This act had been criticized by Republicans who wanted to encourage Chiang Kai-shek to invade the mainland. Once in office, Eisenhower had rescinded part of Truman's order, thus "unleashing" Chiang to attack the Communists. The fact is, the Nationalists were not strong enough to invade, but Eisenhower's act encouraged Chiang to garrison or reinforce some small islands near the Chinese coast—Quemoy, Matsu and the Tachens—as possible bases for assaults on the mainland. In September 1954, in response to Communist shelling of the islands, Chiang's planes raided Amoy on the mainland. Suddenly America's determination to support Chiang threatened to involve it—and the rest of the world—in a nuclear war with Red China.

Congress granted Eisenhower authority to use armed force to repel any Red

"How deep do you think it goes?" Mar. '54

When "dynamic doldrums" struck the American economy in 1953, the Administration was embarrassed. Above, recession-spelunker Eisenhower, as he anxiously peers into the recesses of the cavern, asks the elephant's advice. While some Republicans had denied the existence of a recession, others later claimed credit when it ended— hence the elephant's boast (below).

HERBLOCK

"It never existed—and I killed it" Jul. '54

Chinese attack in the strait, but the Administration indicated it would not defend the offshore islands unless they were assaulted as part of a larger operation to seize Formosa. Nevertheless the situation in the strait remained explosive.

The tension over Quemoy and Matsu seemed part of a pattern in Dulles' handling of foreign affairs. "The ability to get to the verge without getting into the war is the necessary art," he explained. If "you are scared to go to the brink, you are lost. We've had to look it square in the face—on the question of enlarging the Korean War, on the question of getting into the Indochina war, on the question of Formosa. We walked to the brink and we looked it in the face. We took strong action."

This statement created a furor. Critics vociferously challenged the historical accuracy of Dulles' version of these incidents. They also questioned the soundness of a policy of what immediately became known as "brinkmanship" in a world of nuclear terror—a terror given new dimensions by continuing technological developments. In August 1953 the Russians detonated a hydrogen bomb. In the spring of 1954 the United States exploded a bomb one hundred times as destructive as any previous man-made explosion.

The submarine "Nautilus," the world's first atomic ship and sixth U.S. naval vessel of that name, awaits its launching in 1954—"a splash heard 'round the world." The sub cost about $55 million. As knowledge of nuclear technology improved, "Nautilus" was able to steam more than 145,000 miles— mostly submerged—before having to recharge its nuclear reactor.

A^T the same time, a change in Russian policy suggested the possibility of easing tensions. Symbolic of the new turn was the Soviet Union's agreement in May 1955 to a peace treaty that made Austria a neutral state and terminated the long four-power military occupation there.

In July 1955 the heads of the United States, Russia, Great Britain and France met at Geneva in a summit conference that seemed permeated with good feeling. "The United States will never take part in an aggressive war," President Eisenhower told Soviet Premier Nikolai Bulganin. "Mr. President, we believe that statement," Bulganin responded. During the conference Eisenhower—who had advanced an "atoms for peace" plan to a U.N. session in December 1953 in the hope of turning nuclear power to peaceful uses—made a dramatic proposal. He suggested that the United States and the U.S.S.R. give each other complete blueprints of their military establishments and provide facilities for mutual aerial reconnaissance of military installations.

Nothing came of Eisenhower's suggestion, but he exuded such warmth and friendliness that it was impossible for anyone to depict him as a warmonger bent on world conquest. The Geneva parley did little save defer all the hard questions to a subsequent meeting of foreign ministers to be held that fall. But for the moment, Geneva was a brilliant personal triumph for the President.

In the summer of 1955, Eisenhower was at the height of his popularity. A national poll reported that 60 per cent of Democratic voters wanted him as their own candidate. The adulation of Ike rested on more than trust in him as a man of peace. He was also a promoter of domestic tranquility. The partisanship of the late Truman years had been mitigated, the harshness of the McCarthy time had been tempered. The force of his personality and his refusal to agitate issues had helped dissipate the rancor of 1952. "Everybody ought to be happy every day . . ." Eisenhower is reported to have said once. "Play hard, have fun doing it, and despise wickedness."

There was a new spirit of moderation in the United States. In part it resulted from the Eisenhower influence, in part from a number of social changes that had occurred in the postwar decade. One of these was the growth of the managerial-professional class. In 1956 government statistics indicated that, for the first time, fewer Americans were producing things than were engaged in middle-class occupations.

As workers moved up into the middle class, or as the fortunes of the lower middle class were enhanced, they fled the city. From 1950 to 1955, suburbs grew seven times as fast as the central cities. The Republicans were especially strong in this commuter country. In New York's suburbs the G.O.P. polled 70 per cent of the 1952 ballots for President.

In the world of the new middle class, less value was placed on individual achievement, more on a man's capacity to adapt to the standards of the group. The suburban-dweller characteristically was interested not in conquering new worlds but in attending to his own family, garden and home. "A sleeping sickness is spreading among the women of the land," complained Fannie Hurst. "They are retrogressing into . . . that thing known as the Home."

The sense of well-being owed much to the speedy recovery from the recession that had occurred during Eisenhower's early months in office. In September 1955 steel production climbed to 96 per cent of capacity; the continuing migration westward produced a remarkable growth on the Pacific Coast; the construction of the St. Lawrence Seaway brought ocean-going vessels to Chicago and Duluth and promised a bonanza for the Midwest.

The American worker rejoiced in record employment and the highest living standard ever. In 1955, under the pace-setting Walter Reuther, auto workers won from Ford an agreement to receive a substantial proportion of their wages in the first months of unemployment—in effect a partially guaranteed annual wage. Other employers followed suit. In December 1955 the American Federation of Labor and the Congress of Industrial Organizations merged as the AFL-CIO, adding new strength to the union movement.

On September 24, 1955, the President, while vacationing in Denver, suffered a heart attack of "moderate" severity. Americans followed every detail of the President's heartbeat, respiratory rate and intestinal tone. For weeks the President was unable to assume the burdens of office, and a "team" headed by Vice President Nixon in Washington and Sherman Adams at Lowry Air Force Base in Denver carried out some of the President's functions.

The illness seemed certain to limit Eisenhower to a single term of office. But Ike made a remarkable recovery. After a panel of doctors told reporters in February 1956 that the scar on the President's heart muscle had healed, he announced that he would run for a second term. Then in June 1956, he was stricken again—this time with an intestinal inflammation. He was operated on. Soon his doctors were announcing that his health was as good as ever.

WITH its candidates decided on in advance (although Harold Stassen made an abortive attempt to keep Nixon off the ticket), the Republican convention of 1956 went through its paces like a jaded company of actors. Even though Eisenhower's re-election seemed certain, the Democratic convention was more spirited. Competition for the Democratic nomination was stiff; Stevenson had to campaign vigorously in the primaries to defeat a strong bid by Estes Kefauver, and then had to fight off a new challenge in the convention from New York's Governor W. Averell Harriman, who was sponsored by Truman.

After winning the nomination, Stevenson announced, surprisingly, that he was leaving the choice of his running mate to the delegates. Kefauver was

Senator Ralph Flanders of Vermont moved to censure his fellow Republican, Senator McCarthy, in 1954. Although his opponent accused him of "senility," Flanders —who once said he was "antipink, antimink and antistink"— stuck to his guns. The Senate supported Flanders; McCarthy was never again a major political force.

As President, Eisenhower surmounted the personal trials of three serious illnesses, bouncing back each time with amazing resilience. Here seen recovering from his 1955 heart attack, Ike sports five gold Army stars and a silver one awarded by his doctor for "good conduct." His pajamas also bear the cheery message "Much better thanks."

nominated, but only after turning back an unexpectedly strong attempt by the young senator from Massachusetts, John F. Kennedy. Kennedy's showing suggested that for the first time since 1928 the party might be willing to name a Catholic candidate for national office—perhaps even for the presidency.

In the 1956 campaign, both candidates appeared before the country as men of moderation. But Stevenson raised two dramatic new issues. He recommended giving "prompt and earnest consideration to stopping further tests of the hydrogen bomb," and he suggested "that within the foreseeable future we can maintain the military forces we need without the draft."

In pressing these points Stevenson added greatly to Eisenhower's political advantage. To some, Stevenson's position indicated that he was "soft on Communism"; others felt helpless to judge the technical issues involved. Forced to choose between Stevenson's judgment and that of General Eisenhower on what appeared to be military questions, the nation leaned toward the successful soldier. But in the very last week of the campaign, issues arose over which neither candidate had the slightest control.

IN late February 1956 Russian leader Nikita Khrushchev had shocked a secret meeting of Russian Communist functionaries by denouncing Stalin as a monstrous tyrant. The Russian policy of de-Stalinization that followed encouraged Soviet satellites to a show of independence. By October 19, Polish Communists were setting up a new regime modeled on the independent, nationalistic Communism established by Tito in Yugoslavia. Even though Khrushchev flew to Warsaw and threatened suppression by force, the Polish Communists stood up to him. Soviet troops and tanks, moving toward Warsaw, halted before reaching the city, and the Poles won a measure of autonomy. They named the Titoist Wladyslaw Gomulka as chief of their party and voted to expel the Soviet marshal, Konstantin Rokossovsky.

Even more dramatic was the uprising in Hungary. In the last weeks of October the Hungarians overturned their government and brought back ex-Premier Imre Nagy, who promised free elections. The Red army departed Budapest on October 30. For a few days the world thrilled to the thought that the tyranny behind the Iron Curtain was dissolving. But on November 4 the Russian army returned to crush the revolution ruthlessly.

The events in Hungary shattered any illusion that the U.S.S.R. headed an idealistic "people's movement." They also destroyed the pretensions of Dulles' liberation policy. The United States watched helplessly while the courageous Hungarian uprising was crushed. Some Europeans even accused America of encouraging a revolt which it had no intention of supporting.

The same week that the Hungarian revolt was wiped out, the Administration's program to stabilize the Middle East collapsed. In the Middle East there were no easy choices. In that seething region the United States was attempting to maintain the friendship of all the parties: the Arab nations; Britain and France, the imperial powers in the region; and Israel. The entire region was eyed hungrily by the Russians; to forestall any Soviet move, Dulles in 1955 promoted the Baghdad Pact, which joined the northern Moslem bloc—Turkey, Iran, Iraq and Pakistan—to the Western defense system. But when the pact awakened resentment through a vast area from India (hostile to Pakistan) to Egypt (which saw its pre-eminence in the Arab world jeopardized), the United States itself refrained from joining the alliance.

Quemoy and Matsu, two bleak and undesirable islands in the Formosa Strait, became a center of world attention as early as 1949. The Chinese Communists coveted the islands as "stepping stones to Formosa" (above). But even more, they wanted to eject the Nationalists, who threatened to use the islands as bases for attacking the mainland, just a few miles away.

Egypt, strategically located, constituted a special problem. To win Egypt's friendship, the United States urged that the British evacuate the Sudan. Americans also offered to help construct the mammoth Aswan Dam to harness the power of the Nile. Still Cairo showed no sign of being any better disposed to the West. Egypt bought arms from the U.S.S.R., stepped up border raids on Israel, a nation for which Americans felt great sympathy, and recognized Red China. Then Dulles decided to teach Egyptian leader Gamal Abdel Nasser a lesson. He withdrew the American offer on the Aswan Dam.

Outraged, Nasser struck back. On the fourth anniversary of the Egyptian revolution he announced that he had nationalized the Suez Canal. The canal, previously operated by a company controlled by Anglo-French stockholders, had been open to vessels of all nations. Now Nasser closed it to the Israelis and held other users at his mercy.

In the final week of the 1956 election campaign in America, the Middle East crisis erupted in war. On October 29, Israel invaded Egypt for the announced purpose of destroying bases from which the Egyptians had launched their border raids. Two days later Britain and France intervened to drive the Egyptians out of the Suez zone. Within a few days Russia had threatened Britain and France with reprisals unless they withdrew.

Fearful that the Soviets might make good their threat, and angry at the British and French for their gunboat diplomacy, the United States joined with Russia in condemning the military intervention. Under this pressure Britain and France agreed to a cease-fire, and Israeli forces retired. After the cease-fire the American government took the lead in asking for withdrawal of Israeli troops and U.N. supervision of a cease-fire arrangement. In the end the Western alliance had been shaken; the power of the Soviet Union had been confirmed in a new part of the world; Nasser's prestige had been enhanced even though he had been drubbed in the field; and the United States had embittered the Israelis without winning the friendship of the Arabs.

Under ordinary circumstances, all these troubles might have made election difficulties for an incumbent administration. But the Republicans, who had been claiming that only Eisenhower guaranteed peace, now advanced the argument that only the President could be trusted in a time of crisis.

At 7:30 p.m. on election night came disheartening news for the Democrats. Bridgeport, Connecticut, a Democratic factory town, had gone for Eisenhower by a thumping 19,000 votes. Minutes later New Haven, which had never voted for a Republican presidential candidate, gave Eisenhower a 17,000 plurality. It was clear immediately that not only would Ike win—but he would win by a landslide. With 35.6 million votes, the President swept 41 states with an electoral vote of 457 and a popular percentage of 57.4. But the elections had one surprising feature: The Democrats continued to control both houses of Congress, the Senate by two votes, the House by 32.

No one knew quite how to interpret the curious outcome of the election. Of Eisenhower's popularity, there could be no doubt. But what was one to make of the Democratic triumph in Congress? The country, some concluded, wanted both peace and prosperity. It trusted the President to preserve peace and the Democrats to forestall hard times. One thing was clear: Eisenhower had failed to rebuild the Republican party into an instrumentality that could command the support of the nation.

The public generally regarded John Foster Dulles as a remote sort of grand old man who juggled the world in his powerful hands. A New York television audience was startled, then, when comedienne Carol Burnett sang that she was "on fire with desire for John Foster Dulles." An aide to the Secretary of State quickly sent a telegram saying Dulles was "very amused."

An epochal revolution in science

THE nuclear age began in 1945 with a vision of the inferno and was transformed with astonishing speed into the most creative scientific era the world has ever known. Scientists produced drugs and vaccines that ended the threat of terrible diseases, fashioned exotic fuels to propel even more exotic vehicles to the moon and the ocean bottoms, created tiny circuits that opened extraordinary vistas in electronics. Giant computers answered in minutes intricate mathematical problems that would take unaided men hundreds of years to solve. Radioisotopes (many of them beneficial by-products of bomb making) were put to life-giving use in destroying malignant growths.

During the 1960s biologists discovered the structure and workings of DNA, the genetic molecule that determines the traits of every living thing. Control of DNA, a possibility in the next 50 years, implies that man could preselect the sex of children, combat almost any unwanted inherited human condition such as hemophilia, delay the aging process and manipulate genes to reproduce artificially an Einstein or a Hitler.

Yet even the greatest of these feats aroused fears as well as hopes. To many, proliferation of computerized banks of information threatened individual liberties. Nuclear generating stations and seemingly miraculous drugs posed dangers that at first were underestimated. And the growing ability to control genetics raised concern over the ways this unprecedented capacity might be used to influence the future of mankind.

A MODEL of the DNA molecule is displayed by American biologist James Watson *(left)*, and British physicist Francis Crick. The young scientists jointly won a Nobel Prize for their discovery of DNA's structure: a circular ladder with rungs of pairs of chemicals. The number and order of the chemicals determine all heredity, make sure a horse gives birth to a horse instead of a giraffe—or a snail.

A NUCLEAR POWER PLANT in Alabama, shown during construction, is designed to produce 3½ million kilowatts of electricity without depleting the world's increasingly scarce supplies of fossil fuels. But growing public concern over the possibilities of radioactive dangers led to demands for strict safeguards that delayed completion of this and many similar plants.

Probing the seas' depths and the outer edges of space

IN 1957, a group of 66 nations launched an International Geophysical Year as a collective assault on the secrets of land, sea and air. Afterwards, the momentum of the mammoth 18-month research project carried the U.S. into more of its own major geophysical explorations. Among them was the study of the strange world under the oceans. Descending into the earth's last frontier, men challenged this vast, unknown territory that covers 70 per cent of the planet's surface, bears four out of five of all living things, controls weather, provides most of the oxygen men breathe and contains oil and minerals of incredible economic value. A new generation of undersea vehicles, tough-shelled spheres like the vessel below, can resist crushing pressures to probe the ocean bottoms. From their voyages come discoveries that promise fish and plant "farms" as new sources of food for the world's swelling population, new supplies of minerals and fuels as on-shore resources diminish—and a future in which man may return to live and work in the environment that spawned him 300 million years ago.

A HUGE BALLOON, some 170 feet in diameter when inflated, is shown at a Navy launching site in South Dakota. Its flight in 1959 produced valuable data on the planet Venus' atmosphere.

A STAUNCH BUBBLE, the research sub *Deep Star (opposite)*, photographs deep-sea life off Cozumel, Mexico. The craft is maneuvered by controls as intricate as those of a spaceship.

AN EERIE PIPELINE is strung by aquanauts far below the ocean surface as part of an elaborate plumbing system to gather plankton and other microorganisms for examination and study.

Tiny parts for complex tasks; a new kind of light

ONE of the most startling technological developments of recent decades has been in microelectronics. The revolution started in the '50s when scientists reduced bulky vacuum tubes to clusters of pea-sized transistors and continued into the '60s with the development of integrated circuits often no bigger than the "D" on a dime. The complex miniature circuits out-performed transistors by providing a cheaper, lighter, faster, more accurate system for controlling machines as varied as hi-fi sets, missiles, airplanes and computers.

No less striking is the laser (an acronym for "light amplification by stimulated emission of radiation"). Unlike natural light, a laser beam *(below)* does not diffuse its rays in all directions, but retains its tremendous power even when projected over long distances. Feasible applications for the laser include accurate cutting of the hardest metals and improved radio communications. Like radar, the laser beam bounces back off distant objects such as the moon, to let scientists measure the drift of continents and changes in the force of gravity.

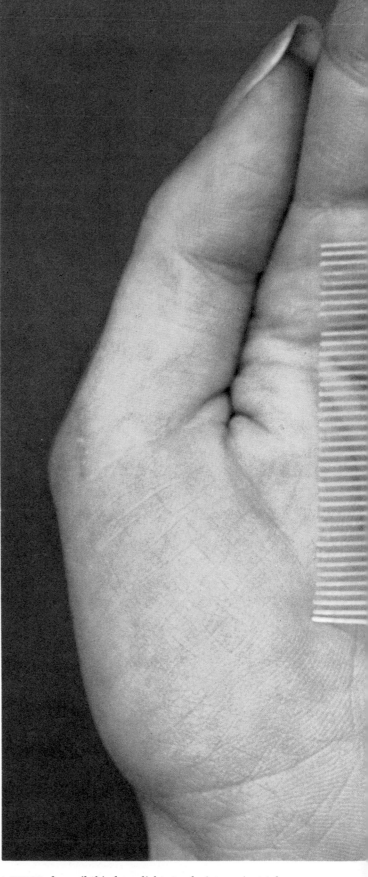

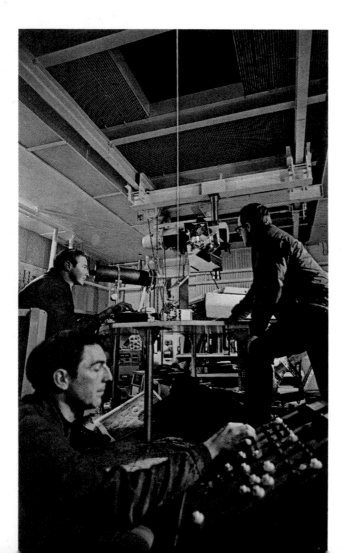

A **BEAM** of pencil-thin laser light streaks into a giant telescope en route to the moon. The telescope widens the beam to five feet; it then spreads to only three miles when it hits its target.

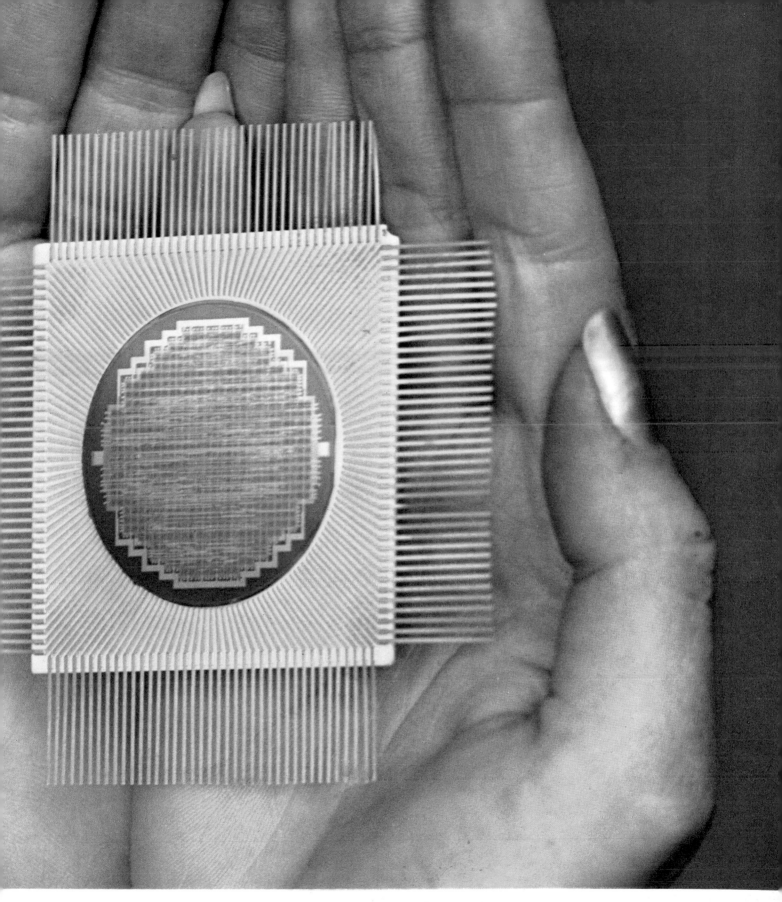

A WAFER etched with minutely detailed electronic circuits does the work of between 1,000 and 4,000 conventional transistors. Replacing previous miniaturized components, this microelec-tronic device was designed, tested and partially manufactured by computers for use in computers. Technologists foresee equal-ly effective circuits as small as the period ending this sentence.

Breakthroughs on healing; transplants of vital organs

I N the '50s and '60s medical science produced a seemingly endless train of achievements. Inspired by the success of penicillin during World War II, postwar researchers developed antibiotics and vaccines to combat previously stubborn illnesses, among them skin ulcers, rheumatic fever, mastoiditis, tuberculosis and measles. New tranquilizing and energizing drugs gave relief to many of the mentally ill who were then able to leave institutions. The mentally well received a boon when hormonologists, searching for ways to induce pregnancy, accidentally discovered an almost infallible oral contraceptive; almost overnight taking the Pill became a ritual for millions of women. In surgery, technology and human skill combined to produce stunning advances.

Complex heart surgery suddenly became routine. Thousands of open-heart operations were performed after the development of mechanical by-pass machines that acted for the heart during surgery. Another invention, the pacemaker, enabled thousands of people with cardiac disease to live normally, their heartbeat stimulated by the rhythmic impulses of a tiny electronic device that was surgically sewn into the walls of their chests. On December 3, 1967, headlines throughout the world trumpeted the news that Dr. Christiaan Barnard of South Africa had made the first successful transplant of a living heart from one human body to another. The widespread attention given to Dr. Barnard's accomplishment—which most laymen felt was a medical miracle—obscured in part a fact well-known to doctors: that surgical replacement of diseased, damaged or worn-out kidneys, livers and lungs by both living and artificial organs had become almost commonplace but that the ultimate answer to failing organs probably lay in artificial substitutes. Medical science in the late '60s looked to the day when surgeons like Dr. Denton Cooley *(below)* would repair or replace human organs as easily as a mechanic installed new parts in an automobile.

REMOVING A PATIENT'S heart prior to its replacement by a donor heart, Dr. Denton Cooley *(center left)*, performs his first heart transplant. Much controversy raged around Cooley, an expert but highly daring heart surgeon who implanted the first completely mechanical heart in a man, and once tried to save a patient by the transplantation of the heart of a sheep. At the age of 47, Dr. Cooley had performed more than 4,000 successful heart-repair operations, including 1,000 on the damaged hearts of tiny infants.

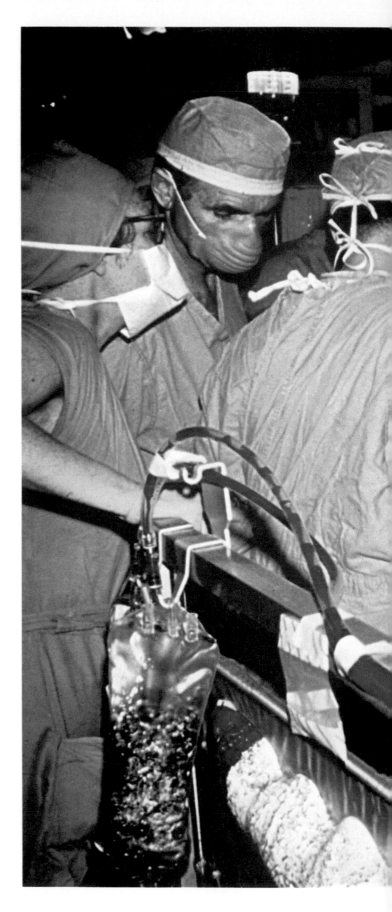

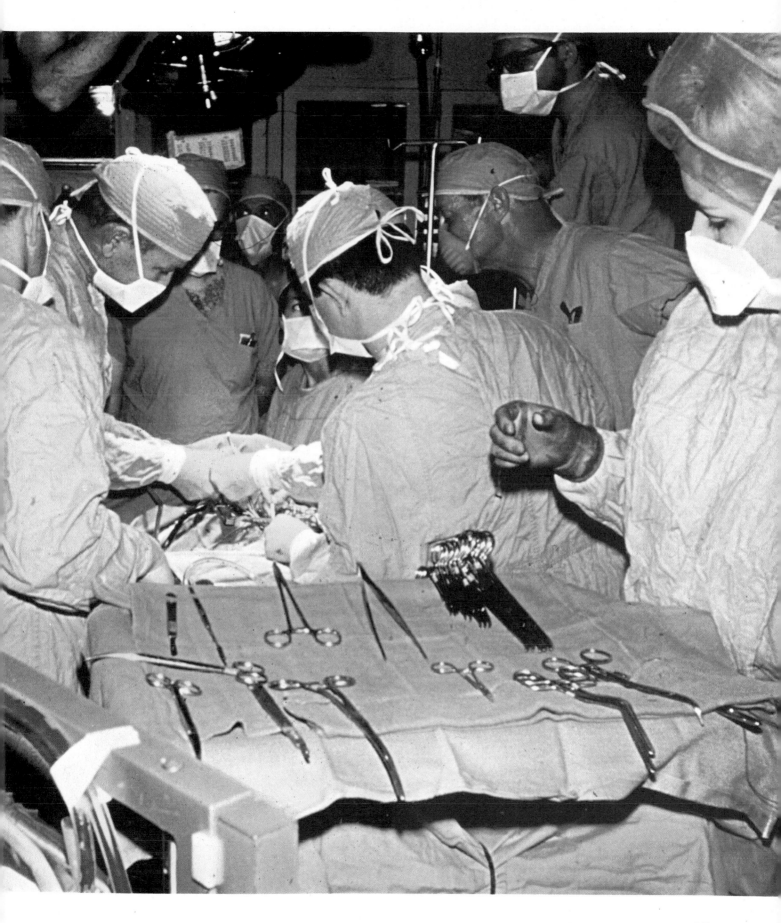

July 20, 1969:
Earthmen on the moon

RUSSIA'S cosmonauts made history with man's first forays into space. In stunning succession, the Soviet Union shot unmanned and manned vehicles into orbit around the earth and then gave the first demonstration of a human "walk" in space. Smarting in second place, the U.S. resolved to eclipse Russia by landing men on the moon before the end of the '60s. To meet this self-imposed schedule, America hurried through a pair of test projects: Project Mercury, a shakedown series of single-man earth-orbiting flights, and Project Gemini, a more sophisticated program that included testing the ability of spacecraft to maneuver and dock while traveling at some 17,500 miles an hour. The success of both test series led to Project Apollo, pointed toward the moon. The key factor in the Apollo flights was the Saturn V rocket, as tall as a 35-story building, heavier than 25 jet liners, the most powerful propulsion machine ever built. On December 21, 1968, Saturn V began hurling the first Project Apollo astronauts into lunar orbit. In May 1969, Apollo 10 flew within 10 miles of the moon, and practiced every moon landing operation except the landing itself. On July 24, 1969, Astronauts Neil Armstrong, Edwin Aldrin and Michael Collins completed the first mission to the moon by men from earth.

AT CAPE KENNEDY Apollo 11 is bathed in floodlights as final preparations are made for its flight. On July 16, 1969, it blasted off and in a perfect mission carried the first men to the moon.

Orbiting through lunar night, Apollo 10 astronauts photographed an earthrise. The line of dark and light cuts across Africa.

ON THE MOON, Edwin Aldrin salutes the flag that he and fellow astronaut Neil Armstrong had planted. At left is *Eagle*, the lunar module. Awed millions on earth, glued to TV sets 239,000 miles away, watched man's first landing on the lunar surface. But by 1972, moon exploration seemed routine, and the final moon trip drew only perfunctory attention from a blasé public.

5. A NATION IN SEARCH OF A GOAL

DURING his second term, Dwight Eisenhower faced new challenges. In his first term, he had conciliated a politically divided nation. Now something more was expected: that he capitalize on his enormous popularity to help solve problems too long postponed. The population explosion was being felt increasingly in schools, hospitals and housing. The blacks' mounting cry for equality made it clear that token integration would no longer suffice. To meet the competition of the Communists, the nation would require a more creative foreign policy and a firmer sense of national purpose.

By the fall of 1952 Soviet policy had begun to move in a new direction. By espousing anticolonialism, it aimed to diminish the power of the West. It began to rely more on economic and political penetration than on military force or subversion. Most important, the Russians showed signs of believing that although Communism would ultimately triumph over capitalism, it might well do so through peaceful competition rather than war.

Crucial to the revised Soviet strategy was the U.S.S.R.'s determination to show that it was the world's leader in technological, economic and scientific development. It sought to prove its boast in two ways: by outpacing America's rate of industrial growth and, in a more spectacular fashion, by taking the lead in the development of rockets and missiles. In 1955 James R. Killian Jr., president of the Massachusetts Institute of Technology, headed a committee of scientists that concluded after examining intelligence reports that the So-

ARMED AND ALERT, Army paratroopers sent by order of President Eisenhower enforce integration of the Little Rock, Arkansas, Central High School in September 1957.

viet Union was overtaking the United States and would soon have "a decided superiority in intercontinental ballistic missiles."

Also deeply involved in the struggle for the allegiance of the new nations of Africa and Asia was a troublesome American domestic issue: civil rights. A country that claimed to speak to the world as the champion of liberty and justice could not continue to deny fundamental rights to its own citizens.

For more than a half century, racial discrimination in the United States had been sustained by court rulings based on an 1896 verdict of the Supreme Court; *Plessy vs. Ferguson* had held that segregation did not violate the 14th Amendment so long as facilities that were separate were also equal. In May 1954 the Supreme Court handed down a historic decision. In *Brown vs. Board of Education of Topeka*, it abandoned the Plessy doctrine and ruled unanimously that segregation in the public schools was unconstitutional. In a subsequent decision, the Court ruled that public-school integration should be pursued "with all deliberate speed."

Partial desegregation of the schools was speedily achieved in some border states, but in the Deep South and in Virginia, resistance was adamant, especially in those areas where the militantly segregationist White Citizens' Councils emerged. In Tennessee John Kasper, a fanatical segregationist from New Jersey, stirred up an orgy of violence. Rope in hand, talking of dynamite, Kasper told a Nashville crowd: "When they fool with the white race they're fooling with the strongest race in the world, the most bloodthirsty race in the world." Early the next day a dynamite blast shattered a wing of a school where a five-year-old black girl had registered the day before.

If the Court's decision was to be enforced, it had to be made clear that the verdict was the law of the land, not merely a caprice of nine men. The President was urged to take action to indicate he supported the Court's ruling as a significant stride forward in democracy. He declined to do so.

In 1960 black college students in the South began the "sit-in" aimed at "whites only" lunch counters, thus triggering a militant, massive campaign against segregation in the South. One writer pointed out that no one objected when blacks and whites stood together—to buy groceries or pay bills. "It is only when the Negro 'sets' that the fur begins to fly," he concluded wryly.

At the beginning of Eisenhower's second term in 1957, not a single child in the Deep South attended a desegregated school. At last a federal court in 1956 ordered Little Rock, Arkansas, to start integration in the 1957-1958 school year. Little Rock seemed an excellent choice. "Jim Crow"—segregated seating —had disappeared on the city's buses, the city had black policemen and its school board was well disposed toward at least token integration. The University of Arkansas had been desegregated since 1948, and several communities in the northern part of the state had integrated their schools without opposition from Governor Orval Faubus.

On Monday night, September 2, 1957, as plans were proceeding for the admission of nine black students to Little Rock's Central High School the next morning, Faubus abruptly dispatched a unit of the state National Guard to the school and told a television audience he was acting to forestall violence. Outraged white citizens, he claimed, were converging on Little Rock, and the city's stores were selling out of knives, "mostly to Negro youths."

The mayor, the superintendent of schools, the police chief and the F.B.I. all subsequently denied that there had been any signs of violence. But Faubus, who may have hoped to improve his prospects for a third term, succeeded in creating the very atmosphere of violence he professed to deplore. The next morning, on the advice of the school superintendent, none of the black children showed up at Central High School.

Alarmed by the consequences of Faubus' defiance of the federal courts, Representative Brooks Hays, an Arkansas moderate, persuaded the governor to telegraph the President requesting a meeting. Eisenhower agreed, and Faubus flew to the President's vacation headquarters at Newport, Rhode Island. After the meeting, the governor appeared to have agreed to an early withdrawal of the troops. No sooner had Faubus returned to Little Rock, however, than he once more adopted a defiant stance. It required another federal court order to compel the governor to withdraw the Guardsmen and permit the black pupils to be admitted. But by now the threat of mob violence, once largely illusory, had become real. Without adequate force, there was no possibility that the children could attend school.

At that point Eisenhower federalized the National Guard and ordered a detachment of the 101st Airborne Division, a Regular Army unit, to Little Rock. At 5 a.m. on September 25, paratroopers stood with fixed bayonets at their posts ringing the school. At 9:25 an Army station wagon rolled up to the school and the nine black pupils were led inside.

THE episode had dealt a heavy blow to America's prestige. When a Ceylonese delegate to the U.N. denounced Soviet intervention in Hungary, a Bulgarian retorted: "Something worse could happen to you if you go to Little Rock." President Eisenhower, who had been almost immune from censure in his first term, now encountered a barrage of criticism from Republicans and Democrats alike, and from every part of the country. The President, they cried, had permitted an explosive situation to erupt without doing anything to head it off. Two months earlier he had said: "I can't imagine any set of circumstances that would ever induce me to send federal troops." Now he had sent in the paratroopers. "The President," commented *The New York Times*, "did, belatedly and powerfully, what he might not have had to do at all if he had previously made his position unmistakably and publicly understood."

Eisenhower studiously avoided taking a position on the Supreme Court decision. He "never told a soul" what he thought about it. He made a point of saying that he had ordered the troops in only because the sanctity of the courts was at stake, not because of "the segregation problem." It was not until 1963 that, as ex-President, Eisenhower finally announced that he considered the Court's desegregation decision "morally and legally correct."

In August 1957 Congress passed the first civil rights law in 82 years. To afford some federal protection to blacks wanting to vote, the measure established a Civil Rights Commission. A second act in 1960 authorized the appointment of federal referees to safeguard voting rights and stipulated that threatening violence to obstruct federal court orders was a crime. With the support of the able Attorney General, William Rogers, the Civil Rights Commission strove to use its powers to expand black suffrage.

Yet congressional action still was of small consequence. More significant in the long run was an episode in Montgomery, Alabama, on December 1, 1955. A middle-aged black seamstress, riding home from a day's work, refused to get up to give her seat to a white man. When she was arrested for defying the state's Jim Crow laws, Montgomery's blacks began a boycott. Led by a young black minister, Dr. Martin Luther King Jr., they employed passive resistance in a campaign to desegregate the city's buses. After 54 weeks the city and the bus company, nudged by a federal injunction, gave in.

Die-hard Southern segregationists like this New Orleans woman responded with rage to token integration of the public schools. Police in some towns attacked black demonstrators with high-pressure fire hoses, vicious dogs and electric cattle prods, thus encouraging extremists—"the duck-tailed, sideburned swaggerers, the rednecked hatemongers, the Ku Klux Klan."

A 1957 cartoon shows Uncle Sam —on the ground with his satellite program still on paper—bowled over by Russia's space accomplishments. After "Sputnik" the U.S. space agency was frequently the object of cynical stories. One told of a reporter who telephoned to ask about its program. "Sir, are you calling for information or with information?" was the reply.

The Montgomery bus boycott indicated a new militancy among Southern blacks, particularly young blacks. On February 1, 1960, four freshmen from a black college in North Carolina sat down at the segregated lunch counter at Woolworth's in downtown Greensboro; when the waitress refused to sell them a cup of coffee, they remained in their seats. In the next 18 months 70,000 blacks and whites joined in sit-ins, wade-ins (at segregated pools and beaches), kneel-ins (in churches) and other movements to end segregation. Blacks and whites also took part in "freedom rides" to put an end to Jim Crow in interstate transportation. They made some progress, but segregation, in both North and South, continued to embarrass the United States. When the finance minister of Ghana bought orange juice at a restaurant near Dover, Delaware, he was not allowed to drink it on the premises because he was black. No one doubted that the United States was changing its laws, but many questioned whether its customs were changing quickly enough.

Ten days after the President dispatched troops to Little Rock, America's complacency received a new jolt: The Soviet Union announced that it had launched *Sputnik*, the world's first successful artificial satellite, into space where it orbited the earth at 18,000 miles per hour at a height of up to 560 miles. This indicated that the U.S.S.R. was far ahead of America in rocketry. At its most optimistic, the United States had hoped to launch a satellite some five months later that weighed less than one eighth as much as *Sputnik*.

Sputnik dealt a mighty blow to what one writer had called "the illusion of American omnipotence," especially in the very area of which it was proudest: technical know-how. The Soviets touted their achievement as proof of the superiority of their system; the uncommitted nations listened attentively.

The shock of *Sputnik* prompted a reassessment of America's intellectual life. United States schools were compared unfavorably (and often unfairly) to Soviet schools, and school boards began to revamp curricula to give more emphasis to science and mathematics. But the Administration responded to *Sputnik* with remarkable complacency. President Eisenhower, asked whether he proposed to appoint a science adviser, said, "I hadn't thought of that."

ON November 3 the Administration had a rude awakening. That day the U.S.S.R. hurled into orbit the much heavier *Sputnik II*, an enormous satellite weighing more than six times as much as *Sputnik I*. Within it was a live dog. This was a stunning achievement. A few days later the Administration announced the appointment of James Killian as special assistant to the President for science and technology; at the same time the government supplemented the Navy's satellite program with the Army's Jupiter-C test rocket.

The Navy's failure to make good with its Vanguard satellite program mortified most Americans. In early December reporters from foreign newspapers arrived at Cape Canaveral (later to be Cape Kennedy) in Florida to watch the United States send its first satellite into orbit, only to see one attempt postponed and another abort. The world press commented derisively. On the last day of January 1958, gloom turned to rejoicing when, at Cape Canaveral, the Army, called in only 12 weeks earlier to save America's face, put the first United States satellite into orbit. As the Jupiter-C missile rose majestically from its launching pad, some reporters cheered. Still, the new *Explorer* satellite was much smaller than the Soviet version. As late as 1959 Khrushchev could jeer: "You send up oranges while we send up tons."

The difference between American and Soviet technical achievements was never as great as some feared. At the time there was widespread concern about "the missile gap," but it subsequently developed that the United States was ahead of Russia in missiles. Moreover, the United States had already marked up some notable technical achievements of its own, including the successful development of an atomic-powered submarine. Nevertheless, the dramatic Soviet advances in space served to embarrass the conduct of foreign affairs in Eisenhower's second term.

Foreign policy during this period was concerned largely with efforts to win the support of the small nations of the world. Two weeks before the start of his second Administration, Eisenhower asked Congress for authority to use troops "to secure and protect the territorial integrity and political independence" of countries requesting aid against "overt armed aggression from any nation controlled by International Communism." This move was aimed specifically at the Middle East, but it failed to take into account the desire of most Middle Eastern nations for neutrality in the Cold War.

I N 1955 Dulles had promoted the Baghdad Pact. Of the Arab states, only Iraq had joined—and a strong but submerged opposition to the pact had developed in that country. In July 1958 the pro-Western government of Iraq was overturned in a military coup and its leaders slain. The rebellion was led by initially pro-Nasser elements, and it appeared to threaten the governments of Jordan and Lebanon. At Lebanon's request, Eisenhower immediately dispatched 9,000 Marines and paratroopers to that country. Britain sent forces to sustain the government of King Hussein of Jordan.

The Lebanon action precipitated an international crisis that brought the world very close to war. Khrushchev threatened to intervene, Mao made his voice heard and Nasser attempted to play the Russians off against the West. In the end a United Nations resolution eased the immediate crisis, but there was little substance left of the Eisenhower policy. By the time the American troops were withdrawn, Lebanon had a neutralist president and prime minister, and for the time being both Nasser and the Soviets had enhanced their power in the Middle East.

While the American troops were deployed in Lebanon, a new crisis developed in the Far East. On August 23, 1958, Red China began a major bombardment of Quemoy. Though the Joint Chiefs of Staff held that the offshore islands were not essential to the defense of Formosa, Dulles felt that any use of force by the Communists in the western Pacific was a menace to world order and that it was a "vital interest" of the United States to fight back. Once again the world seemed to tremble on the brink of war. American warships escorted Chiang's transports to the three-mile limit off Quemoy; the Seventh Fleet, equipped with nuclear weapons, plied the Formosa Strait; Dulles suggested that the United States might bomb the Chinese mainland if Formosa or Quemoy were attacked or threatened. America's allies were deeply disturbed by this position, and Dulles received biting criticism at home. Senator Herbert Lehman declared that "not a single American life . . . should be sacrificed for the defense" of these islands.

On September 30 Dulles announced his willingness to encourage negotiation. He declared that the United States had "no commitment of any kind" to help Chiang back to the mainland and that any hopes for his return were "highly hy-

By the time the U.S. Atlas intercontinental missile became the fifth successful American satellite in 1958, the post-"Sputnik" gloom had lifted. Commenting on the use of an Atlas communications satellite to beam President Eisenhower's Christmas message back to earth, a visiting Russian scientist said: ". . . we haven't thought of doing anything like that yet."

pothetical." Eisenhower went even further; Chiang's buildup of troops on the islands, the President asserted, was "a thorn in the side of peace." After a three-day conference in Taipei, Dulles and Chiang issued a joint statement on October 23 in which Chiang renounced the use of force to regain control of the mainland of China.

As crises mounted—Little Rock, *Sputnik*, Lebanon, Quemoy—there was unusually severe criticism of the President, primarily on grounds that he seemed to be following a policy (as he himself put it) of "not making decisions until after the event reaches you." Political analyst Samuel Lubell found that even Ike's admirers were grumbling: "Things are in an uproar, but what is Eisenhower doing? All you read about is that he's playing golf. Who is running the country?" When Eisenhower took a 10-day vacation trip to Georgia early in 1958, he was subjected to sharp criticism, some of it from periodicals that had been his warmest supporters. On November 25, 1957, Eisenhower had suffered a third illness, a mild stroke that caused a temporary speech impediment; this time the country's sympathy was mixed with concern about the President's ability to meet the demands of his office.

A commemorative stamp, which used the same star motif as the Alaskan flag designed by an Indian child, marked the entry of the first state not contiguous to U.S. territory. The 49th state, rich in fur, fish, gold, oil and untapped resources, Alaska was bought from Russia in 1867 for two cents an acre.

AT the same time that Eisenhower was facing a rising tide of criticism of his leadership, his Administration was hurt by scandal. Eisenhower had come to office as the leader of a "crusade" for decency in government. But before long the Administration was rocked by a series of disclosures. Before the dust settled, a series of high-placed officials had handed in their resignations: Secretary of the Air Force Harold E. Talbott; the chairman of the Interstate Commerce Commission; the public buildings administrator; the General Services administrator.

Of all the Administration officials, the closest to Eisenhower was Assistant to the President Sherman Adams. Callers at the White House noted how frequently the President told them: "Take it up with Sherman." When critics complained that Adams had too much power, Eisenhower responded angrily: "The trouble with these people is they don't recognize integrity."

In 1958 a congressional subcommittee came up with some startling revelations. It reported that a Boston textile manufacturer named Bernard Goldfine had paid for a vicuña coat and had also picked up several hotel bills incurred by Adams, a longtime friend. The presidential assistant, it seemed, had interceded for Goldfine when the manufacturer got into trouble with the Federal Trade Commission and the Securities and Exchange Commission. Adams' transgressions were not of a major kind, but they carried directly into the White House and made a mockery of the Eisenhower "crusade." Since fur coats had been a symbol of the Truman scandals, the episode of the vicuña coat was especially embarrassing.

Hawaii became the 50th state on August 21, 1959. The stamp shows eight of some 20 Hawaiian islands (only seven are inhabited) and a native warrior of earlier times. After Mark Twain visited the 1,600-mile chain in 1866, he called it "the loveliest fleet of islands that lies anchored in any ocean."

Eisenhower rebuffed demands that he dismiss his aide. "I need him," the President said. Adams hung on until September 22, intensely unpopular with G.O.P. leaders and a target for Democrats. At last he resigned, but he had stayed on long enough to keep the issue alive into the 1958 campaign.

Even before Adams' fall from grace, Republican election prospects had been poor. Late in 1957 the economy had taken its deepest plunge since the war. The auto and steel industries laid off thousands of men. Unemployment climbed to 7.7 per cent of the total labor force, the highest rate since 1941.

The Administration, which had taken steps to counter the milder recession of 1953-1954, moved more slowly this time. It forestalled tax cuts and refused to approve substantial pump-priming proposals; the government, Eisenhower explained, was giving "the private citizen and private enterprise a helping hand —not a federal wheelchair." The economy did not straighten itself out until a good deal of potential output had been lost. Even when industrial recovery was achieved, unemployment remained stubbornly high. In November, as the country went to the polls, nearly four million Americans were out of work. In the farm belt, where grain prices had been falling through the Eisenhower years, Benson's policies were more unpopular then ever.

In the last two weeks of the fall's congressional election campaign, Eisenhower attempted to rally his party, declaring that the country faced a choice between "left-wing government or sensible government." But the country sent the Republicans down to a thunderous defeat. The Democrats widened their margin in the Senate from a narrow 49-47 to a stunning 62-34. Their 282-153 House majority was the greatest since F.D.R.'s landslide in 1936.

Three weeks after the elections, Alaska added its first two senators and its lone representative to the Democratic holdings. Admitted to the Union as the 49th state on January 3, 1959, Alaska had an area more than twice that of Texas and a population smaller than the least populous state, Nevada. In August 1959 Hawaii joined the Union as the 50th state and sent one Republican and one Democrat to the Senate and a single Democrat to the House.

For almost six years one of the most popular Presidents in American history had been in office, yet his party found itself in the minority and losing ground with every election. The *Wall Street Journal* asserted: "The responsibility for this disaster, when you come right down to it, must rest on President Eisenhower. It was he who had the sense of direction and lost it; it was he who should have nurtured a party to support his ideas and did not."

The elections shattered the Republican right wing. The "Class of 1946," the conservatives first elected to the 80th Congress, all but vanished. The most notable exception to the trend against the G.O.P. was the victory of the liberal Republican Nelson Rockefeller, elected governor of New York by a half-million-vote margin after a campaign in which he took pains to dissociate himself from the Eisenhower Administration.

After assessing the election returns, *The New York Times* concluded: "Manifestly we are in for a liberal swing. Let us have no doubt of that." Dwight Eisenhower thought otherwise. He now used his influence to turn pending legislation in a conservative direction. A notable example of this was his role in shaping the Labor Reform Act of 1959, a measure that grew out of a Senate investigation of the Teamsters' Brotherhood, the largest union in America. The McClellan committee, with young Robert Kennedy as its counsel, unearthed an appalling pattern of corruption and charged that Teamster President David Beck might have misappropriated $320,000 in union funds. Beck did not stand for re-election, but as his successor the Teamsters chose James Hoffa, who was in equally bad repute with the Senate committee. As a consequence, the Teamsters were ousted from the AFL-CIO.

On the basis of the hearings, Robert Kennedy's elder brother John, the senator from Massachusetts, drafted a bill aimed chiefly at protecting the rights of rank-and-file union members. But with strong backing from the President, Congress amended the measure to add new restrictions on unions. The main ef-

By the spring of 1958 the country was deep in a serious recession. Cartoons like this one captured the mood of many Americans. So did wry definitions of the difference between recession and depression. "A recession," went one joke, "is when you lose your job, a depression is when I lose mine."

fect of the Labor Reform Act of 1959 was to leave strong unions like the Teamsters virtually untouched but to damage weaker unions and impede the spread of unionization in unorganized industries.

At the same time that the President was acting more aggressively in domestic affairs, he was showing a new willingness to take the reins in foreign policy. In April 1959 Dulles resigned; five and a half weeks later he died of cancer. His successor, Christian Herter, was not given an opportunity to dominate foreign-policy making, as Dulles had. With both Dulles and Sherman Adams gone, Eisenhower exercised more personal leadership than ever before.

The world situation confronting the President offered new challenges and new possibilities. On the one hand, the Russians seemed exceptionally truculent. In November 1958 Khrushchev made another attempt to drive the West out of Berlin; throughout 1959 the fires of the Berlin controversy smoldered. But at the same time the U.S.S.R. showed a new eagerness to reach an agreement with the United States.

IN January 1958 the United States and Russia signed an agreement providing for cultural exchanges on a large scale. By the summer of 1959 it sometimes seemed as if everyone in both countries was being exchanged: Nine U.S. governors were touring the Soviet Union, and Soviet First Deputy Premier Frol R. Koslov was visiting America.

While the U.S.S.R. displayed the first big exhibition of Soviet progress in science, industry and culture in the United States since 1939, Vice President Nixon flew to Moscow to open an American exhibition in a Russian park. In Moscow Nixon and Khrushchev got involved in several face-to-face debates, the most renowned of them in the model American kitchen at the U.S. exhibit. Although the quarrels revealed Khrushchev's infinite capacity for boorishness, real and feigned, the world was heartened by the fact that leaders of the two countries were at least talking to each other.

In September 1959 the Soviet premier arrived in the United States for a tumultuous 13-day tour. At the outset he displayed bad temper at a Washington press conference, and he behaved with ill grace at Hyde Park, where he was rude to Mrs. Roosevelt. In California he complained at not being permitted to go to Disneyland (police feared for his safety), and when Hollywood arranged for him to see the filming of Can-Can, he denounced the dancing as immoral ("a person's face is more beautiful than his backside").

But once Khrushchev reached San Francisco, the mood changed. Both he and his hosts mellowed. At the end of his visit, the premier spent three agreeable days with Eisenhower at the President's Maryland retreat, Camp David. "Let us have more and more use for the short American word O.K.," the premier urged. Khrushchev dropped his ultimatum on Berlin, and Eisenhower looked more favorably on a summit meeting. The world began to talk of "the spirit of Camp David" as it once had of the "spirit of Geneva."

In return for the premier's visit, the President made plans to go to Russia in June 1960. Meanwhile he undertook a series of unprecedented trips. In December 1959 he traveled 22,000 miles in 19 days, seeing 11 nations from Spain to India. In February he made a good-will tour of Latin America.

In 1958 Eisenhower had told reporters: "There is no place on this earth to which I would not travel, there is no chore I would not undertake, if I had any faintest hope that by so doing, I would promote the general cause of world

Nelson Aldrich Rockefeller inherited much from his grandfathers —oil billionaire John D. Rockefeller and potent Senator Nelson Aldrich. After 18 years in appointive posts, Rockefeller decided that only elected officials could make major policy—so he ran for governor in New York and was elected.

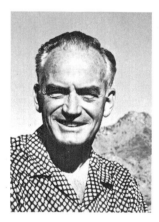

A conservative Republican who won decisively in 1958 was Arizona Senator Barry Goldwater. He flew his own plane around the state and campaigned in slacks and a sports shirt. A personable store owner and Air Force reserve officer, he overcame a two-to-one Democratic lead in registration.

peace." Much of the world seemed to sense how profoundly he was dedicated to the cause of peace. In India he was showered with flowers, and he was greeted with signs reading: "WELCOME PRINCE OF PEACE."

Eisenhower's reception encouraged new hopes for world peace. As the time for the summit meeting neared, expectations soared higher than at any time since the beginning of the Cold War.

On May 5, 1960, only 11 days before the scheduled summit meeting, Premier Khrushchev reported to the Supreme Soviet some startling intelligence: Four days before, an American plane had been shot down over Russian territory while on a mission of "aggressive provocation aimed at wrecking the summit conference." The premier did not hold Eisenhower directly to blame, but suggested that "Pentagon militarists" had ordered the flight. Cleverly Khrushchev had baited his trap for the American government.

The Americans obligingly walked into it. Perhaps, the National Aeronautics and Space Administration suggested on May 5, the plane was a high-altitude U-2 that, while engaged in weather research over Turkey, had strayed across the border. In any event, the State Department's press officer emphasized on May 6: "There was absolutely no—N-O—no—deliberate attempt to violate Soviet air space, and there never has been."

The very next day Khrushchev sprang his trap by revealing that the Russians had captured the pilot of the U-2, Francis Gary Powers, alive; that he had been shot down 1,200 miles inside the U.S.S.R.; and that he had confessed that he was on a spy mission that had started in Pakistan and was to end in Norway.

Caught in a lie, the State Department now conceded that Powers was on a flight of "surveillance" and that such missions had been undertaken for four years, ever since the U.S.S.R had rejected the President's "open skies" proposal at Geneva. Yet it indicated that "the authorities" had not sanctioned the flight. Two days later, on May 9, the department reversed itself once more: The President himself had authorized the U-2 program.

On May 15 the Big Four gathered in Paris amid considerable tension. At their first session on May 16, Khrushchev insisted that if Russia were to participate in the conference, not only must the espionage flights cease, but the United States must apologize for "past acts of aggression" and punish those responsible. Blustering and crude, he accused Eisenhower of "treachery" and a "bandit policy" and suggested that the summit meeting be postponed for six to eight months in the hope that another American President "would understand that there is no other way out than peaceful coexistence." In a studied insult, the premier withdrew the invitation he had extended to Eisenhower to pay a reciprocal visit to the U.S.S.R.

T HE President sat through Khrushchev's tirade in a controlled fury, then rejected the premier's ultimatum, although he said the overflights had ended. When the leaders assembled the next day, Khrushchev was not there. The summit meeting, freighted with such high hopes, had been torpedoed.

At an explosive press conference before he left Paris, the Soviet dictator pounded the table, again insulted the United States and warned that any nation that permitted the United States to use it as a base for overflights would be subject to "shattering" blows.

In the dark year of 1960, the U-2 fiasco was only one of a series of disastrous

After Eisenhower's lavish White House reception for Nikita Khrushchev in 1959, the Soviet premier toured America, joking and bubbling proverbs. But in California his good humor turned to anger when he was denied a visit to Disneyland. "Have gangsters taken hold of the place . . .?" he growled.

While Francis Gary Powers, shown with a U-2 model, was in a Russian jail, his father recalled his first flight. "He got out of the plane, told me, 'Left my heart up there and I'm going back to get it.' Well . . . it must be a long way up there . . . he's been up to 100,000 feet and he hasn't brought it back."

developments that damaged American prestige in many parts of the world: Asia, Africa and, most particularly, Latin America.

Under Truman and Eisenhower, Latin America had largely been neglected unless a threat of Communism was posed. In 1954 the United States intervened to help overturn a pro-Communist regime in Guatemala, but Dulles showed little interest in the massive economic development schemes Latin Americans desired. And Eisenhower antagonized democratic leaders when he conferred the Legion of Merit on the dictators of Venezuela and Peru.

In April 1958, after both these dictators had been overthrown, Vice President Nixon set out on a good-will tour of Latin America. In Uruguay he was showered with anti-U.S. pamphlets. In Peru mobs of youthful demonstrators shouted, "Get out, Nixon!" When, against the advice of security officers, he drove to the 400-year-old University of San Marcos, students stoned him.

WORSE was still to come. In Venezuela the Vice President and his wife were met with howls of hatred and were spat upon. In a working-class suburb of Caracas, Nixon's motorcade was mobbed. The crowd ripped off the American and Venezuelan flags, hurled huge stones that shattered the safety-glass windows and attempted to overturn the Vice President's car.

No longer was there any possibility of Nixon's continuing his tour as scheduled; the only question was whether he could be gotten out of Caracas alive. Eisenhower ordered paratroopers and Marines flown to U.S. bases in the Caribbean. They were not needed, but it required six truckloads of soldiers to escort Nixon's bulletproof limousines to the airport.

At home Nixon was praised for his valor, but the Administration was denounced for so misjudging Latin American opinion as to send the Vice President on a trip to countries in which he would be subjected to such indignities. Nixon's tour, wrote Walter Lippmann, was "a diplomatic Pearl Harbor." Few doubted that the Communists had instigated the rioting, but the Communists succeeded only because they were exploiting real grievances. Nixon commented: "The people there are concerned, as they should be, about poverty, misery and disease." The Administration now gave increasing thought to aiding economic progress in Latin America and to encouraging democrats rather than dictators. But some feared that this change of heart had come too late.

Events in Cuba suggested that these fears were well founded. On January 1, 1959, rebels under the bearded Fidel Castro overthrew the brutal Batista regime that had first come to power in 1933. The revolt was greeted warmly in the United States. But within six months Castro had begun to deliver anti-American tirades. He conducted mass trials and executions and established a Communist-leaning dictatorship. With Castro's support, the Soviet Union was able to achieve its first effective penetration of the Western Hemisphere. In February 1960, after a nine-day visit to Cuba, Soviet Deputy Premier Anastas Mikoyan agreed to purchase Cuban sugar and to grant the island a $100 million credit. Castro's successful defiance of the United States served as an exciting stimulant to other pro-Soviet rebels throughout Latin America.

As events in Latin America seemed to outrace Washington's policy, the United States took comfort in the fact that there were still nations that seemed firmly in the Western camp. Of these, none was stauncher than Japan, a country whose friendship had been carefully nurtured since 1945. To cement these cordial relations, President Eisenhower planned to visit the island empire. In June

A violent attack on Richard Nixon's car, stalled by jeering, spitting Venezuelan left-wing "students," ended his 1958 mission to South America on a sour note. After his narrow escape, Nixon commented: "If the four men who broke the windows were students, they've been in college more than 20 years."

1960 came a shocking rebuff. Following an outbreak of anti-American riots, the Japanese cabinet decided to ask the President to call off his proposed visit for his own safety. Correspondent Richard H. Rovere wrote from Washington: "If there has ever been a moment of national failure and humiliation comparable to the present one, no one in this dazed capital can identify it."

The unrest in Asia and in Latin America was one phase of the revolution of rising expectations that was shaking the whole globe. On June 30, 1960, in the same month that Eisenhower was barred from Japan and while Cuban-American relations were reaching a crisis, the Belgian Congo celebrated its independence. Within two weeks it was in chaos; tribe turned upon tribe, native upon European. Congolese troops mutinied against their Belgian officers, some fleeing Belgian refugees were dragged from cars and beaten, white women were raped. After an urgent session of the U.N. Security Council, Secretary-General Dag Hammarskjöld (who was later to die in a plane crash in Northern Rhodesia) dispatched an emergency U.N. force, made up of units from Ghana, Tunisia, Morocco and Ethiopia, to restore order.

The session of the U.N. General Assembly that began in mid-September 1960 was a showcase for the forces of change that marked Eisenhower's last months in office. No longer did the Western world dominate the U.N.: the Afro-Asian nations now constituted the largest voting bloc. At this one session, no fewer than 16 new African countries were admitted to the organization. To Manhattan came leaders of nations either independent of the United States or antagonistic to it—including Khrushchev and Castro. The Communist leaders seemed bent on assaulting not only the dignity of the United Nations but all of the traditions of peaceful negotiation. At one General Assembly meeting, Khrushchev noisily banged his shoe on the table to indicate displeasure; in his turn Castro harangued the Assembly for hours. When, in February 1961, news reached the outside world that the Congolese leader, Patrice Lumumba, had been murdered by his rivals, American blacks stormed the U.N. Security Council. The violence unleashed at the U.N. revealed a world that seemed to be moving quite out of control, a world in which the United States no longer enjoyed its former pre-eminence.

Khrushchev lost his temper often during the fall session of the U.N. in 1960. The translation of his description of one delegate reads: "A jerk and a lackey." His famous shoe pounding performance is satirized in this newspaper cartoon, captioned: "Is Big Insult, Asking Me To Free MY Colonies!"

PUZZLED by the fact that the United States seemed to have lost the initiative in world affairs, the country engaged in an intensive self-examination to see if there was something amiss in American society. Most of the introspection came to a common conclusion: that the United States urgently needed a clearer sense of national purpose. More than a year earlier George Kennan had given an address in Washington that aroused widespread comment. "If you ask me," Kennan observed, " . . . whether a country in the state this country is in today: with no highly developed sense of national purpose, with the overwhelming accent of life on personal comfort and amusement, with a dearth of public services and a surfeit of privately sold gadgetry, with a chaotic transportation system, with its great urban areas being gradually disintegrated by the headlong switch to motor transportation, with an educational system where quality has been extensively sacrificed to quantity, and with insufficient social discipline even to keep its major industries functioning without grievous interruptions—if you ask me whether such a country has, over the long run, good chances of competing with a purposeful, serious and disciplined society such as that of the Soviet Union, I must say that the answer is 'no.'"

The executions that followed Castro's revolution in 1959 led to this Bill Mauldin cartoon. In it the Cuban comforts a doomed man: "Think what could happen to you if we weren't idealists." Mauldin added: "Fidel came out of the hills like Robin Hood and . . . began acting like the Sheriff of Nottingham."

Two leading 1960 Democratic presidential hopefuls, Senators Hubert Humphrey of Minnesota and Lyndon Johnson of Texas, exchange greetings. Johnson was nominated for Vice President. Humphrey, an ex-pharmacist who visited at least one drug store wherever he campaigned, went back to the Senate.

In 1960 LIFE and *The New York Times* ran a number of articles on the quest for a national purpose, and Eisenhower created a Commission on National Goals to examine the prospects for the next decade. A report issued by the Rockefeller Brothers Fund insisted that it was necessary to define the national purpose in order to win the Cold War and argued that a democracy could "do more than respond to the initiatives taken by its enemies."

Much of the ensuing national debate focused on dissatisfaction with the quality of American life. Many observers argued that the pressures of a bureaucratized society were snuffing out the aspirations of the freewheeling individual and that the modern American did not seek self-expression but approval through conformity. The young people who made up the "Silent Generation" of the 1950s seemed to live in a world of shrunken ambitions. They appeared to be obsessed with security; they looked not for worlds to conquer but for a place on the ladder of a corporation or tenure in a university or a civil-service permanency in the government. They showed little interest in public issues; "their minds," complained a professor, "are as quiet as mice."

NOT long before the uproar over the deterioration of the national character, one of the nation's best known young people had been the modest, intelligent Charles Van Doren, then an instructor at Columbia, who had a long run as a contestant on the NBC quiz show "Twenty-One." He was snowed under with letters telling him that he, for one, was an idol the younger generation might emulate. Then evidence was made public that the shows, which were ostensibly unrehearsed contests, had in fact been rigged. Testifying before a grand jury, Van Doren denied any part in any crookedness. But a House subcommittee conducted its own investigation—and on November 2, 1959, Van Doren finally admitted that he had cheated from the very outset. Disgraced, Van Doren offered his resignation; Columbia immediately accepted.

Much of the criticism that emerged from the debate on national purpose was directed at President Eisenhower. The President, it was said, had not only justified political apathy and made indifference to politics respectable, but had failed to meet the crucial issues of the times. "Under the leadership of the President we are promoting private prosperity at the expense of national power," Walter Lippmann protested. "As a result the influence of the United States as a world power is declining." Soviet successes in the space race focused criticism on a consumer-oriented economy that could turn out powerful and ostentatious automobiles but apparently lagged in rockets and missiles.

The debate over national purpose insinuated itself into the contests for both major party nominations in the 1960 campaign. To avoid a floor fight at the Republican convention, Richard Nixon, leading contender for the G.O.P. nomination, agreed to a platform draft modified to meet the demands of New York's Governor Rockefeller, who had been notably critical of the record of the Eisenhower Administration. Although both the Old Guard and the Eisenhower forces were dismayed by Nixon's willingness to compromise, the Vice President secured the Republican nomination by acclamation.

The contest for the Democratic nomination also revolved around the issue of national purpose. Two of the leading contenders for the presidency, Senator John F. Kennedy of Massachusetts and Senator Lyndon B. Johnson of Texas, had been criticized by Stevensonian Democrats for unwillingness to join issue sharply with Eisenhower's policy of moderation and, some thought, stagnation. They were challenged for the nomination by Minnesota's bold, lo-quacious Senator Hubert Humphrey.

The busiest schedule of primary campaigning was Kennedy's. But over him hovered the shadow of an earlier campaign: the election of 1928, when, for the first time, a Roman Catholic had made a serious bid for the White House. Ever since the defeat of Al Smith that year, it had been considered axiomatic that a Catholic could never be elected President. However, historians noted that many who had voted against Smith did so not only because he was a Catholic but also because he represented the threat of the immigrant slum dwellers of the big city. Kennedy was cut from quite different cloth. Although his great-grandfather, Pat Kennedy, had settled in Massachusetts only a century before, the Kennedys had moved upward swiftly; the senator's father had served as ambassador to the Court of St. James's. "Jack," said Massachusetts Governor Paul Dever, "is the first Irish Brahmin."

Fighting to overcome the handicap of his religion, Kennedy suffered an ominous setback in the first of his significant primary contests—with Humphrey in Wisconsin. Kennedy did take six of the state's 10 districts, but he lost all four of the heavily Protestant districts. He would have to fight Humphrey all over again in West Virginia, which was 95 per cent Protestant.

In West Virginia Kennedy's managers pulled out all the stops—they exploited the senator's war record, they played crude courthouse politics, they spent money with a lavish hand. Everywhere Kennedy turned he confronted the religious issue, and he boldly met it head-on. "I refuse to believe that I was denied the right to be President on the day I was baptized," Kennedy cried. This turned out to be a shrewd tactic; even West Virginians who admired Humphrey turned to Kennedy to demonstrate that their state was not guilty of intolerance. "You could see them switch," noted a pollster.

O N May 10 Kennedy won so decisive a victory in West Virginia that Humphrey withdrew from further competition. That same day Kennedy captured Nebraska. After that, it was all downhill. By convention time Kennedy had such a commanding lead in delegates that every attempt to block him failed. Kennedy won and selected Lyndon Johnson as his running mate.

Many of those who had been disturbed by the country's apparent lack of national purpose had difficulty working up enthusiasm over either presidential candidate. People wore buttons saying "Neither," and one commentator remarked: "I don't see how either of them can win."

There was a widespread feeling that the political philosophies of both candidates were founded less on principle than on expediency. The commentator Eric Sevareid, arguing that the two men were ambitious opportunists who lacked deep conviction, declared: "The 'managerial revolution' has come to politics, and Nixon and Kennedy are its first completely packaged products. The Processed Politician has finally arrived."

Some observers tempered their criticism of Nixon with sympathy. "Richard M. Nixon," author Theodore H. White wrote, "is a man of major talent—but a man of solitary, uncertain impulse." Suspicious and moody, Nixon was eager to be liked yet slow to give his trust. A prey to self-pity (he told an Ohio audience of how he had never gotten the toy train he had wanted as a child), Nixon gave the appearance, White noted, of being "one of life's losers." On election night, Kennedy would be in his summer home on Cape Cod surrounded

Long before he became a leading figure in the 1959 television quiz scandals, contestant Charles Van Doren wrote of "the bright little circle of light in which the quiz show contestant basks. . . . All is certainty there." Van Doren himself never knew concern; he was given all the answers in advance.

by family, while Nixon would await the returns in a California hotel room, a man homeless even in his own state.

Much of the criticism of Kennedy centered on his "coldness." "Let me put it this way," one senator remarked. "If my dear old mother were to fall and break her leg, Hubert Humphrey would cry, but I'm not so sure about Jack." Many liberals also mistrusted him because he had never taken a public stand against McCarthyism despite ample opportunity to do so.

During the campaign Kennedy, with his boyish good looks and his flashing smile, dispelled some of the impression that he was a man of impersonal detachment; he had even more success in demonstrating that he was a thoughtful man of deeply held convictions and one who shared the concern over the nation's apparent aimlessness.

But he still had to overcome two great handicaps: prejudice against his religion and the fact that Nixon was better known and believed to be more experienced. Kennedy hoped to defer the religious issue to the closing weeks of the campaign; this hope was quickly dashed. Early in September a group of Protestant churchmen under the aegis of Norman Vincent Peale, probably the best-known Protestant clergyman in the country, raised doubts about the ability of any Catholic to commit himself fully to the Constitution. Kennedy met the issue directly. He accepted an invitation from the Greater Houston Ministerial Association to discuss his religious views. He spoke eloquently and directly: "I believe in an America where the separation of Church and State is absolute—where no Catholic prelate would tell the President (should he be a Catholic) how to act, and no Protestant minister would tell his parishioners for whom to vote—where no church or church school is granted any public funds or political preference—and where no man is denied public office merely because his religion differs from the President who might appoint him or the people who might elect him." Before Kennedy concluded, the audience, which had been sullen and suspicious at the outset, broke into applause.

I F the religious issue had not been killed, it had been muted. Yet Nixon still led Kennedy at the polls and appeared the probable winner, though by a hairsbreadth. Nixon claimed a wide experience, while Kennedy seemed a stripling who, it was said, was challenging for the White House too soon.

When Nixon agreed to debate Kennedy in a series of national telecasts, the Vice President and his lieutenants were certain that Nixon would enhance his advantage. The Vice President had used the medium to good effect in 1952, and he could now count on a phenomenally large audience. In the 1950s the number of American families who owned television sets had risen from 4.4 million to 40 million, 88 per cent of the nation's families. Millions of Americans—estimates ran as high as 70 million—tuned in to watch the first contest.

The outcome was a major surprise. While Nixon seemed constantly on the defensive, obsessed with scoring debater's points against his rival, Kennedy ignored the Vice President and spoke directly to the nation, enunciating his major theme of national purpose: "I think it's time America started moving again." While Kennedy appeared calm and self-possessed, Nixon seemed tense and haggard (TV cameras were unkind to his features).

Although three more debates followed, they were largely unilluminating encounters in which various issues were so fuzzed over that neither man's position was distinct; it was the first debate that made its mark and, many thought, de-

An exaggerated view of Nixon by the famous British cartoonist Ronald Searle cruelly emphasized the Republican candidate's ski-jump nose. Searle joined the entourages of both parties during the 1960 presidential campaign, reported that "Nixon's nose is an absolute treasure" for caricaturists. Below and on the opposite page are campaign buttons of both candidates.

termined the outcome of the election. Almost all observers agreed that Kennedy had scored a clear triumph; at the very least, he had drawn even with Nixon and could no longer be dismissed as a callow upstart.

In an election that promised to be so close, both candidates faced a crucial tactical decision: whether to appeal to the black voter or to Southern whites. Of all Democratic contenders, Kennedy had been least popular with blacks before the convention. Nixon, on the other hand, had won favor by his commendable record on civil rights. But during the campaign Nixon lost his advantage by attempting to court both black voters and Southern whites at the same time; in the end he failed to poll his full strength with either.

ON October 19 Martin Luther King, along with 52 other blacks, was arrested for taking part in a sit-in in an Atlanta restaurant. The others were released, but King was sentenced to four months' hard labor and spirited away to the state penitentiary. Many doubted that King would emerge from jail alive. Even before his arrest, some Southern governors had warned Kennedy that if he ever intervened in King's behalf, he would lose the South. But Kennedy called Mrs. King long distance to express his concern. The next morning the candidate's brother Robert telephoned the Georgia judge who had set sentence. On October 27 King was released from prison, alive and well. Nixon, who had had a similar opportunity to act, remained silent.

King's father, a Baptist minister who had opposed Kennedy on religious grounds, announced: "I've got a suitcase of votes, and I'm going to take them to Mr. Kennedy and dump them in his lap." On the Sunday before the election, a million pamphlets on the King affair were distributed outside Negro churches. In the election black voters gave Kennedy his margin of victory in at least three states, with an electoral count of 55.

On election night the first returns indicated a Kennedy landslide. Connecticut, which had gone for Eisenhower by over 300,000 votes in 1956, went to Kennedy by a wide margin. At 11 p.m. Kennedy already had 241 of the 269 electoral votes he needed. But the last 28 votes came painfully hard. Ohio, where Kennedy had been greeted with frenzied cheering, went to Nixon.

It was not until dawn that the Kennedy margin seemed ample. At 5:45 a.m. in Washington, the chief of the Secret Service, charged with safeguarding the life of the President-elect, turned away from his television screen, which showed Michigan putting Kennedy over the top. Minutes later 16 agents in Hyannisport, Massachusetts, set out in borrowed cars for the Kennedy home. Kennedy had been elected—but in the tightest race since Harrison's victory in 1888. Out of a record vote of more than 68 million, Kennedy won by less than 120,000—slightly less than two-tenths of one per cent. A shift of 32,500 votes (4,500 in Illinois, 28,000 in Texas) would have elected Nixon.

Still Kennedy had won a remarkable victory. He had overcome the handicap of his religion, his "inexperience" and his "immaturity" to defeat the candidate backed by America's most popular hero of the generation.

But at the same time that the nation elected Kennedy, it chose a less liberal Congress than that elected in 1958. By adding a handful of seats to the G.O.P. contingent in both houses, it strengthened the conservative coalition and denied the President-elect a secure working majority. The country seemed to be searching for a national identity, but it still did not sense any special urgency that would inspire a massive liberal upsurge.

Caricaturing Kennedy was more difficult, Searle said. "All you have to work with is the hair. It took me the better part of a week before I could get the hang of his face." Here the nominee imbues fund raising with lofty idealism by telling guests: "You are not paying $100 a plate for the privilege of eating . . . you are paying to maintain the freedom of the world."

UNDER FIRE from Red Chinese gun batteries on the mainland, Nationalist soldiers guard the offshore island of Quemoy in September 1954. Red threats to invade Quemoy, Matsu and Taiwan brought Nationalist raids on the mainland from Quemoy.

A search for peace at the summit

AFTER a decade of cold war, the summer of 1955 saw a dramatic manifestation of the international thaw as Stalin's successors met President Eisenhower at Geneva. In the first news conference ever of a Soviet Premier, Bulganin promised to make every effort for peace. Bounding into Geneva, party boss Nikita Khrushchev exclaimed: "Things are different now." No one knew quite what to expect. The U.S. delegation brought along more than 10 trunkloads of documents because, said an aide, "You have to be prepared for anything." In the talks, Eisenhower confided to the Soviets, "I have had enough of war." Later he astonished everyone by offering to trade blueprints of military bases with Russia and to open the skies of each country to aerial inspection.

The new "spirit of Geneva" brought no immediate disarmament or disengagement along cold-war frontiers Matsu and Quemoy (above). The ensuing years would more than once bring the world, as Secretary of State Dulles put it, "to the brink" of war. But at Geneva, summit diplomacy became a symbol of a new effort to check the threat of nuclear holocaust, to move toward peaceful coexistence. The transition was not to be easy or particularly successful. In translation, Nikita Khrushchev's contemptuous boast, "We will bury you!" seemed very ominous. Secretary Dulles would continue to threaten aggressors with "massive retaliation." The arms race would go on. Though disappointed in the end, Eisenhower never faltered in the search for peace: "My God," he once said, "we have to simply figure a way out of this situation."

PEACEMAKERS, President Eisenhower and Premier Bulganin chat cordially during the Geneva meeting. Bulganin set a warm mood by pinching the cheek of a U.S. guard.

After defeating the French at Dienbienphu on May 7, 1954, Ho Chi Minh's Vietnamese troops mop up the battered fortress. This panorama

Years of atomic stalemate —and brushfire wars

WHEN the U.S. and Russia exploded their first hydrogen bombs only nine months apart, the two nations seemed to stand stalemated, neither daring to tip what Churchill called "the balance of terror." Yet it often took extraordinary restraint for Ike to resist employing the awesome arsenal at his command.

The first test came in Indochina. When their Dienbienphu base was threatened by Communist forces, the French asked Ike to supplement the financial support already given by the U.S. with air strikes. Eisenhower refused, having previously concluded that air action "would comprise an act of war and would also entail the risk of having intervened and lost." Ike did send additional technicians. When he left office in 1961, there were only some 800 military advisers in Vietnam.

American restraint was tested again in 1956. In October Hungarian "freedom fighters" rose against Soviet rule. Also in October Israeli forces, soon joined by French and British troops, made an abortive attack on Egypt in response to the earlier nationalization of the Suez Canal by Egypt. Meanwhile, Soviet armed forces crushed the revolt in Budapest. For all its nuclear might, the U.S. could neither dissuade its friends nor deter its opponents from waging small, "brushfire" wars. As Eisenhower had warned: "Any notion that 'the bomb' is a cheap way to solve things is awfully wrong. It ignores all the facts of world politics. . . ."

BRITISH TROOPS guard the Suez Canal as a ship burns. The Israelis crossed the Sinai in six days and British planes bombed Port Said. But world pressure forced British, French and Israelis to withdraw.

—five pictures pieced together—shows captured American-made materiel, three trucks being loaded with gas cans and two 105-mm howitzers.

BUDAPEST REBELS fire rifles in a vain effort to down a Russian plane on November 3, 1956. The next day, thousands of Soviet tanks rolled into Budapest and smashed all Hungarian mass resistance in days.

117

Reviving the spirit of peaceful coexistence

As Eisenhower won a second term—while occupying armies camped in Budapest and along the Suez Canal—the spirit of Geneva was at its nadir. Patiently the President began again. To restore some stability to the revolt-torn Middle East, Ike dispatched troops in July 1958 to guard Lebanon's pro-Western President Chamoun against a Communist-inspired coup. But significantly, and against the advice of some of his military advisers, Eisenhower limited the action to Beirut and its airfield. He noted: "If the Lebanese Army were unable to subdue the rebels when we had secured their capital and protected their government, I felt, we were backing up a government with so little popular support that we probably should not be there."

Nearer to home shores Ike was worried about Communist penetration in Cuba, where Fidel Castro was waging a revolution against the Batista dictatorship. Despite warnings from the Central Intelligence Agency about Castro's politics, Eisenhower adopted a hands-off policy. When Castro, victorious, executed many Batista supporters, shocked Americans were further angered by his comment: "If the Americans do not like

what is happening, they can send in the Marines. . . ."

The American policy of restraint began paying dividends. In April 1958 the Russians unilaterally suspended testing of nuclear weapons. Ike's first reaction was, "I think it is a gimmick." But by fall he imposed a one-year moratorium on U.S. tests. In July Vice President Richard Nixon went off to Moscow, to a U.S. exhibition there. Touring a model ranch house with Khrushchev, Nixon engaged the Russian in a widely publicized "kitchen debate." "Is it not far better," Nixon asked, "to be talking about washing machines than machines of war . . .?" In September Khrushchev arrived in the U.S. for a two-week tour. When he returned home, he later confided: "In America they pay the unemployed more than we pay some of our workers."

As his visit ended, Khrushchev sat down with Ike at the President's retreat, Camp David. In three days of talks, he withdrew the latest Soviet threat to Berlin, while Ike agreed to another summit. "Like mountain summits," he cautioned, "political summits are normally barren. . . ." But, with hopes for peace renewed in "the spirit of Camp David," a new summit was planned.

Standing at attention behind their flags, Eisenhower and Khrushchev

FIDEL CASTRO delivers a speech during his triumphant march to Havana. "Power does not interest me, and I will not take it," he said. "From now on, the people are entirely free."

Arriving at the airport in Beirut in July 1958, a contingent of American troops unloads its gear from an Air Force flying boxcar.

observe ceremonies at Andrews Air Force base as the Soviet Premier begins his American visit. In background: Khrushchev's giant TU-114 jet.

A final failure for Ike's "personal diplomacy"

ON May 1, 1959, two weeks before the summit was to convene in Paris, an American U-2 spy plane, flying over Russia at 65,000 feet, was shot down. When the conference opened, Eisenhower's long search for peace at the summit ended as Khrushchev delivered a bitter personal attack on the President, face to face.

Following the crash of the plane, Washington shifted from outright denial of espionage to unprecedented candor—as Eisenhower took full responsibility for the U-2 flight. Khrushchev, possibly to bolster Soviet leadership of world Communism as U.S.S.R.-China tensions increased, charged the U.S. with "reviving the dead rat" of cold war. The flights, retorted Ike, were a result of Russia's "fetish of secrecy and concealment."

Ironically, the Paris summit collapsed over the issue that, five years earlier, had inspired the spirit of Geneva —aerial inspection. The U-2 flights began after Russia rejected Eisenhower's "open skies" proposal at Geneva.

Throughout Eisenhower's years in office, he had urged disarmament plus inspection. Only with such mutual surveillance, he felt, could the nuclear powers take practical steps toward peace. He had consistently tried to hold down his own defense budget. "I am getting a little tired," he once snapped at a Congressman, "of having to defend myself against the charge of being out to wreck the Army." As Eisenhower realized, the longer the arms race went on the harder it was to halt. "One of the most serious things about this defense business," his Secretary of Defense, Charles Wilson, warned Congress, "is that so many Americans are getting a vested interest in it." Eisenhower would repeat the warning about "the military-industrial complex" in his farewell speech. Yet as he left the wrecked Paris summit, there was little more he could do to bring disarmament.

In Paris Khrushchev withdrew an invitation to Eisenhower to visit Russia. Instead, Ike set off on a goodwill tour of Asia. Soon after anti-American rioting in Tokyo forced cancellation of his visit there, Ike headed home to complete his term and pass the torch to a new President—who would begin again the search for peace.

U-2 WRECKAGE, displayed (above) in the Chess Club of Moscow's Gorky Park, included such items as the Pratt & Whitney J57 jet engine. Also displayed were pilot Francis Gary Powers' possessions—among them his social security card and half a pack of cigarettes.

JAPANESE, protesting Ike's visit, forced its cancellation. However, he went from Manila to Taiwan aboard an American cruiser. When Chinese Reds shelled the off-shore islands, a reporter quipped, "Ike's the only Chief of State who ever got an 80,000 gun salute."

A GRIM PRESIDENT, Ike leaves the building where the Paris meeting collapsed. Khrushchev, departing, joked: "Only my face is ruddy. Eisenhower's is white. And Macmillan's has no color."

AN EARTHY PREMIER, Khrushchev, having broken up the summit meeting, shows French woodcutters his skill. Before the conference, Khrushchev joined a French farmer scything hay.

6. THE NEW FRONTIER

O N January 20, 1961, John Fitzgerald Kennedy was inaugurated as the 35th President of the United States. The inauguration ceremonies, which took place in a numbing 20-degree cold, demonstrated how far the nation had come in recognizing that minority groups should have a prominent place in national life. "The Star-Spangled Banner" was sung by Marian Anderson, a black; years before, the Daughters of the American Revolution had refused to rent their concert hall to this world-famous contralto, solely because of her race. The invocation was delivered by a Roman Catholic prelate, Richard Cardinal Cushing from Kennedy's home city of Boston. The new Administration recognized the importance, too, of the intellectual in American public life. More than 150 writers, artists and scholars were invited to the inauguration, and for the ceremonies Robert Frost, America's most renowned contemporary poet, prepared a special dedicatory preface to his poem, "The Gift Outright."

In his eloquent inaugural address, the new President showed a sharp awareness of the fact that his election marked a new era in American history. "Let the word go forth from this time and place, to friend and foe alike," he said, "that the torch has been passed to a new generation of Americans—born in this century, tempered by war, disciplined by a hard and bitter peace, proud of our ancient heritage—and unwilling to witness or permit the slow undoing of those human rights to which this nation has always been committed, and to which we are committed today at home and around the world. . . .

MARTYRED PRESIDENT, John F. Kennedy, first Chief Executive to be born in the 20th Century, sits at his desk in the picture he chose as his official color photograph.

"The energy, the faith, the devotion which we bring to this endeavor will light our country and all who serve it—and the glow from that fire can truly light the world.

"And so, my fellow Americans: ask not what your country can do for you —ask what you can do for your country.

"My fellow citizens of the world: ask not what America will do for you, but what together we can do for the freedom of man."

As the leader of "a new generation of Americans," Kennedy set a style for his Administration marked by youth, grace and "vigor." The first President born in the 20th Century, he appointed a Cabinet whose average age was eight years younger than Eisenhower's. One Washington correspondent wrote: "He surrounded himself with bright, handsome, gay people, all activists, who worked and played hard . . . and perhaps removed the presidency for all time from the log-cabin tradition. Kennedy presented a picture of total urbanity, the first true reflection in the presidency of America at the mid-century, a country of city dwellers long gone from Main Street."

Kennedy saw his role as not only that of Chief Executive but as tastemaker and impresario. Here was a President who quoted Madame de Staël on "Meet the Press" and whose Postmaster General had published a novel. Mrs. Kennedy had won *Vogue's* Prix de Paris in 1951 with an essay in which she named as the three men she would most like to have known Baudelaire, Wilde and Diaghilev. Kennedy, however, understood that history would judge his presidency more by the changes he wrought in substance than in style.

The President approached foreign affairs, his most challenging assignment, with two different and somewhat contradictory assumptions. Disapproving Dulles' moralistic rhetoric, he sought to develop a range of flexible responses —one that would take into account the divisions within the Communist camp, the aspirations of the emerging nations in Asia, Africa and Latin America, and the fact that Europe would no longer play second fiddle to the United States. In November 1961 Kennedy stated that "we must face the fact that the United States is neither omnipotent nor omniscient—that we are only six per cent of the world's population . . . and that therefore there cannot be an American solution to every world problem." The new President hoped to defuse the Cold War and pressed for an arms-control agreement. But he also insisted that he would restore the United States to the position of pre-eminence he said had been lost under Eisenhower.

Before Kennedy even took office, he had become implicated in a chain of events that would give him a rude lesson in the intractability of the world. Shortly after his election the Central Intelligence Agency informed him that it had been training and arming anti-Castro exiles in Guatemala, Texas and Florida for an invasion of Cuba. Startled by the news, Kennedy reluctantly gave his approval, in part because plans were highly advanced, and in part because it appealed to the audacity of the New Frontiersmen. On April 17, 1961, the invaders landed and soon were overwhelmed by Castro's forces at the Bay of Pigs on Cuba's southern coast. Critics differed about whether Kennedy had blundered more in failing to supply adequate air power, in trusting the CIA, which botched the job, or in endorsing so outlandish a scheme. Afterwards, the President said: "All the mysteries about the Bay of Pigs have been solved now but one—how could everybody involved have thought such a plan would

At the Kennedy inauguration, Robert Frost faltered while reading a special preface to his poem, "The Gift Outright," because he was bothered by the sun's glare. Vice President Johnson tried unsuccessfully to shield the papers. As the assemblage looked on with concern, Frost straightened up and vigorously recited the poem itself, which he knew by heart.

THE GIFT OUTRIGHT

The land was ours before we were the land's.
She was our land more than a hundred years
Before we were her people. She was ours
In Massachusetts, in Virginia,
But we were England's, still colonials,
Possessing what we still were unpossessed by,
Possessed by what we now no more possessed.
Something we were withholding made us weak
Until we found out that it was ourselves
We were withholding from our land of living,
And forthwith found salvation in surrender.
Such as we were we gave ourselves outright
(The deed of gift was many deeds of war)
To the land vaguely realizing westward,
But still unstoried, artless, unenhanced,
Such as she was, such as she will become.

succeed. I don't know the answer, and I don't know anybody else who does."

The Bay of Pigs disaster apparently convinced Khrushchev that the President was too indecisive to resist Russian ambitions in Central Europe. That summer the Soviet leader repeatedly threatened to sign a treaty with East Germany that would cut off Western rights of access to Berlin. To stop the outpouring of refugees into West Berlin the East Germans built a hideous wall across the city. Kennedy responded by calling up reserves, asking for large additional military funds and sending a battle force of U.S. soldiers down the autobahn across 110 miles of Communist territory to Berlin. As tension built, thousands of Americans constructed air-raid shelters and newspapers ran horrifying debates about the right of a man to shoot any neighbor who wanted to crowd into his shelter. By January 1962, however, the crisis had diminished. While Kennedy appears to have overreacted, especially by encouraging the shelter mania, he had also resisted advice to knock down the Berlin Wall, for he knew that such action might have provoked a disastrous war.

In the months that followed, Kennedy sponsored an enormous military build-up. He attempted to substitute for Eisenhower's emphasis on nuclear power a more flexible fighting capability with an arsenal "ranging from the most massive deterrents to the most subtle influences." The government stepped up by 50 per cent the total of long-range bombers on ready alert, placed greater reliance on Polaris missiles carried by submarines and on the Minuteman missiles in underground silos, and trained troops for paramilitary warfare.

On May 5, 1961, the United States became an added starter in the "space race" when Alan B. Shepard's capsule soared off the launching pad at Cape Canaveral and returned safely. That same month, Kennedy announced a project to land a man on the moon "before this decade is out," largely to gain points in the Cold War. Some faulted "moondoggling" as a diversion of funds from urgent terrestrial problems, but the space effort won a popular following when on February 20, 1962, John H. Glenn Jr. became the first American to orbit the earth. But the Russians were still considerably ahead in space technology.

Savoring the moment of celebration, John F. Kennedy and his wife Jacqueline attend the main inaugural ball on January 20, 1961. Despite a heavy snowfall that made travel difficult, thousands of guests gathered at five separate Washington balls to cheer the new President. Each ball was so crowded—12,000 attended the armory affair shown above—that many guests never got to dance at all.

KENNEDY, who had deplored Dulles' "brinkmanship," not only came to the brink but peered over the precipice in the fall of 1962. When Russian vessels in Cuban ports unloaded missiles, fighter planes and patrol boats in addition to Soviet instructors and technicians, the President, slow at first to believe that offensive missiles were being emplaced, resisted pressure to take forceful action, since Russia insisted the missiles were only defensive. In mid-October, however, American aerial photographs of Cuba revealed launching pads being built for intermediate-range missiles that could devastate cities almost as distant as Seattle. Some of his advisers wanted to launch an air strike, and others preferred to trade Cuban missile bases for the closing of obsolete American missile bases in Turkey. Kennedy chose a middle course: to impose a "quarantine" on shipments of military equipment to Cuba and to warn the U.S.S.R. that any nuclear attack from Cuba on any part of the Western Hemisphere would result in a "full retaliatory response upon the Soviet Union."

The President's policy of firmness with restraint prevailed. As Russian ships steamed toward the Caribbean where American naval vessels had orders to intercept them, many feared that doomsday might be only hours away. But after some complicated communications, the two powers reached an understanding: the Soviet Union would remove offensive weapons, the United States

Kennedy and Khrushchev beam as they enter the American Embassy in Vienna in June 1961 to begin their talks. The cheerful mood faded when Khrushchev threatened to seal off West Berlin in December, and Kennedy said that America would meet force with force. At the close of their tension-filled talks Kennedy spoke grimly to Khrushchev, "It will be a cold winter."

The wall dividing East and West Berlin is reinforced by East Berlin police in September 1961 to end escape attempts. In August, to dam the flood of refugees from the Communist sector seeking freedom in the West, East German leader Walter Ulbricht had suddenly ordered the barrier erected. It tore the city in half, blocking subway lines, splitting friendships and families.

would pledge not to invade Cuba. By hindsight Kennedy was criticized for risking a holocaust over a relatively small increase in the threat to American security, but most hailed the President's mastery of "eyeball to eyeball" diplomacy. The President, for his part, knew better than to push his advantage. When Castro refused to grant on-site inspection, Kennedy did not insist, and even though Cuba's action freed him from his non-invasion pledge, he kept the spirit of the bargain by ordering the interception of expeditions launched by anti-Castro Cubans based in America.

In other areas of the world, Kennedy encouraged more peaceful and constructive new departures. Unlike Dulles, he recognized the folly of trying to coerce neutrals into choosing sides in the Cold War. He altered the emphasis of foreign aid in the direction of economic rather than military assistance. Under his leadership, Congress stepped up Food for Peace shipments to nearly $1.5 billion yearly and bought $100 million worth of U.N. bonds to finance the Congo venture. But the best showcase of the Kennedy administration in the underdeveloped world was the Peace Corps, started in 1961 and directed by the President's brother-in-law, R. Sargent Shriver Jr. Enormously enthusiastic young men and women were soon building roads in Tanganyika, fighting a typhoid epidemic on the Caribbean island of St. Lucia, teaching midwifery in Colombia, nursing natives in North Borneo and adopting a Bolivian leper colony.

MORE than a year before the Cuban missile crisis, the President had launched the most far-reaching program ever directed at Latin America: the Alliance for Progress. At an Inter-American Economic and Social Council meeting in Punta del Este, Uruguay, the United States proposed a ten-year, $20 billion investment in "controlled revolution." If Latin American nations would agree to carry out urgently needed social and economic reforms, the United States would contribute the lion's share of the cost of the program. However, while every nation but Cuba joined the *Alianza*, progress came slowly.

In Southeast Asia as in Latin America, Kennedy inherited troubles. He improved matters in Laos, where he abandoned the ineffective regime that Eisenhower had sponsored, but at the same time reserved the threat of military intervention to deter the Communists. A neutral, if unstable, tripartite regime removed Laos as a chess piece in the Cold War, at least for the moment. But in Vietnam Kennedy left matters worse than he had found them.

Kennedy's error lay in seeking to impose a military solution on a complex political situation. When Ho Chi Minh's Communist government in North Vietnam increased aid to the Viet Cong in the South, Kennedy dispatched military "advisers" to bolster the Saigon regime of Ngo Dinh Diem. However, Washington was becoming increasingly disenchanted with the tyrannical Diem circle and after a coup d'état on November 1, 1963, during which Diem and his brother were assassinated, the President hastily recognized the new government, arousing suspicions that the Administration had played more than a passive role in the incident. At times, too, Kennedy harbored doubts about America's role. "In the final analysis," he had said in September 1963, "it is their war. [The Vietnamese] are the ones who have to win it or lose it."

The President also encountered unexpected difficulties in Europe. To create a "Grand Design" that would improve American and European economic relationships, he pushed hard to gain passage of the Trade Expansion Act of 1962 empowering him to reduce or eliminate tariff duties. But his efforts were frustrated when France's President Charles de Gaulle blackballed the admission of Great Britain to the Common Market.

Despite the numerous setbacks he had sustained, Kennedy in his last months in office succeeded in approaching his goal of building a more peaceful world. In June 1963 he warned Americans "not to see only a distorted and desperate view of the other side" and recommended a re-examination of "our attitude toward the Soviet Union." In response to Kennedy's approaches, the U.S.S.R. agreed to a nuclear test-ban treaty with the United States and Great Britain. For the first time, the President noted, the world had taken a step toward getting "the genie back in the bottle." The same spirit of harmony that accompanied this pact led to the installation of a "hot line" between the White House and the Kremlin to lessen the possibility of an accidental war and an invitation to the U.S.S.R. to take part in a joint venture to explore the moon.

In domestic affairs even more than in foreign policy, Kennedy knew frustration as well as achievement. Only on occasions was he able to overcome the conservative coalition of Southern Democrats and Northern Republicans that hobbled him as it had his three predecessors in office. The President asked for massive federal aid to education, a new Department of Urban Affairs and Housing, mass transportation legislation and medical care for the aged. On all of these programs, he met defeat.

Critics charged that Kennedy failed to rally the country behind his "New Frontier" proposals, that he did not give enough attention to relations with Congress and that he was too self-protective to risk defeat. But others pointed out that he had established exceptionally effective liaison with Congress through his assistant, Lawrence O'Brien, and they doubted that there was more Kennedy could do to arouse the nation.

Furthermore, Kennedy could take pride in a not insubstantial legislative record. Among other things, Congress extended old-age pension and unemployment benefits, raised the minimum wage, enacted a drug safety law, established a program to retrain jobless workers, adopted a Federal Water Pollution Control Act and appropriated money for public housing, mental health and aid to depressed areas. In 1962, the same year that the Supreme Court required the reapportionment of legislative districts on the "one-man, one-vote" principle, Congress sent to the states for ratification the Twenty-fourth Amendment to wipe out the poll tax as a bar to voting in elections to federal offices.

B Y a series of measures, Kennedy stimulated economic growth and pulled the country out of the recession that depressed the nation when he took office. Thus began the longest peacetime expansion of the economy in modern American history. To curb inflation the President proposed wage-price guidelines. When he and Secretary of Labor Arthur Goldberg convinced the steel workers' union to agree to a non-inflationary contract, Kennedy felt he had won a significant victory for economic stability. He was outraged when Roger M. Blough, Chairman of the Board of U.S. Steel, announced a price rise of six dollars a ton, and other companies followed suit. Convinced that he had been gulled by the steel magnates, the President favored them with an expletive that led *The New York Times*, for the first time in its 111 years, to report this profanity in a news story. Threatened by a series of reprisals, the steel firms backed down.

The President recognized that new medicine was called for if a full-employment economy was to be achieved. Although personal income was

Jubilant John Glenn smiles broadly as he is welcomed aboard the U.S.S. "Randolph" in February 1962, after completing the first American orbital space flight. His feat followed tests in which apes were sent into space for short journeys. Back at home, Colonel Glenn reported the words of four-year-old Caroline Kennedy when he met her: "Where's the monkey?"

Deferring to Kennedy's demands to remove the weapons, Soviet missiles being shipped back from Cuba to the U.S.S.R. in November 1962 are uncovered for inspection by Americans on nearby ships. Nuclear war had been so close that the President and his wife considered and finally decided against her leaving the White House in order to be closer to her shelter.

127

reaching new heights and gross national product rose nearly 20 per cent under Kennedy, unemployment stood at a disappointingly high 5.5 per cent late in 1963, in part as a consequence of automation. He recommended to Congress a multibillion dollar tax cut to spur investment and consumer purchases and urged businessmen to abandon the "myths" of orthodox economics.

In the civil rights field, Kennedy started out by emphasizing executive rather than legislative action, because he was convinced that an attempt to secure civil rights legislation would not only be fruitless but would provoke Southern resistance to other Administration measures. The President named blacks to high federal posts and set up a Committee on Equal Employment Opportunity to coax big defense contractors to hire members of minority groups. Under Attorney General Robert Kennedy, the Civil Rights Division of the Department of Justice filed more suits to secure voting rights for Southern blacks in its first year than the Eisenhower Administration had in three years. In 1961 the Justice Department negotiated and litigated to end Jim Crow practices at airports and interstate bus and railroad terminals.

The Kennedy brothers met defiance in Mississippi the next year when they came to the aid of a black veteran who sought admission to the state university. Despite federal court orders compelling the registration of James H. Meredith, Governor Barnett interposed himself and deployed state police to keep the institution lily-white. On September 30, 1962, the President dispatched to Oxford several hundred U.S. marshals, who were met by a vicious mob. To quell the riot Kennedy sent in troops. Two people were killed and nearly 200 injured before Meredith could be registered at Ole Miss.

Although the Kennedys were abused by white racists for their action, black leaders lamented both the failure of the Administration to press for civil rights legislation and the President's procrastination in issuing an edict banning discrimination in public housing.

The tempo of the civil rights movement quickened with the centennial celebration of the Emancipation Proclamation in 1963. Martin Luther King Jr. stated: "We're through with tokenism and gradualism and see-how-far-you've-comeism. We're through with we've-done-more-for-your-people-than-anyone-elseism. We can't wait any longer. Now is the time." When Dr. King led a demonstration in Birmingham, Alabama, that spring, the world was horrified by the brutality of the police response. But the demonstrators prevailed. All over the South the mold of segregation was cracked—at universities, motels, department stores and public recreation areas.

Dallas, where President Kennedy was killed in November 1963, seemed gripped by irrational violence that fall. Adlai Stevenson, attacked there in October by spitting, screaming right-wing extremists (above), warned the White House of an "unpredictable madness" in the air and suggested canceling the President's visit. Lee Harvey Oswald (below center), who killed Kennedy, was in turn shot by Jack Ruby (holding pistol) two days after the assassination. Ruby's reported explanation was as senseless as the violent events of the preceding weeks: "I did it to spare Mrs. Kennedy the agony of a prolonged public trial."

HOWEVER, in Alabama, one of two states with totally segregated school systems, Governor George C. Wallace pledged to stand in the doorway to block any black who sought to enter the state university. When Vivian Malone and James Hood attempted to register at Tuscaloosa in June 1963, the Governor barred their way. In contrast to President Eisenhower's passivity in 1956 when Autherine Lucy tried to attend the University, Kennedy once more federalized the National Guard, and Wallace gave in. A week later, the President asked Congress for legislation against racial discrimination and segregation.

Yet neither Kennedy's appeal nor the peaceful methods of Martin Luther King won adoption of the civil rights measure or banked the fires of violence. Two hundred thousand people took part in a "March on Washington" that summer, but Congress made clear that it would not pass the civil rights bill in

1963. Even more disturbing were the ugly acts of violence—the cowardly murder of Medgar Evers, head of the NAACP in Mississippi, and the bombing of a Birmingham church that killed four black girls. Many feared that wanton violence would spread like an ugly stain to every area of American life.

On Friday, November 22, 1963, at 11:40 a.m., President Kennedy's plane landed at Love Field in Dallas, Texas, a city that harbored many members of the "Radical Right." But as the presidential motorcade traveled through the streets of the city the crowds were warmly responsive. "You certainly can't say that the people of Dallas haven't given you a nice welcome," Mrs. John Connally, the wife of the Governor of Texas, said to Kennedy. A moment later, at 12:30 p.m., the crack of rifle shots split the air. The President, mortally wounded, was rushed to a hospital; minutes later he was pronounced dead. That same dreadful weekend, the grief-stricken nation was interrupted in its mourning for the fallen President by still another murder. Millions of Americans, their gaze focused almost compulsively on television screens, watched with horror as Jack Ruby, a Dallas nightclub operator, gunned down Lee Harvey Oswald, who had been arrested as the President's assassin. A commission headed by Chief Justice Earl Warren later reached the conclusion that Oswald, a 24-year-old ex-Marine who had once expatriated himself to the Soviet Union, was a lone killer. Although critics of the commission charged that Kennedy was the victim of a conspiracy, they have yet to produce persuasive evidence.

While her husband's casket is prepared for the trip to Arlington Cemetery, Mrs. John F. Kennedy waits at St. Matthew's Cathedral in Washington. With her are her children Caroline and John, and her brothers-in-law Edward (at left) and Robert. President Kennedy was buried on the peaceful hillside where he had once told a friend, "I could stay here forever."

EVEN before Kennedy's body had been laid to rest, students had begun to assess his career. Some asserted that whatever might have been the result had he lived his record was so brief that historians had to write him off as a minor figure. The political scientist Clinton Rossiter, who admired Kennedy as a "copybook President," said sadly, "As a President, he will, alas, be remembered as one to whom greatness . . . was denied," because death "claimed him long before his hour. . . ." Others said this was one of those rare instances when a man's style marked him for greatness. *Le Figaro* of Paris commented: "What remains as the loss . . . is a certain feeling of possibilities, of an *élan*, and—why not say it?—of an impression of beauty. These are not political qualities, but surely they are enduring legendary and mythological qualities."

Still others argued that Kennedy's tenure represented more than a triumph of style. In *A Thousand Days*, Arthur M. Schlesinger Jr., who had served on the President's White House staff, concluded: "Yet he had accomplished so much: the new hope for peace on earth, the elimination of nuclear testing in the atmosphere and the abolition of nuclear diplomacy, the new policies toward Latin America and the third world, the reordering of American defense, the emancipation of the American Negro, the revolution of national economic policy, the concern for poverty, the stimulus to the arts, the fight for reason against extremism and mythology. . . . He re-established the republic as the first generation of our leaders saw it—young, brave, civilized, rational, gay, tough, questing, exultant in the excitement and potentiality of history."

Some critics who had taxed Kennedy for his reluctance to fragment the nation in order to secure legislation now had second thoughts. Perhaps, they said, he had understood too well how thin was the crust of civilization.

To his successor, John F. Kennedy left the awesome task of uniting a country rent by divisions; to posterity he bequeathed the memory of his grace and of his faith that reason could, in the end, conquer the brutal forces of violence.

IN DEFIANCE of a court order, Mississippi Lieutenant Governor Paul Johnson *(in hat)* blocks U.S. Marshal James McShane *(center)* from enrolling a Negro student, James H. Meredith, *(right)*, at the University of Mississippi in 1962. When white students rioted on the campus, 16,000 troops were dispatched—and Meredith was then admitted.

From civil rights to civil strife

ONE hundred years after President Lincoln proclaimed the Negro's emancipation, some 200,000 black and white Americans marched to the mall of the Lincoln Memorial in Washington, D.C., and heard the Reverend Martin Luther King Jr. say, "I still have a dream . . . that one day this nation will rise up and live out the true meaning of its creed: 'We hold these truths to be self-evident, that all men are created equal.' " Another more militant black leader was not so sanguine or patient. "I don't see any American dream," said Malcolm X, "I see an American nightmare." In a turbulent era of protest and progress, America was to share both the dream and the nightmare.

In the segregated South, thousands of young, non-violent civil rights workers singing "We shall overcome" were staging sit-ins, jail-ins, boycotts and protest marches. Their efforts—and the violent response of Southerners and their sheriffs—roused the nation's conscience and spurred major new civil rights legislation. But in the North, where discrimination was often more subtle and more stubborn, non-violent protest gave way to long, hot summers of rioting in scores of cities. In Watts, a sprawling Los Angeles ghetto, "We shall overcome" was replaced by a new cry—"burn, baby, burn."

After studying the riots of 1967, the Kerner Commission warned: "Our nation is moving toward two societies, one black, one white—separate and unequal." Even as black mayors won election—from Ohio to Mississippi —young blacks were rejecting white society. With Martin Luther King's murder in 1968, many proclaimed that the civil rights movement was dead.

IN PROTEST, some 200,000 black and white Americans gather at the Lincoln Memorial in the 1963 "March on Washington," demanding the redress of black grievances.

A "non-violent" revolution in the Deep South

ON February 1, 1960, four black college students sat down at a "white" lunch counter in Greensboro, North Carolina. Within two weeks, there were sit-ins in 15 Southern cities. Within a year, over 50,000 people had demonstrated in 100 cities, and 3,600 had been jailed. As Southern segregationists fought back, civil rights workers were beaten and shot, their homes and churches bombed. In Birmingham, when Martin Luther King led a mass protest in 1963, Public Safety Commissioner Eugene "Bull" Connor turned police dogs and fire hoses on the demonstrators—and when a black church was bombed, four small girls at Sunday school were killed.

Responding in outrage, Congress in 1964 passed a civil rights bill that desegregated public facilities everywhere. "The civil rights movement," President Kennedy said, "owes Bull Connor as much as it owes Abraham Lincoln." In Selma, Alabama, 8 months later, the violent police response to blacks seeking the vote prodded Congress to pass a sweeping voting rights law. The results were dramatic. In 1969, six years after Mississippi NAACP director Medgar Evers was slain, blacks elected his brother Charles mayor of Fayette, Mississippi.

YOUNG CASUALTIES in the 1963 Birmingham protests (above) are stunned by a stream from a high-pressure hose used to break up demonstrations. Demonstrators were also bitten by police dogs. After a black church was bombed, a 12-year-old girl was hospitalized (right) to remove glass splinters in her eyes. Her sister was one of the four young Sunday-school students who were killed in the blast.

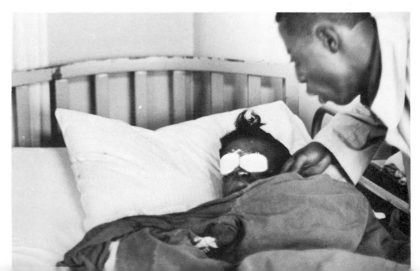

STATE POLICE break up a black voting rights march from Selma to Montgomery, Alabama, with clubs, tear gas and bullwhips *(above)*. The incident, on March 7, 1965, brought hundreds of supporters, black and white, to Selma to lend their support to the marchers. Two of them—a Detroit mother of five and a Boston minister—were murdered. The Reverend Martin Luther King Jr. and his wife *(below, center)* concluded the march to Montgomery on March 25, 1965. At the state capitol, King said: "If the worst of American life lurked in the dark streets, the best of American instincts arose passionately . . . to overcome it."

Flash fires of frustration in the black ghettos

ARSONISTS' WORK, a raging fire guts a block of retail stores in the Los Angeles Watts ghetto during 1965 rioting. As rioters burned retail shops, flames also spread to black-owned homes.

RIOT VICTIM, 12-year-old Joe Bass Jr. lies bleeding on a Newark street during 1967 disorders. He was wounded in two places by a shotgun blast when a policeman fired at a fleeing looter.

THE rights Southern blacks fought for in the 1960s were taken for granted in the North. Watching the 1963 protests in Birmingham, a Black Muslim leader said: "It . . . doesn't amount to anything to be able to sit down at a lunch counter and have a hot dog with a white man. We don't want the hot dog, we want the lunch counter. . . ." Slum housing, joblessness, run-down schools proved all too resistant to non-violent protest, despite a wave of city hall sit-ins, rent strikes and school boycotts. Suddenly, in 1964, when a white policeman shot a black youth, New York's ghetto erupted in a five-day riot. For the next several summers, similar incidents sparked violent ghetto insurrections from coast to coast.

Watts in 1965, Cleveland in 1966, Newark and Detroit in 1967, Washington, D.C., in 1968—these and scores of other cities counted millions of dollars in loss and nearly 200 deaths as riots spread. As the ghettos burned, snipers fired at police and troops while looters sacked stores in what New Jersey's Governor called "a holiday atmosphere." Voicing the new mood of the ghettos, one incendiary young black, H. Rap Brown, proclaimed: "Violence is necessary. It is as American as cherry pie."

AGAINST THE WALL in Watts, blacks caught on the street after curfew are searched by a plainclothesman brandishing a gun at the height of the disorders that hit Watts during 1965.

LOOTING A STORE, Chicago blacks react to Martin Luther King's murder in April 1968. In Washington, D.C., one of 168 cities hit, stores were looted two blocks from the White House.

A new era: reconciliation or armed revolt?

Roused by the civil rights struggle in the South and the civil disorders in the nation's ghettos, Americans began to address the problems of poverty and injustice that underlay their affluent society. Federal, state and city programs proliferated in a "war on poverty," while many leaders of large corporations spearheaded drives to recruit and train the "hard-core" unemployed. Progress could be seen in statistics showing that by the late 1960s only one third of Northern blacks still lived in the black ghettos, while nearly one third of all black families had an annual income exceeding $7,000.

This progress, however, was most visible among the black middle class. Poorer blacks, especially the young, faced continuing despair. In 1967 the Commission on Civil Rights reported that 75 per cent of all black grade-school pupils in metropolitan areas were in predomi-

nantly black schools, while more than a quarter of all black teen-agers seeking work could not get a job. It was to attack this problem that Martin Luther King in 1968 reoriented his civil rights drive and launched a "Poor People's Campaign." He planned to lead a host of the poor, white and black, to Washington—there to pitch a tent city and demand economic aid from Congress.

In 1968, too, Senator Robert F. Kennedy began a campaign for the presidency with an appeal that won support from ghetto blacks and poorer whites alike. When both King and Kennedy were assassinated, in April and June, 1968, their new approach to social reconstruction, which enlisted the poor of both races, was abruptly set back. In the ghettos, young militants found new cause for disillusion—and, for many, a new reason to heed spokesmen urging blacks to arm and segregate themselves.

POOR PEOPLE, led by Reverend Ralph D. Abernathy, built a Washington, D.C., "Resurrection City" *(left)* in 1968, after Martin Luther King's death. Although thousands of demonstrators came to Washington, the "Poor People's Campaign" failed.

REACHING OUT, Robert F. Kennedy won strong support from blacks and was often met with cries of "soul brother" as he campaigned for the presidency. With local black leaders *(right)*, he toured Watts. The day after this picture was taken, he was slain.

ARMED MEN, Black Panther Party members, invade the California State Capitol at Sacramento *(below)* in 1967. With other revolutionary black groups, the Panthers maintained that the blacks would only gain their rights by urban guerrilla warfare.

7. THE GREAT SOCIETY

Mr. Speaker, Mr. President, Members of the House, Members of the Senate, my fellow Americans: All I have I would have given gladly not to be standing here today," the new President began. Sworn into office five days earlier on the plane bearing John F. Kennedy's body back to Washington, Lyndon Baines Johnson had determined to show that American institutions could survive a disaster that would have shaken less stable governments. On November 27 in his first presidential address to Congress, Johnson emphasized continuity. He recalled that the fallen President in his inaugural had urged the nation: "Let us begin." Then Johnson declared: "Today, in this moment of new resolve, I would say to all my fellow Americans, let us continue."

If Johnson deferred to the Kennedy program, he also quickly stamped the L.B.J. brand on the national government. Washington correspondents described this imperious, egocentric, power-hungry man as a "ponderous, protean Texan, with the forbidding look of a chain-gang boss. . . ." Yet the new President was almost pathetically anxious for affection; he was forever pulling polls out of his pocket to prove that people loved him. His favorite text was a paraphrase of Isaiah: "Come, let us reason together." Instead of pitting rival groups against one another or wrangling with Congressmen, the Great Persuader would—and for a time did—win their cooperation.

Although some of the Kennedy circle were appalled by the new President's style, even Johnson's sternest critics conceded his parliamentary acumen. In

IN AN ANGRY MOOD, Lyndon Johnson denounces the 1965 racial violence in Alabama. As President, he used his legislative experience to push his program through Congress.

rapid order this former Majority Leader drove through Congress bills to aid college construction and safeguard wilderness areas, and the Urban Mass Transportation Act to improve one of the worst rail commuter systems in the world. He persuaded Congressmen to approve the plan that Kennedy had proposed for an $11.5 billion tax cut. By the summer of 1964 Johnson could boast that more than 72 million Americans were at work, a record high.

In his first address to Congress Johnson had said: "We have talked long enough in this country about equal rights. We have talked for one hundred years or more. It is time now to write the next chapter, and to write it in the books of law." The first resident of a Southern state to serve as Chief Executive since Andrew Johnson in 1865, he met fierce sectional resistance. But Northern Democrats led by Hubert Humphrey, with the aid of Republican leaders like Senator Everett Dirksen, succeeded in invoking cloture to break a Southern filibuster on civil rights for the first time in history. The Civil Rights Act of 1964 banned Jim Crow in places of public accommodation; strengthened Washington's hand in extending suffrage and quickening the pace of school desegregation; and authorized federal bureaus to withold funds from federally assisted projects that practiced racial discrimination.

N OT content with winning approval for the "New Frontier," Johnson also developed his own legislative slogans. When in his State of the Union message of January 1964 he called for a "war on poverty," he borrowed a Kennedy phrase he soon made his own. Beginning with the Economic Opportunity Act of 1964, Congress authorized such anti-poverty experiments as Head Start, Neighborhood Youth Corps, Job Corps and VISTA, all aimed at young people, and community action programs to allow the poor to participate in operating government projects. In spring 1964 Johnson made his goal the "Great Society." This tagline "was symbolic of the new President," wrote Congressman Richard Bolling. "It was expansive, implied a state of affairs already achieved, and was hyperbolic, like the tall tales of Mark Twain."

To gain adoption of his Great Society program, Johnson required a smashing election victory that would alter the composition of Congress; in 1964 the Republicans obliged him. G.O.P. candidates for a quarter of a century had been moderates acceptable to the internationalist Eastern wing of the party; now the party chose a man of the Right, Senator Barry Goldwater of Arizona, reckoning that it could afford to write off the populous Northeast by putting together an unprecedented alliance of the South and West. Goldwater was expected to attract a big turnout of conservative nationalist voters who had stayed home rather than vote for past "Me Too" Republican candidates.

Less a politician than an idealogue, Goldwater went out of his way to demonstrate the purity of his doctrine. He not only refused to openly repudiate the John Birch Society but assured the San Francisco convention that "extremism in the defense of liberty is no vice!" He told students that the federal government should not aid education. One of only six Republican Senators to vote against the civil rights bill, he made "violence in the streets" readily recognized as a code word for racial discrimination. In Knoxville, Tennessee, he advocated the sale of TVA to private utilities. An opponent of Johnson's "no win" policy in Southeast Asia, Goldwater, an avid jet pilot, informed a reporter, "I'd drop a low-yield atomic bomb on Chinese supply lines in North Vietnam." His uncompromising stands convinced many voters that he would undo

A haggard Lyndon Johnson, watched by a desolate Jacqueline Kennedy (right) and his wife, Lady Bird, takes the oath of office after John Kennedy's death. The ceremony took place on the presidential plane at the Dallas airport; the only photographer present raced to process his films and prove to an anxious world that an orderly transfer of power had taken place.

the reforms of the past generation and could not be trusted with the Bomb.

With 43 million votes to Goldwater's 27 million Johnson ran up the biggest popular majority in history. Goldwater won the electoral votes of only his own Arizona and five Deep South states; for the first time the South made up the main bloc of G.O.P. electoral votes. Goldwater dragged so many conservative Congressional candidates to defeat that Johnson secured a firm majority for his program. By depriving the conservative bipartisan coalition of the pivotal role it had held since 1938, Goldwater's loss had the ironic consequence of smoothing the way for the adoption of Great Society legislation.

The new Congress added two more Cabinet posts: a Department of Housing and Urban Development (to which Johnson named the first black Cabinet member, Robert C. Weaver) and a Department of Transportation. Congress not only approved Medicare but Medicaid (which provided medical care for the poor) and a multimillion-dollar program for medical research. It implemented the Great Society's concern with "quality," by creating a National Foundation for the Arts and the Humanities and enacting the Highway Beautification Act. To aid the consumer, it passed the Truth in Packaging Act and, largely as a consequence of muckraker Ralph Nader's prodding, traffic and highway safety acts. It ended biased restrictions on immigration, voted funds for the depressed Appalachian region and introduced, on a limited scale, such innovations as model cities and rent supplements. A former teacher, Johnson took special pride in Congress' billion-dollar appropriation for the 1965 Elementary and Secondary Education Act and in its approval of federal aid to higher education, a cold-war GI Bill of Rights and a National Teacher Corps.

When civil rights protests led by Dr. Martin Luther King Jr. in Selma, Alabama, early in 1965 led to the deaths of three demonstrators, Congress responded to the national outcry by enacting the Voting Rights Act of 1965, which authorized direct federal intervention to protect the Negro's suffrage. In the next few years voting examiners enrolled 460,000 blacks in five states in the Deep South. The percentage of blacks registered to vote in Alabama jumped from 14 per cent in 1960 to 53 per cent in 1968. Blacks now sat on the Supreme Court (Justice Thurgood Marshall) and on the Federal Reserve Board. By the end of Johnson's term, there were black mayors in Cleveland, Ohio, and Gary, Indiana, and Edward W. Brooke of Massachusetts, a Republican, had become the first black Senator since Reconstruction.

Yet Johnson had hardly begun his Great Society program when developments abroad raised disturbing threats. Less than three weeks after his Inaugural Address in January 1965, the President faced a crisis in Southeast Asia triggered by Viet Cong mortar attacks on an American base at Pleiku.

Barry Goldwater (above) won the 1964 Republican nomination for President amid the screaming delight of his fervent followers, who interrupted moderate Nelson Rockefeller with verbal onslaughts. But despite Goldwater's optimistic slogan, he aroused little enthusiasm in the nation. Johnson quickly sensed victory and happily pursued his favorite activity, handshaking (below), a ritual he gave the name of "pressing the flesh."

W HEN he took office, Johnson had inherited Kennedy's woes in Vietnam. During his first term he respected his predecessor's commitment but did little to expand the war. In August 1964, when two United States destroyers were attacked in the Gulf of Tonkin, the President ordered a retaliatory assault on North Vietnamese bases and won a Congressional resolution authorizing him both to repel attacks and "to prevent future aggression." But his response was measured and he emphasized that "we still seek no wider war." Johnson's great triumph as a "peace" candidate in the 1964 elections gave him the opportunity to extricate the nation from the Vietnam quagmire.

But Johnson, whose approach to foreign affairs was shaped during the Roo-

Early in his presidency, Lyndon Johnson was faced with crises in Southeast Asia and the Caribbean. In August 1964 carrier-based jets (above) responded to North Vietnamese action against American destroyers by bombing the North. In April 1965 Marines were sent to the Dominican Republic to crush an allegedly pro-Communist uprising (below). Johnson said, "It's just like the Alamo. . . . Well, by God, I'm going to go."

sevelt era and hardened by the Cold War, had long since set a different course. In the spring of 1961 he had warned against permitting the "vast Pacific" to become a "Red Sea" and of pulling back our defenses to San Francisco. When, several months after the Pleiku incident, he landed marines in the Dominican Republic, he revealed a disposition to oversimplify the nature of the Communist challenge and to rely on a disproportionate amount of force. By the time the Dominican crisis had eased, many were asking whether after having voted against Goldwater, a "super-hawk," they had gotten his equivalent.

IN Vietnam the war quickly careened out of control. The President ordered an air strike against North Vietnam in February 1965 as retribution for the Viet Cong attack on Pleiku, since he regarded the V.C. simply as agents of the North. But within a month, bombing planes were "going North" without any pretense of making a retaliatory response and the first United States combat units had disembarked. In the next three years, American planes unloaded more bombs on Vietnam, South as well as North, than had fallen on all enemy targets in World War II, and United States forces in Vietnam, some 25,000 when Johnson took office, had grown to more than half a million—with an enormous rise in casualties.

As the cost of the war rose, the President heard a rising chorus of criticism. Hawks wanted restraints lifted on the bombardiers' targets, even at the risk of bringing China and Russia into the conflict. At least as late as the spring of 1967 polls indicated that most of the country was hawkish. But "doves" raised a greater threat to the Johnson coalition because, unlike the hawks, who were strongest among conservative Republicans, the doves included many of the top Democrats in the Senate, among them the Chairman of the Foreign Relations Committee, J. William Fulbright, the Majority Leader, Mike Mansfield, and the junior Senator from New York, Robert F. Kennedy.

The Johnson Administration vigorously defended itself against its critics. Secretary of State Rusk, a legacy of the Kennedy Administration, insisted that the United States had to honor its treaty commitments, for if it did not, no nation would ever trust this country again. Should South Vietnam fall, he argued, the Red Chinese would swarm over and topple all the independent governments of eastern Asia like dominoes and the Communists would start "wars of national liberation" throughout the third world. To pull out of Vietnam would—like the appeasement of Germany at Munich in 1938—invite a subsequent war at a far greater cost. Since the Communists refused to respond to peace feelers and even to bombing halts, only an intensification of the bombing, said Rusk, would bring the enemy to the negotiating table.

The doves, in return, pointed out that the SEATO pact had no specific military obligations, and they scoffed at "the domino theory" as a misreading of the character of the struggle in Vietnam. The doves viewed the conflict as principally a civil war; indeed, the Viet Cong had won control of the countryside before there was any large-scale infiltration from the North. The doves believed that the Hanoi government, far from being a pawn of Peking, might evolve into a Titoist kind of independent Communist regime if the United States did not throw North Vietnam into the arms of Mao Tse-tung. They scoffed at the Munich analogy; even if the United States withdrew from Vietnam, and few doves favored so drastic a course, it was absurd, they maintained, to think that the Red Chinese would pursue the Americans all the way to California.

If the President really wanted an end to the war, the doves asserted, he should call off the bombing and show a willingness to bargain with the Viet Cong.

The Vietnam imbroglio shattered the "consensus" Johnson had carefully put together. Civil rights leaders like Martin Luther King Jr. broke with the President for giving the war a higher priority than the Great Society. Many college students despaired not only of the Administration but of the political system. In the Senate the most ardent advocates of the Great Society turned against Johnson. Even more alarming to the President was the growing evidence of the political consequences of the war. In 1966 the Democrats lost three seats in the Senate and 47 in the House, and on November 30, 1967, Senator Eugene J. McCarthy, a scholarly politician, announced he would challenge Johnson for the presidential nomination in several Democratic primaries.

In the first three months of 1968 Johnson's world fell apart. On January 23 the U.S.S. *Pueblo*, an intelligence-gathering vessel, was captured by North Korean gunboats. One week later, the Viet Cong's *Tet* offensive revealed that despite all the expenditure of lives and money not even the American embassy compound in Saigon was safe. On March 12 Senator McCarthy, who had not been regarded as a serious contender, ran up a stunning 42 per cent of the vote in New Hampshire's primary, and four days later Robert Kennedy entered the campaign against the President.

On March 31 Johnson delivered a major television address. He announced that he was sharply restricting bombing of the North and was inviting Hanoi to enter into negotiations, a bid which the North Vietnamese soon accepted. He concluded with a stunning refusal to run for another term. Johnson's withdrawal did not bring peace either abroad or at home. While the negotiations droned on in Paris the slaughter in Vietnam continued. In the United States violence shook urban ghettos, college campuses and political conventions.

R ACE riots had agitated Northern cities as early as the summer of 1964, but they failed to prepare the country for the violence that erupted in the Watts district of Los Angeles the following summer. In one of the worst racial disturbances in American history, 34 died, 1,032 were injured. The next two "long, hot summers" saw outbreaks in scores of cities, the most terrible in Detroit where 43 lost their lives. The havoc substantiated James Baldwin's words in his prophetic *The Fire Next Time*: "To be a Negro in this country and to be relatively conscious is to be in a rage almost all the time."

By 1966 the movement for black rights had shifted from the South to the Northern cities and from an emphasis on desegregation to the new battle cry of "black power." An ambiguous term, black power sometimes meant no more than determination to play the kind of Tammany politics the Irish had found advantageous. But more and more frequently it signified hatred of "whitey," a term covering all whites, and a reliance on violence. The doctrines of the black nationalist spokesman Malcolm X, who was murdered in 1965 by Black Muslim former associates, were taken over by young militants who formed such new groups as the Black Panthers. In 1966 the Student Nonviolent Coordinating Committee, once dedicated to peaceful ways of racial progress, fell into the hands of a new cadre who made a mockery of the organization's title. Yet if black firebrands and snipers were the most conspicuous element in the riots, the President's National Advisory Commission on Civil Disorders, headed by Governor Otto Kerner of Illinois, pinned

"Backlash"   From *The Herblock Gallery*
Simon & Schuster 1968

By the end of 1966 the cost of the Vietnamese war—almost $2 billion a month—had led Washington to impose sharp cuts on domestic spending. The budget was cut to the bone, and as cartoonist Herblock pointed out, among the victims of budget-paring were the prospects of the Great Society.

Catholic priests Philip Berrigan (left) and his brother Daniel burn stolen draft records in 1968 as a protest against the Vietnam war. The Berrigans, leaders of a radical pacifist group (the Catonsville Nine), were jailed for this incineration, which was set off with napalm made from an Army recipe.

143

H. Rap Brown is led into court in July 1967 to be charged with inciting a riot in Cambridge, Maryland. While head of the Student Nonviolent Coordinating Committee, he changed its policy, and in 1969 dropped "Nonviolent" from its name to reflect the growing militance in the black community.

Black firebrands Eldridge Cleaver (left) and Stokely Carmichael had preached violent revolution before fleeing the U.S.—Cleaver in 1968 to avoid a murder charge, Carmichael in 1969 to go into voluntary exile. By 1975 Cleaver had returned to stand trial and Carmichael had touted Pan-Africanism on U.S. campuses.

the chief blame on whites who profited from or tolerated the ghetto squalor.

Against discouraging odds Dr. Martin Luther King Jr. continued to believe that gains could be made through non-violent means. Awarded the 1964 Nobel Peace Prize in Norway, he had many warm admirers in white America. On April 3, 1968, the 39-year-old minister told a Memphis meeting: "Like anybody, I would like to live a long life. . . . But I'm not concerned about that now. . . . I've seen the Promised Land. I may not get there with you, but I want you to know tonight that we as a people will get to the Promised Land." The following evening as he stood on the balcony of a motel Dr. King was murdered by a bullet fired from across the street. James Earl Ray, a white escaped convict, was subsequently sentenced to a 99-year term for the crime.

Although Dr. King's death was an irreparable loss, the country responded to it in contradictory ways. His sermons on non-violence were ignored when black rioters rampaged through 168 cities and towns at a cost of 46 lives. However, on the day after he was buried in his adopted city of Atlanta, the House passed and sent to President Johnson for approval the Civil Rights Act of 1968, which aimed to prohibit discrimination in some 80 per cent of the nation's housing. The law also imposed penalties for crossing state lines to incite riots.

D R. KING'S murder, coming only four days after L.B.J.'s withdrawal, gave a new urgency to the campaign of Robert Kennedy. Condemned by some as a ruthless opportunist, the New York Senator had a greater following in the smoldering ghettos than any other candidate. After winning the Indiana primary he was defeated by Senator McCarthy in Oregon; his hopes for the Democratic nomination all hinged on his winning the California primary on June 5, 1968. Shortly before midnight Kennedy got exhilarating news—on a single day he had taken both California and South Dakota. A tough fight against Vice President Hubert Humphrey, the Administration's candidate, still lay ahead, yet never had the future seemed so promising. He told his jubilant supporters at Los Angeles' Ambassador Hotel: "I think we can end the divisions within the United States, the violence."

But as Bobby Kennedy walked from this meeting through a kitchen passageway, he was fatally wounded by a shot fired by a 24-year-old Jordanian immigrant, Sirhan Bishara Sirhan, who was infuriated by the Senator's pro-Israeli stand. Senator Edward Kennedy chose one of his brother's favorite passages from George Bernard Shaw to conclude his moving funeral oration at St. Patrick's Cathedral: "Some men see things as they are and say 'Why?' I dream things that never were and say, 'Why not?'" Only 42, the father of ten children with another on the way, Robert Francis Kennedy was buried in a hillside grave in Arlington beside his brother, another victim of an assassin's bullet.

The murders of Senator Kennedy and Dr. King shocked America into a critical self-examination. Some commentaries exaggerated the propensity for violence in the United States, a country that in many respects was distinguished for the stability of its institutions. Yet there was cause enough for concern. Even the college campus, for centuries a peaceful sanctuary, was the scene of bombings, arson, intimidation and other outrages.

Turbulent squalls also buffeted the 1968 presidential campaign. The new American Independent Party offered Governor George C. Wallace as a candidate who would restore "law and order," a phrase that signified anything from racial segregation to criticism of an "overly permissive" Supreme Court to anti-crime crusades. But Wallace's own rhetoric suggested less law and order than vigilantism. And his running mate, retired Air Force General Curtis LeMay, who resented the nation's "phobia" about using nuclear weapons, sounded like a character in *Dr. Strangelove*, the doomsday movie.

The turmoil had even more fateful consequences for the Democrats, whose convention at the Chicago Stockyards reverberated to the clamor of Senator McCarthy's "Children's Crusade." McCarthy's young enthusiasts and the followers of Senator George McGovern of South Dakota, who had inherited some of the Kennedy support, complained that the convention was undemocratic and boss-ridden, even though the conclave broke new ground by seating black delegates from the Deep South, abrogating the unit rule and giving opportunity for debate on Vietnam. In downtown Chicago, peace demonstrators, some of them spoiling for a fight, battled with Mayor Richard J. Daley's club-wielding police who savagely mauled innocent spectators. By the time the delegates got around to nominating Hubert H. Humphrey for President the party had been so badly divided that the Vice President faced an uphill struggle.

Since both Humphrey and his Republican rival Richard Nixon took a "hard line" on Vietnam, there were many voters who felt that these two veteran politicians offered no meaningful choice. Nixon's name also recalled disagreeable memories of the Joe McCarthy era, an association that was emphasized when he chose the blundering Governor of Maryland, Spiro T. Agnew, as his running mate. Humphrey, on the other hand, had made a shrewd move when he picked the able Senator from Maine, Edmund S. Muskie, to run with him, and many Democrats grudgingly remembered the Vice President's sterling performance as the leader of Senate liberals for two decades. When in the last week of the campaign Johnson announced he was halting the bombing of North Vietnam, Humphrey almost caught up with his Republican opponent.

I N one of the closest races in history, Richard Nixon, with 31.8 million votes (43.4 per cent), nosed out Hubert Humphrey who polled 31.3 million votes (42.7) per cent). Nixon did better in the electoral vote, 301 to 191, by carrying most of the West and running unexpectedly well in the upper South. Humphrey found his strongest following among lower income groups, especially black voters, in the big cities. But so far had the "Solid South" disintegrated that the Vice President took only one Southern state, Texas. Wallace made one of the best third-party showings in history with 9.9 million votes (13.5 per cent) and 46 electoral votes, all from the South, but he did not do as well among Northern blue-collar workers as had been anticipated.

As the dreadful year of 1968 ended the country's prospects seemed to many to be uninviting. Some recalled Adlai Stevenson's words 15 years earlier: "The ordeal of the Twentieth Century—the bloodiest, most turbulent era of the Christian age—is far from over." Yet if the recent era had been a time of turmoil and defeat, it had also been a period of social gain. From 1960 to 1968 the number of people living in poverty was reduced almost by half. The worst eventuality of all—a nuclear holocaust—had been avoided. If Americans had to endure a troubled time, they also lived in an era which posed the most challenging questions. As John F. Kennedy observed, "Our problems are manmade—therefore, they can be solved by man. . . . For, in the final analysis, our most basic common link is that we all inhabit this small planet. We all breathe the same air. We all cherish our children's future. And we are all mortal."

AGNEW AND NIXON

HUMPHREY AND MUSKIE

WALLACE AND LEMAY

As the 1968 presidential campaign neared its end, only Nixon and Agnew, buoyed by support at the Republican Convention, were still optimistic. Humphrey and Muskie had yet to heal the party divisions revealed at the violence-ridden Democratic Convention. George Wallace was also in trouble: his running mate General Curtis LeMay had said: "A nuclear weapon is just another weapon. . . ."

HUNTING for Viet Cong northeast of Saigon in 1964, a unit of mountain tribesmen from South Vietnam is led by an American Green Beret "adviser." Trained in counterinsurgency tactics, Green Beret troops recruited and led local forces. Successive U.S. Administrations hoped in this way to avoid using conventional troops in combat.

The war that defeated L.B.J.

During the five years that Lyndon Johnson was President the war in Vietnam denied him his chief goals: the building of a liberal consensus in America and the fashioning of a Great Society. American participation in the Vietnamese trouble began before he took office, for both Eisenhower and Kennedy had sent military "advisers" to help South Vietnam repel pro-Communist Viet Cong forces that were being aided by North Vietnam, Russia and China. Johnson affirmed this commitment two days after Kennedy's assassination, saying to a diplomat, "I am not going to be the President who saw Southeast Asia go the way China went." But while he continued Kennedy's policy of limited aid, he responded to North Vietnamese torpedo-boat attacks on American ships in the Gulf of Tonkin in August 1964 by getting from Congress broad powers to combat aggression. Nevertheless, successfully campaigning that fall for the presidency, Johnson said the United States is "not about to send American boys nine or ten thousand miles away from home to do what Asian boys ought to be doing to protect themselves."

Within a month of his inauguration, Johnson may have regretted his pledge not to expand the war. By February the Viet Cong were mounting greater attacks on American bases, infiltration of soldiers from the North was increasing and the shaky Saigon government, which had changed leaders numerous times following the coup that toppled President Diem in November 1963, seemed about to go under. Johnson, deciding that a policy of restraint was no longer possible, began massive bombing of the North and committed American troops to active combat for the first time. Thus, early in 1965, began the process that was to destroy Lyndon Johnson's hopes and turn his nation against him.

A FIERY SUICIDE on a Saigon sidewalk horrifies Sunday morning bystanders, who stare at the dying Buddhist monk. During 1963 seven such immolations in protest against the persecution of Buddhists by dictatorial President Diem portended the rebellion that broke out on November 1, 1963. Vietnamese generals led the uprising, killed Diem and set up a new government.

147

The piteous victims of an endless war

EVERY weekday evening of the mid-'60s, around dinnertime, millions of Americans watched films on television of recent fighting in Vietnam. People at home became familiar with the everyday, unheroic face of combat: an injured GI being carried to a rescue helicopter, an old woman dying of wounds inflicted by stray machine-gun rounds. Appalled by the gruesome parade of casualties, Americans became deeply involved in the war and the realization grew that behind a screen of optimistic government statements lay unpleasant realities. They learned how Vietnam's steep hills, thick jungles and leech-infested rivers made fighting difficult. They learned of *punji* spikes (poisoned bamboo slivers hidden

along trails to pierce soldiers' boots) and other tricks of guerrilla warfare. They learned the strange names of places—Con Thien, Dak To, Khe Sanh—where Americans fought battles that sent casualty rates soaring.

Progress toward an often promised victory was painfully slow. Even by the end of 1968, when troop commitments had jumped from 25,000 in 1963 to 540,000 and three commanders, Paul Harkins, William Westmoreland and Creighton Abrams, had tried their hand at winning, the Viet Cong still controlled much of the countryside. Parents with sons in Vietnam and taxpayers footing the huge bill began to feel as if they were trapped on a treadmill, running hard but not going anywhere.

HELPING a Marine, a corpsman braves enemy shelling on a burned-out slope to apply a compress to a casualty; seconds later, realizing the man was dead, the medic raced to the aid of another victim. The incident occurred in the Khe Sanh valley, a key point on the North Vietnamese infiltration route into the South where Americans were later to survive a lengthy siege.

COMFORTING his distraught family after two battles on successive days devastated their village and killed many friends and relatives, a Vietnamese looks around as if unable to believe the danger has finally passed. He and his family were lucky to survive unharmed: by early 1968, hundreds of thousands of the civilians in South Vietnam had been killed or wounded.

A FLAMING SHROUD engulfs a thicket where planes have dropped napalm on Viet Cong. The grisly effects of the blazing, sticky jelly were widely condemned by Americans at home.

DEAD VIET CONG, slain within the supposedly secure grounds of the American embassy in Saigon, are inspected by Ambassador Ellsworth Bunker on the day the *Tet* offensive began.

A glut of problems
for a wartime President

PRESIDENT Johnson kept promising that peace was just ahead. But peace was elusive, and people frustrated by the slow war turned into critics who noted that Johnson passed quickly over such troubling issues as the use of napalm to burn villages suspected of harboring the enemy. When the Viet Cong, supposedly on the run, launched their bloody *Tet* offensive in February 1968, the credibility gap—the gulf between Johnson's promises and what the nation saw—never seemed wider.

In addition, the nation was haunted by the specter of the rising death toll, at times 500 Americans a week in early 1968; the war was also damaging the budget: It cost $25 billion in 1967 alone and was helping to raise consumer prices by more than three per cent a year. L.B.J.'s support dropped away sharply. In March 1968 a poll showed that only 26 per cent of Americans—compared with 83 per cent in 1965—approved his conduct of the war and only 36 per cent—compared with 80 per cent in 1964—had general confidence in him as President.

A HARSH CRITIC of Vietnam policy, Senator J. William Fulbright of Arkansas used the powerful Senate Foreign Relations Committee to voice dissatisfaction with the war in Vietnam.

The brutal shooting by South Vietnam's police chief of a Viet Cong prisoner, shown grimacing as the bullet hits, outraged Americans.

Protests, smashing defeat and a surprise speech

S ENATOR Eugene McCarthy's victory in the New Hampshire Democratic primary of 1968 was the surprise of the year. Promptly labeled "The Unforeseen Eugene," the introverted, scholarly peace candidate captured 20 out of 24 delegate votes from Lyndon Johnson, who had at his disposal all the muscle of an incumbent President. The depth of the opposition to L.B.J., previously aired largely in demonstrations by activists, had now been tested at the polls and the situation was clear: many Americans were fed up with Johnson and the war.

The President got the message. Soon after the primary, concluding a television speech that announced a partial halt in the bombing of North Vietnam, he roused viewers out of Sunday evening drowsiness with the words: "I shall not seek, and I will not accept, the nomination of my party for another term as your President." The old pro had admitted defeat, overwhelmed by the longest, most unpopular war in America's history.

GREETING SUPPORTERS in St. Louis in 1968, Senator McCarthy charms students. The peace candidate attracted so many young people that his effort was called "the children's crusade."

A protest honoring America's first Congresswoman, Jeannette Rankin, files by the Capitol to dramatize a plea to end the war.

DEEP IN THOUGHT, Lyndon Johnson polishes the speech announcing that, in an effort to heal the "division in the American house" and to achieve peace in Vietnam, he has withdrawn from the presidential race of 1968. On March 30 he worked late on the speech, his deeply lined face revealing fatigue and concern. The next evening he went before the nation with his address.

8. A CONSTITUTIONAL CRISIS

THE Nixon Administration opened on a muted note. The new President appealed for an end to the noisy dissension of 1968: "We cannot learn from one another until we stop shouting at one another." For Richard Nixon, the role of conciliator was new, for he had made his way as a battler who viewed his long political career as a succession of crises. For the moment, it seemed possible that Nixon, now 56, was a changed, more settled man.

Yet this quiet beginning was deceptive; the matching-up of Nixon and the Presidency was to prove fateful. The office had greatly expanded under Lyndon Johnson, not only in its authority over war and peace but in its control of the domestic economy. Nixon, while rhetorically invoking a return to limited government, was, in fact, deeply susceptible both to the use of executive power and to its expansion to constitutional limits and beyond. In this contradiction lay the seeds of the gravest American governmental crisis in a century.

That crisis lay years ahead; in 1969, aware that he faced opposition majorities in both houses of Congress, Nixon seemed to be constructing a centrist, caretaker government, one that was designed to slow down and moderate the Great Society programs rather than discard them.

But on his own Nixon secured many of his objectives in his first administration—their value to the nation depending, in many instances, on the political bias of the observer. The South had contributed heavily to Nixon's election and might be looked to for more help in his re-election; it would be rewarded by a

STERN AND COMPOSED in the White House Rose Garden, Richard M. Nixon weighs a 1970 Middle East alarm in the heady, pre-Watergate period of his presidency.

Black and white Denver children enter a school desegregated by a series of court orders dating back to 1954. Busing to achieve integration aroused the ire of many whites and some blacks around the country, but Denver had a special problem: a Hispanic minority demanded separate, ethnically oriented bilingual schools.

slowdown, if not a reversal, in governmental pressure for racial equality. "Law and order" would be enforced. Inflation would be curbed. A new political coalition would be forged, bringing together white Southerners, urban Catholics and other Democratic conservatives under a Nixon-Republican banner.

Such were the Administration's objectives at home, as they were enunciated or as they gradually manifested themselves in the first years. Abroad, an end would be sought to American participation in the Vietnam war; "peace with honor" was to be the formula. In place of the rigidly anti-Soviet stance of the Cold War, foreign policy would be made more flexible and brought in line with contemporary realities of power.

THE two policies, domestic and foreign, were entangled. A breakthrough in one area sometimes bolstered a weakness in the other; a goal abroad could justify an unpopular act at home. Most important, at home as well as abroad, the executive power was unilaterally broadened, and in the process that power was more and more centralized in the White House.

When the Administration began, Americans appeared ready for respite from conflict. In August of 1969, however, the government sided for the first time with Southerners seeking a delay in ending segregated, dual-school systems. But when the case reached the Supreme Court in October the Court ruled unanimously that school desegregation must proceed "at once," thus going beyond the famous 1955 criterion of "all deliberate speed."

Even before this rebuff, Nixon had become determined that the ideological character of the Court had to be changed in order to modify what conservatives viewed as its extreme bias. But of seven conservative jurists he nominated to fill three vacancies on the Court, only three—Harry Blackmun, Lewis Powell Jr. and William Rehnquist—were clearly qualified.

The attempt to influence the Supreme Court toward closer alignment with the Administration view was only one of several struggles over ideology. The departure of L.B.J. and Nixon's moderate public position on Vietnam had to a great extent defused the anti-war issue, but in April of 1970 the Administration abruptly extended the ground fighting into Cambodia. The supercharged atmosphere of the 1960s immediately returned. The peace movement came back to life on campuses, violently. Within days, blood was shed: an Ohio National Guard company fired on a demonstration at Kent State University, killing four students and wounding 11. More violence occurred when construction workers beat marching students in the streets of New York City. Two black students were killed by Mississippi state police at Jackson State College.

The Administration's reaction to the uproar was ambiguous. In a statement following the Kent State shooting, Nixon expressed the hope that the nation's campuses would oppose a "resort to violence." Later, however, he seemed to equivocate. He paid an unexpected, conciliatory, pre-dawn visit to demonstrators at the Lincoln Memorial; he conferred with college presidents and he created a commission on campus unrest. Then a harder line was taken. Vice President Spiro Agnew, who had earned public attention in 1969 when he attacked peace activists as "an effete corps of impudent snobs," moved further into the limelight by blasting an array of Administration social targets, including rock music, the drug culture, permissive child-rearing and network television news.

Thus began an extraordinary mid-term election campaign in which even the President took a hand. Administration forces were trying to build on their victory of 1968. According to a thesis they adopted from *The Emerging Republican Majority*, a book by Kevin Phillips, a former Nixon campaign aide, a party realignment had begun to take shape in that election year. A new majority would be created under Republican leadership, Phillips asserted, including disaffected Democrats, for whom the Republicans now held out the hope of "law and order." By election day, the economy had joined ideology as an issue. The Administration had tried to curb inflation with tight-money measures. The result by mid-1970 was a country near recession.

The voting failed to produce decisive gains for either party. Although the White House boasted of victory, the Republicans could claim only a net of two seats in the Senate; they had lost a net of nine seats in the House and a net of 11 governorships. It was an irritated, impatient President who faced the new Congress. Now he would rely more on the power of the Presidency rather than plead for Congressional cooperation. Henceforth much of the executive power was to be exercised by Nixon's principal assistants—H. R. Haldeman, White House Chief of Staff, and John Ehrlichman, Chief Assistant for Domestic Affairs—zealous and devoted but politically inexperienced men who controlled access to the President and freely acted for him. Friction with Congress increased as the President used the pocket veto. Although he was forbidden by law to veto any single item in appropriation measures passed by Congress, Nixon accomplished that end by impounding funds for programs he opposed.

Doubts about Presidential power were intensified by events related to the Vietnam war. The disclosure of a massacre in the village of My Lai, in which over 100 South Vietnamese civilians had been deliberately slain by American forces, had set off waves of revulsion throughout the United States and led to new criticism of the Administration. Then came the publication in various newspapers of the Pentagon Papers, a secret government compilation of the origin and development of American involvement in Vietnam that chronicled a cynical misleading of the public. The Nixon Administration—though not involved in the machinations disclosed—reacted swiftly, strongly and fatefully. It obtained injunctions to stop newspapers from publishing the Papers. A divided Supreme Court ruled that the newspapers could resume publication.

Public interest in the Papers was intense and the public reaction largely one of dismay over the revelations. More important was the traumatizing effect that the unauthorized publication had on the Administration and on the President himself. Determined to stop further disclosure of secret materials, the White House set up a clandestine intelligence unit under the direction of John Ehrlichman. There was no precedent or authority for establishing the "Plumbers"—so-called because their mission was to stop leaks—and they quickly overstepped the bounds of legal government activity, but their crimes did not come to light until the Watergate investigation one year later.

WHILE newspaper front pages were headlining the Pentagon Papers, the business pages reported disquieting news of a still-ailing economy. Late in the summer of 1971, with the next Presidential election little more than a year away, Nixon made dramatic moves. He announced that the United States dollar would no longer be redeemable in gold. He imposed a 10 per cent surcharge on imports; later the dollar was officially devaluated by 8 per cent. And on August 15 he imposed economic controls. The pace of inflation slowed.

Despite such determined actions in domestic affairs, the Nixon Adminis-

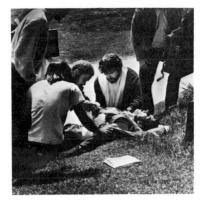

Friends tend a mortally wounded Kent State University classmate, one of the four students killed on May 4, 1970, by Ohio National Guardsmen who fired shots into a crowd protesting the U.S. invasion of Cambodia. Five years later, an Ohio jury ruled that the shooting of the unarmed students was justified self-defense. When parents of the dead students sued for damages in 1976, they were rebuffed with the same verdict.

Their fists raised militantly, convicts take over New York State's Attica prison in September 1971. Begun with relatively minor demands, the uprising resulted in a bloody shoot-out when police stormed the prison; 29 inmates and 10 hostages were killed. Five years later, with only two inmates having been convicted, all of the remaining charges were dismissed against the inmates and the sole policeman who had been indicted.

tration had little cause to feel confident of the upcoming election results:
* The "Southern strategy" had alienated civil rights advocates.
* The anti-war activists were gaining public favor.
* Devaluation of the dollar and imposition of controls, though at least partially effective in stabilizing the economy, had angered many traditionalists.

In foreign affairs the situation was different. The real strength in the direction of foreign policy, as in the direction of domestic policy, lay in the White House. Here the planning authority was vested in a National Security Council headed by Henry Kissinger. As he saw it, the world was entering an "era of negotiation." During this time the bipolarity of the Cold War—the United States vs. the Soviet Union—seemed about to give way to a many-sided situation on the model of the 19th Century balance of powers in Europe. Vietnam, in the meantime, remained the problem it had become in President Johnson's time: a war locked in stalemate.

Nixon was committed to ending the American involvement in Vietnam, but without appearing to lose the war or sacrificing America's South Vietnamese ally. Late in 1969 he announced a plan for what came to be called Vietnamization—replacing American ground forces with South Vietnamese troops. This strategy appeared to be winning time for the President: as the United States ambassador in Saigon put it brutally, it changed the color of the corpses on the battlefield. Thus it came as a shock when, on April 30, 1970, Nixon announced an extension of the war into Cambodia. He spoke as though throwing down a gauntlet, "We will not be humiliated. We will not be defeated . . . I would rather be a one-term President and do what I believe was right than to be a two-term President at the cost of seeing America become a second-rate power."

Nixon took dramatic and surprising steps elsewhere abroad, turning his back on long-held positions. Since 1949, American policy on China had been based on a refusal to recognize the Communist government in Peking while supporting the myth that the regime on Taiwan was the real government of China. Nixon had endorsed this policy, but now he decided to reverse it, announcing that he would himself travel to the mainland Chinese capital. In the fall of 1971, the United States dropped its opposition to Peking's admission to the United Nations, and stood by as Taiwan was expelled.

Nixon made his historic journey to the Far East in February 1972. In television pictures broadcast via satellite, Americans saw a once-undreamed-of, face-to-face meeting of Nixon and Chairman Mao Tse-tung, watched the President as a tourist at the Great Wall and looked on as he toasted Premier Chou En-lai. Nixon returned home to the greatest and broadest acclaim of his term.

Like the trip to Peking, Nixon's journey to Moscow was the first by a President in office. Its most significant accomplishment was the conclusion of one phase of the Strategic Arms Limitation Talks (SALT). Winding up two years of SALT discussions, the nations agreed to a treaty restricting antiballistic missile sites and freezing the number of certain types of missiles.

THE President's trips to the Communist capitals helped serve the cause of international stability but did nothing to ease the sorest overseas dilemma, the war in Vietnam. In fact, the war seemed momentarily to thrust the trip to Moscow in jeopardy. On May 18, 1972, shortly before Nixon took off, he announced he was stepping up the pressure on North Vietnam by placing the country under blockade and mining the port of Haiphong. It was a gamble that

This handshake of Le Duc Tho and Henry Kissinger marked a declaration of truce in January 1973 in the drawn-out Vietnam war. In October the two negotiators won the Nobel Peace Prize, but Le Duc Tho refused his award and Kissinger accepted his by proxy. Both had reason to be skeptical: by May of 1975, North Vietnam had accomplished a full-scale military conquest of the South.

might have touched off a reaction in Moscow, Hanoi's chief ally. The gamble worked: Moscow remained passive, the action benefited Saigon and it won Nixon support at home. What the Nixon forces had called the "silent majority" of Americans, truculent and impatient over the long, drawn-out, divisive war, cheered the blockade.

From the President's point of view, it was high time. In mid-1971 a Gallup poll had showed that for the first time less than 50 per cent of the people backed the President. Another poll showed him trailing Democratic Senator Edmund Muskie of Maine as a candidate in the campaign ahead. No doubt his dramatic moves on the economy and his new China policy as well as the steps toward *détente* with the Soviet Union improved his standing.

The Democratic primary contests had already caused sharp reversals. Senator Muskie, all but conceded the nomination at the start of the year, slipped badly after his margin in New Hampshire fell short of forecasts. His rapid decline had been hastened by spying and campaign "dirty tricks" that, it was later revealed, had been carried out by Nixon supporters. By the end of April, only Minnesota Senator Hubert Humphrey and South Dakota Senator George McGovern, who had risen swiftly from an apparently hopeless position, remained.

McGovern narrowly defeated Humphrey in the California primary and took a commanding lead in the number of National Convention delegates committed to him. His staff had made superb use of changes in convention procedure that gave the McGovernites the weapons with which to outflank the regular party organizations and, by convention time, to bring the Democratic left—the anti-war wing—into control of the party.

Raspy-voiced Janis Joplin wails a eulogy to sensuality, anguish and hard drugs in 1969. Joplin's near-fanatical youthful following was stunned when the high priestess of the drug culture died of an overdose of heroin later in the year. In the '70s, heroin usage leveled off but marijuana went middle class and prices quadrupled—one ounce of high-quality grass went for $150, a price that topped the going rate for gold.

THE turbulent, exuberant Democratic convention of 1972 was like none before it. Many who had protested in the streets of Chicago in 1968 were now inside the hall at Miami Beach. Women, blacks and the young (18-year-olds had won the vote in 1971) abounded in the delegations. The old bosses, the labor leaders and even party officials hung uneasily on the fringes or stayed away. McGovern's forces slickly parried all challenges, adopted a liberal platform and won the nomination on the first ballot.

But from that moment, McGovern's campaign began to unravel. First there was disaster in the choice of a Vice-Presidential nominee: a week after the convention, McGovern's choice, Senator Thomas Eagleton of Missouri, acknowledged he had been hospitalized three times for nervous exhaustion. McGovern asserted that he was "1,000 per cent" behind Eagleton, but only days later removed him and substituted the former Peace Corps head, Sargent Shriver.

Meanwhile, the Nixon campaign for re-election had taken shape as a massive effort for the President that paid little attention to other Republican nominees. Rather than work through the party, the White House set up the Committee for the Re-Election of the President, widely known as CREEP, and an adjunct finance committee, both headed by former cabinet members. The finance committee raised more money than the re-election committee was able to use—in excess of $60 million, with $10.6 million received in secret before the date set by a new federal election law requiring disclosure of contributors.

McGovern found himself on the defensive. He had to refute charges that he held extreme views on drugs, sex and race and what had once been his strongest issue, opposition to the war, had eroded even before Kissinger dealt it a blow in October by announcing—prematurely—that peace was "at hand."

Pickets in Houston, Texas, protest one of the first widely distributed movies to depict explicit sexual acts. Pornography, shielded by Supreme Court rulings on freedom of speech, became a two billion dollar a year industry in the 1970s. But by 1973 the Court had retreated, upholding a community's right to set standards for acceptable activities, and in 1976 it ruled that commercial sex could be contained with zoning laws.

A troubled electorate, its doubts reflected in a comparatively low turnout, gave Nixon a near-record 520 electoral votes out of 538. He was the first Republican to sweep the South, and his 60.7 percentage of the vote trailed Lyndon Johnson's 1964 landslide by only three tenths of a percentage point. Explanations for the sweep varied. Some analysts argued that the once-dominant New Deal coalition was in retreat before new ideologies. Others noted that Nixon had been able to picture himself as "the peace candidate," although the cease-fire in Vietnam did not come until a week after his second inaugural. Finally, McGovern turned out to be a dismal failure as a candidate.

As the extent of Nixon's victory became clear, it would have taken a seer of extraordinary powers to predict that the sweetness of triumph was to sour so swiftly or that a squalid little incident, its origins close to the President himself, would burgeon into scandal unequaled in American history. Not even the most hardened cynic could have imagined that an event that Ron Ziegler, the Presidential press secretary, was to brush aside as "a third-rate burglary attempt" would have such fateful consequences.

The train of circumstances later collectively called Watergate was set in motion more than four months before the election with a bungled break-in of the Democratic National Committee headquarters in the Watergate office-hotel-apartment complex in Washington, D.C. At about 2 a.m. on Saturday, June 17, 1972, Frank Wills, a guard at the building, noticed a door latch taped open to permit access from the subbasement garage. He called police, who quickly captured five well-dressed men in the Democratic Committee offices. An incredible story began to unfold.

The burglars were unusual. For one thing, they carried not only sophisticated electronic wiretapping equipment, cameras and film, but the keys to two Watergate Hotel rooms and $1,754 in cash, of which $1,300 was in $100 bills. The police were impressed: "We felt it was just a little bigger than the average burglary." A hint of how much bigger soon emerged. Four of the men were anti-Castro activists said to have CIA ties; the fifth, James McCord, was a retired CIA man whose current job was chief of security for CREEP. Then police found address books that listed "Howard E. Hunt," "W. House" and "W. H." followed by White House telephone numbers; Hunt, another former CIA agent, was a White House consultant.

Waiting in another room in the hotel as the police arrested the burglars was Gordon Liddy, general counsel of CREEP. Liddy was in his office early the next morning to destroy incriminating documents in a shredding machine, in the first of what was to be a series of frantic efforts to suppress the White House connection with the break-in. Then he called his boss, Jeb Magruder, who later testified, "I do not think there was ever any discussion that there would not be a cover-up." Late on Monday afternoon Magruder met with former Attorney General John Mitchell, now director of CREEP (ironically, at Mitchell's Watergate apartment) and, according to his own story, asked what he should do with papers on an extensive CREEP espionage project, of which the Watergate break-in had been but one part. According to Magruder, Mitchell answered: "Maybe you ought to have a little fire at your house tonight." Magruder did.

The White House ordered further moves: destruction of all documents connecting the President or his staff with Watergate, and a public relations campaign to divert attention from the break-in. John Dean, Counsel to the Presi-

H. R. Haldeman zealously controlled access to the Oval Office, admitting, "Every President needs his s.o.b. and I'm Nixon's." The crew-cut former advertising executive, who amused himself on diplomatic missions by taking home movies of Nixon, redecorated the White House's West Wing in crisp Federalist style and kept fires crackling in every fireplace.

Rigid, efficient John Ehrlichman, who ranked in third place in the Nixon hierarchy, neither drank nor smoked and detested imperfection. "Your Nixon pin is upside down," he once barked at a White House speech writer. At home, Ehrlichman was a devoted father who cited the day he became an Eagle Scout as one of the proudest moments of his life.

dent, wearing surgical gloves, cleaned out Hunt's White House safe, and gave the politically sensitive documents to Patrick Gray, acting head of the FBI, intimating (Gray reported later) that for national security reasons they should be destroyed. Gray agreed; later he also kept Dean—and through Dean, the President—posted on a probe of Watergate begun by the FBI. Paradoxically, while Gray was unwittingly aiding the cover-up, his FBI agents were tracing the origins of the break-in, and it was only a matter of time before the $100 bills would lead to CREEP—and thence to highly questionable White House activities of long standing.

I N retrospect, it seems clear that those activities stemmed from what Elliot Richardson, a five-year member of the Nixon Administrations, said was the fatal flaw of this Presidency—"the proclivity . . . to perceive critics and opposition as 'enemies' and the willingness to 'adopt tactics used against an enemy' in handling such criticism." The White House obsession with "enemies" created an atmosphere in which any schemes to protect the incumbent and discredit opponents seemed justified. In the first half of 1969, for example, the White House hired two former New York City policemen to set up a private intelligence system partly to investigate the sexual, drinking and family problems of political opponents. Within a few months the ex-cops had installed an illegal wiretap on one newsman—while the FBI was tapping others—to trace leaks of proposed foreign policy. Other leaks, past and potential, were sought by the White House undercover group known as the Plumbers. Howard Hunt and Gordon Liddy, who joined the Plumbers in 1971, tried, unsuccessfully, to discredit Daniel Ellsberg—former Special Assistant to the Assistant Secretary of Defense for Internal Security Affairs and the man who had released the Pentagon Papers—by raiding Ellsberg's psychiatrist's office to find evidence that would discredit his patient. A few months later, Liddy and Hunt brought their talents to CREEP.

Liddy, described by a former associate as "a wild man," amazed his superior at CREEP, Jeb Magruder, from the beginning. One day, Magruder put his hand on Liddy's shoulder and chided him for his delay in submitting some reports, to which Liddy responded: "Get your hand off me or I'll kill you." From almost anybody else, these words would have been a joke, but Magruder was understandably taken aback.

It was in this environment of hare-brained plots and eroded integrity that preparations for the re-election campaign began late in 1970. Nixon, fearing that the Democrats might outspend him in 1972, ordered the collection of as much money as possible. His fund raisers called on officers of large corporations and "suggested" contributions appropriate to the size of the firms. In one of the most flagrant examples of the *quid pro quo* contributors might expect, an influential group of dairymen made a $2 million pledge; Nixon then supported a rise in the level of the federal milk subsidy. As the arm-twisting proceeded, corporations that could be affected by regulatory agency action contributed as much from fear of what might happen to them if they did not give as from hopes of what they might get if they did. The money poured in, much of it in crisp, presumably untraceable $100 bills. Checks were another matter. To avoid exposing their contributors, some checks were "laundered"— passed through several hands. The last payee would arrange to send cash back to CREEP. Several such checks were converted to $100 bills in Miami by Ber-

In the happier days before Watergate, Martha and John Mitchell snuggle before a formal dinner in St. Louis in 1970. Few people credited her gossipy charges— made in midnight telephone calls to reporters—of crimes in the White House. But after she died in 1976, estranged from her husband, an anonymous admirer had a large floral arrangement sent to her funeral spelling out the words, "Martha was right."

A major figure in the Watergate scandal, Presidential Counsel John Dean at one time considered entering the ministry; instead, he chose law. Six months after beginning his career at a communications law firm, he was fired for secretly counseling a client's competitor. Even so, Dean landed a series of jobs that led to the White House in 1970. After a brief 1974 jail term for Watergate crimes, he became a lecturer, journalist and best-selling author.

nard Barker, an old friend of Hunt's. A number of these bills were deposited in CREEP's safe and used for such clandestine operations as a $250,000 plan for political espionage against the Democratic National Committee set up by Liddy. He asked Hugh Sloan, CREEP's treasurer, for an advance of $83,000 in cash. In an incredible coincidence, the unsuspecting Sloan reached into his safe and gave Liddy some of the same $100 bills that he had received from Barker's Miami bank. Two months later, some of these bills would be found in the possession of the Watergate burglars.

THESE bills were troubling Nixon and Haldeman, as they sought ways to stop the FBI from pursuing the break-in trial. Hugh Sloan was asked to commit perjury if questioned by the FBI about cash paid to Liddy. Sloan refused, resigned, retained a lawyer and told his story to the United States Attorney. After this crack in the structure of deceit, the cover-up took yet another tack. Jeb Magruder placed full blame on Liddy and Hunt, and a grand jury found his perjured testimony convincing. On September 15 the five burglars plus Hunt and Liddy were indicted.

But it took more than perjury to continue the cover-up. Hush money was now flowing to the burglars on a schedule that envisaged nearly $450,000 to be paid—ostensibly for bail, legal fees and family expenses. This agreement kept the burglars quiet through the election campaign, and McGovern's attempts to make Watergate an issue failed.

Yet the edifice of lies and pay-offs had already begun to crumble, owing in part to the suspicions of some observers and in part to circumstances unforeseeable by any of the conspirators. While many of the nation's news programs, magazines and newspapers were treating the break-in as insignificant, calling it the Watergate caper, Bob Woodward and Carl Bernstein, two *Washington Post* reporters who had covered the Watergate story from the start, were fascinated by coincidences linking the burglary to the White House. The "Woodstein" stories gradually uncovered a web of White House entanglement in the case, and they reached a climax with their October report that Watergate "stemmed from a massive campaign of political spying and sabotage conducted on behalf of . . . the White House." Although these stories had no immediate discernible effect on public opinion, they were effective in keeping pressure on the White House.

More dramatic in its impact was an unrelated disaster that coincidentally recalled attention to Watergate and produced a number of side effects. A few days after Howard Hunt received his final payment of hush money, his wife died in an airplane crash; in her purse was found $10,000 in those ubiquitous $100 bills. While the mystery of the money fascinated news watchers, the tragedy threw Hunt into deep despair; he decided to plead guilty to the charges of burglary and rely on executive clemency to avoid jail. To ensure Hunt's continued silence, Nixon agreed that Hunt and Liddy could be promised clemency. In January, Hunt, Liddy and four of the five burglars were found guilty. Judge John Sirica, however, was not altogether satisfied: he felt that the prosecutors had not gotten to the bottom of the case.

There were others who sniffed a rat. Representative Wright Patman, for one, had attempted during the election campaign to investigate the break-in, but the White House had persuaded his committee members to stifle that effort. This action so angered Senator Edward Kennedy that he started his own investigation, and by February 7, 1973, the Senate was sufficiently impressed by his findings to set up a Select Committee on Presidential Campaign Activities with Senator Sam Ervin of North Carolina as chairman.

The White House publicly announced that it would cooperate with the Committee's investigation, if it was handled in "a nonpartisan way," but privately—Dean later reported—it planned "to restrain the investigation and make it as difficult as possible to get information and witnesses . . . the ultimate goal would be to discredit the hearings and reduce their impact by attempting to show that the Democrats have engaged in the same type of activities."

Even before hearings of the Ervin Committee began, other threats to the cover-up emerged. Patrick Gray, during an appearance before the Senate Judiciary Committee, volunteered the information that the White House had been given records of the FBI investigation of the break-in. Then Hunt, faced with a March 23 date for sentencing by Judge Sirica, demanded $132,000 from the Administration, failing which he would have to "review his options."

Dean told Nixon that his latest problem was serious: "We have a cancer—within—close to the Presidency, that's growing." The continued blackmail, he said, was likely to cost a million dollars over the next two years. To which Nixon calmly replied, "We could get that." It did not become necessary: Hunt was given $75,000, which sufficed to keep him quiet for a while.

ANOTHER cancer close to the Presidency had been growing quietly for more than a year and was soon to erupt into a new scandal. Vice President Spiro Agnew, self-billed apostle of law and order, was under federal investigation for possible law violations starting in his pre-White House political career. On October 10, 1973, he resigned his office, pleaded no contest to a tax-evasion charge and was sentenced to three years' probation and a $10,000 fine. Two days later, Nixon nominated House Minority Leader Gerald Ford to the office.

At the same time, matters of even more far-reaching consequence were compelling Presidential attention. A new war had broken out between Israel and the Arab states, and it had reached a critical stage for Israel. Nixon decided that the Israelis must be aided to prevent an Arab victory that would make the Middle East a Soviet preserve. The Israelis managed to achieve a military stalemate. Yet the Arabs won a significant political victory through the use of a powerful economic weapon: a total embargo on oil exports to the United States and some other nations, accompanied by a spectacular rise in the price of crude oil. In the United States, the price of gasoline and substitute energy sources took a breathtaking leap; although the gasoline crisis would fade by spring, the underlying energy crisis seemed to be permanent. The rate of inflation soared, and recession threatened. All the industrialized nations of the Western world suffered a damaging impact on their economy, though the underdeveloped oil-poor nations were the hardest hit. The underdeveloped yet oil-rich nations were the only ones that gained. Suddenly, the balance of world power had changed: the Arab states had unprecedented influence. Even after the first shock waves of the crisis faded, the potential significance of Arab control over much of the world's petroleum supplies remained, a time bomb looming over the Western nations—and over the future of the United States as a power in an economically revolutionized world.

On the domestic scene, the Watergate crisis refused to go away. In spite of lavish hush money, and in spite of the lack of evidence to link the President

Watergate judge John Sirica, an ex-boxer, had a reputation for toughness. Champion Jack Dempsey said of his friend's handling of the Watergate trials, "He's a better fighter now than he ever was." Indeed, the stiff provisional sentences that "Maximum John" handed down were crucial to resolution of the crisis.

Puritanical Archibald Cox was the sixth man offered the job of special prosecutor by Elliot Richardson, who had studied labor law under Cox at Harvard. Cox's Watergate staff, who were primarily Ivy Leaguers, complained that the aloof professor conducted his briefings "like the dullest, driest seminars back at Harvard."

Alexander Butterfield, the former Deputy Assistant to the President, told of the secret recordings of Presidential conversations that assured Nixon's downfall. When Ervin Committee staffers casually asked about the recordings Butterfield said, "I was hoping you fellows wouldn't ask me about that." Then he dropped his bombshell.

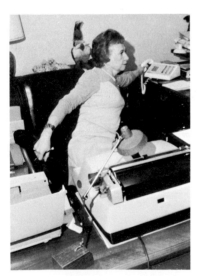

Toe on the tape machine's foot pedal, hand on the telephone, Rose Mary Woods, Nixon's fanatically loyal long-time secretary, recreates her alleged accidental erasure of crucial evidence from a Nixon tape. Her demonstration came after other White House staffers had attributed the gap to some form of "sinister force."

directly to the scandal—the "smoking gun" that Nixon's supporters insisted had to be found before he could be considered guilty—the President's men were uneasy. It might be best, Haldeman advised, to find a scapegoat who would permanently draw any attention away from the President. Nixon chose John Dean and urged him to write a statement that could explain away Watergate and clear the President. Dean sensed his personal danger. He procrastinated until Nixon insisted that he go to Camp David and finish the job.

It was at that point that the already eroded structure of the cover-up began to come apart. While Dean was driving to the Presidential retreat on March 23, he heard a radio report: McCord had admitted to Judge Sirica that, under political pressure, the defendants had committed perjury to protect higher-ups involved in the Watergate break-in. This confession was to win McCord a relatively light sentence. And when the other defendants remained mute, Judge Sirica meted out extremely severe sentences, which he said he would review only if they testified openly and completely. Dean returned to Washington, retained a lawyer and arranged to talk with the United States Attorney.

Dean was not alone as he looked for shelter: Herbert Kalmbach and Charles Colson, former Special Counsel to the President, were already retaining lawyers. On April 14 Magruder talked to the prosecutors.

Dean, meanwhile, was bargaining with the prosecution team and lobbying his case with the press. To preserve the cover-up Nixon told his two most trusted aides—Haldeman and Ehrlichman—that they, as well as Dean, had to go. On April 30 he announced the resignation of all three plus Attorney General Richard Kleindienst, who had been under fire earlier for his role in the settlement of a major antitrust suit. Kleindienst was replaced by Elliot Richardson, former Secretary of Defense.

Richardson appointed as Watergate Special Prosecutor a respected Harvard Law School professor, Archibald Cox, who vowed that he would follow every trail in pursuit of the truth, even to the Oval Office in the White House.

Nixon again made a blanket denial of unlawful activity. Nonetheless, public opinion had swung toward the belief that Nixon *had* been involved. On June 25 Dean testified at a public session of the Ervin Committee; he clearly believed that the President was implicated. National attention became riveted on the question that Senator Howard Baker kept asking: "What did the President know and when did he know it?" Only Nixon himself could answer and—in a manner that galvanized the American people—he did.

FRIDAY, July 13, 1973, was an inauspicious day for Richard Nixon. On that day, speaking to the Ervin Committee, Alexander Butterfield, formerly Deputy Assistant to the President, revealed the existence of an elaborate if unsophisticated system of tape-recording equipment in the Cabinet Room and in Nixon's offices at the White House, the Executive Office Building and Camp David. This disclosure sealed Nixon's fate.

It is now clear that without the tapes—which contain much of the evidence to support the story told in these pages—Nixon might never have been linked conclusively with Watergate. But once the tapes became public, there was no way for him to avoid his downfall. Why, then, did he not destroy them? A likely explanation is that he never seriously entertained the possibility that his right to the privacy essential to leadership might be vulnerable to invasion by law; he apparently was convinced he could not be forced to give them up. When Cox's subpoenas for nine tapes were accepted on July 23, the tapes became potential evidence, the destruction of which would have been a criminal act. Nixon now could only fight to hold onto them.

Cox's subpoenas signaled the start of a momentous court struggle. Nixon's attorney, Charles Alan Wright, contended that under executive privilege the President could refuse to obey the subpoenas, or the necessary Presidential privacy established by the Constitution would be endangered. Cox's response was that "there is no exception . . . from the guiding principle that the public, in pursuit of justice, has a right to every man's evidence." Sirica upheld Cox.

ON the day that Nixon nominated Gerald Ford as successor to Agnew, the Court of Appeals affirmed Sirica's decision on the tapes and stayed its order five days to permit an appeal to the Supreme Court. On Friday, October 19, Cox rejected a plan that would have given him access only to edited transcripts of the tapes and would have forbidden him to subpoena any more White House material. The next day Nixon called on Attorney General Richardson to fire Cox, Richardson refused and resigned. Then Deputy Attorney General William Ruckelshaus was fired when he, too, refused to dismiss Cox. Finally, Solicitor General Robert Bork, serving as Acting Attorney General, did dismiss the Special Prosecutor. That evening the White House announced what was promptly christened the Saturday Night Massacre: Richardson's resignation, the firing of Cox and Ruckelshaus, and the abolition of the office of the Special Watergate Prosecution Force.

An avalanche of letters, telegrams and telephone calls overwhelmed official Washington within hours. The next Tuesday, impeachment resolutions were sent to the Judiciary Committee of the House of Representatives for "speedy and expeditious consideration." Even Republican stalwarts wavered. To still the clamor, Nixon reversed himself and agreed to give the tapes to Sirica.

From then on, no matter what Nixon did, nothing seemed to help. He appointed Leon Jaworski, considered a conservative, as Special Prosecutor. But Jaworski, convinced that Nixon was guilty of indictable offenses, pursued the investigation as aggressively as Cox. Then, when the tapes were finally surrendered, two were unaccountably missing; the suspicion persisted that they had been destroyed. At a meeting with Republican Senators, Nixon said that he would not resign because he had not been convicted of any crime.

What many had a hard time realizing was that Nixon and his people were not interested in changing their standards, for they were still treating Watergate as a public relations problem, just as they had ever since June 1972, when—three days after the break-in—Nixon had ordered a "PR offensive to top this."

Implicit in this attitude was a philosophy of government that had been put into practice decades earlier, but now had been brought to an intolerable extreme. From Franklin Roosevelt's time on, the concept had grown of an "imperial presidency." A steadily growing White House staff had assumed functions formerly the responsibility of Congress and the executive departments; a corollary of this shift in power had been the use of agencies like the FBI and the CIA, in ways not always ethical or legal, to implement goals pursued by the incumbent President. For Nixon's White House staff, the essential good was to keep Nixon in office as a bulwark against external threats. For Richard Nixon himself, according to an interesting theory set forth in *The Time of Illusion*, a study of the Nixon era by Jonathan Schell, the primary goal was the preserva-

Silver-haired Peter Rodino, Chairman of the House Judiciary Committee that recommended the impeachment of Richard Nixon in 1974, first ran for Congress in 1946 when Nixon was making his own initial Congressional bid. Nixon won, and Rodino lost. Elected two years later with the assistance of Newark's large Italian-American vote, Rodino had a career marked by ethnically oriented actions such as his drive to make Columbus Day an official national holiday.

Democratic nominee Jimmy Carter listens intently to President Gerald R. Ford during their first televised debate in Philadelphia in September 1976. He had begun his drive for the Presidency barely three years earlier, virtually unknown. In 1973, when he appeared on the TV show "What's My Line?" no one recognized him. "You seem to have a certain aura about you," said one panelist. "Do you recruit nuns for a living?"

tion of a credible image of American power and the willingness to use it. Since, wrote Schell, neither the United States nor the Soviet Union desired nuclear war, credibility must be augmented by national support for limited wars, such as Vietnam. But domestic anti-war movements undermine a nation's credibility; therefore, any action to destroy such dissidence is justifiable if it preserves the appearance of monolithic national support for the war. Hence Nixon's "enemies" list. Hence the willingness of the White House to engage in questionable activities in order to protect the President and maintain his authority. Hence the necessity for continued PR treatment of national issues.

THE possibility of impeachment now seemed very real. And nemesis came even closer when John Doar, appointed chief counsel of the House Judiciary Committee by Chairman Peter Rodino, presented a report that defined impeachable offenses in a broad manner. Nixon countered that criminality, not merely improper actions, had to be demonstrated to justify impeachment. A few days later Haldeman, Ehrlichman, Mitchell and other former Administration officials were indicted for conspiracy, lying and obstructing justice. If they were found guilty, Nixon might well be found guilty, too. Then, by his own definition, he would be impeachable.

Jaworski subpoenaed 64 Nixon conversations on April 18. To avoid complying, Nixon issued edited transcripts of 46 of the tapes. As soon as they were examined and compared with tapes already released, some glaring discrepancies showed up between the tapes and the transcripts; even worse, the whole tone of the transcripts—even with "expletives deleted"—was so sleazy, cheap and vulgar that a wave of revulsion swept the country.

On May 5 Jaworski offered a compromise in the tape dispute: if Nixon supplied 38 specific tapes of the 64, that would be enough; if he refused, Jaworski warned him that he probably would have to disclose the fact that Nixon had been named by the grand jury as an unindicted co-conspirator with Haldeman, Ehrlichman and Mitchell. Nixon refused and moved to quash the Jaworski subpoenas. When Sirica upheld the subpoenas, Nixon went to the Court of Appeals. Jaworski then appealed directly to the Supreme Court on the ground of the "imperative public importance" of the issues. On May 31 the Supreme Court agreed to hear the case. It was argued on July 8. Early on July 24, a Court official suggested that representatives of both the White House and the Special Prosecutor be present that day. When Nixon, in San Clemente, heard this he phoned Special Counsel Fred Buzhardt in Washington and told him to listen to the June 23, 1972, tape, on which "there may be some problems."

Buzhardt listened and was appalled. The tape proved that only six days after the break-in, Nixon was fully aware of the details of the crime, of Mitchell's probable part in it and of the roles of Liddy and Hunt; moreover he could be heard ordering a cover-up and giving instructions for the FBI and the CIA to aid in the cover-up. Here was the "smoking gun" directly involving the President in the crime. Buzhardt told Nixon's aides "it was all over."

At about the same time Chief Justice Warren Burger was reading an 8-0 opinion upholding Jaworski's demand for the tapes. It concluded that the claim to executive privilege "cannot prevail over the fundamental demands of due process of law in the fair administration of criminal justice." It was the penultimate blow. By July 30 the Judiciary Committee, in affirmation of the Constitution and vindication of the political process, had voted to submit three articles of impeachment to the House of Representatives. At last Nixon recognized that he had lost almost all his support in Congress.

On August 9 he resigned, the first President to do so, and flew off to exile in his California residence at San Clemente.

G ERALD R. Ford took office with the good wishes of most Americans, who hoped he would restore their belief in Presidential integrity. However, when he pardoned Nixon for "all offenses . . . he . . . committed" during his tenure, Ford's credibility plummeted. Republican candidates in the November elections had to combat the cries of "Deal!" that revived Watergate as an issue; Democrats gained seats.

In the 26 months that followed his inauguration, Ford's domestic policy was essentially negative. By November 1970 he had vetoed 66 measures, including a number intended to alleviate the worst recession and highest unemployment since the Depression. Paradoxically, Ford's term saw some of the highest federal deficits in history, one of the facts that turned conservatives toward Ronald Reagan as their 1976 candidate. GOP right-wingers also disliked the Nixon-Ford-Kissinger policy of *détente* with Russia. After Ford imposed embargoes on grain exports, his support among conservative farmers waned. By early 1976 he faced the real possibility that he would be the first incumbent in 40 years to be denied renomination by his party. As he battled Reagan down to the wire, Ford claimed important accomplishments: a nation at peace, a reduction in the unemployment rate, inflation curbed. Ford won the nomination, but it was close.

The Democrats had previously nominated James Earl "Jimmy" Carter Jr., formerly Governor of Georgia but a political unknown nationally, who had defeated far better known Democratic aspirants in a series of primary victories. In the primaries, Carter had struck a responsive note with his promise that, as President, he would restore to that office honesty, compassion and respect for individuals. This approach had been far more effective with voters than his position papers on important issues.

Carter started out far ahead in the polls; Ford was considered the underdog, trailing at one point by 33 per cent. Then an indiscreetly worded interview by Carter was published in *Playboy* magazine and his apparent margin, already lessening, decreased even more. The race became even closer after the first of three television debates, which Ford seemed to win. In a suspenseful conclusion, Carter, who had chosen a definite asset to the ticket in his running mate, Senator Walter (Fritz) Mondale of Minnesota, unseated Ford by the narrow electoral margin of 297 to 241 votes and a 3 per cent edge in the popular vote. The South, for the first time since the 1848 election of Zachary Taylor, had brought in one of its own in an anomaly, supporting Carter against its ideological bent. The South was thus reintegrated into national politics.

Yet it was the blacks, particularly in the South, who tipped the balance for Carter. He was seen as a man who had lived among them, understood them, fought for their civil rights and—unlike Ford—actively sought their support. They responded by giving Carter an unprecedented 94 per cent of their vote.

Carter, as he approached the beginning of his term, faced complex problems: the economic recession and continuing inflation; tension in the Middle East; the probability of further oil-price hikes as the Arab states exercised their economic muscle; and—most important of all—the restoration of the American public's faith in government.

President Ford rebuts challenger Jimmy Carter during their first debate. Affable Jerry Ford, lauded as a "Congressman's Congressman," had been catapulted into power by the Watergate scandal. He spent one of the happiest afternoons of his first year in the White House taking a group of Soviet cosmonauts to a firemen's picnic in a Washington suburb. But he also managed to restore a calm integrity to the Presidency.

CHRONOLOGY *A timetable of American and world events: From 1945*

WORLD EVENTS	POLITICS	MILITARY and FOREIGN AFFAIRS	ECONOMICS	SCIENCE	CULTURE, RELIGION and SOCIAL EVENTS
1945 United Nations organized 1945 Arab League formed 1945 Attlee becomes British Prime Minister 1945-47 American-British French-Russian Council of Foreign Ministers holds several meetings on peace treaties 1945-49 Nuremberg War Crimes trials 1946 Russians withdraw from Iran 1946 Italy a republic 1946-48 Trial of Japanese war leaders 1946-49 Greek Civil War 1947 Palestine partitioned 1947 Soviet control of East Europe consolidated	1945 Harry Truman becomes President after death of Roosevelt 1945 New York establishes first state antidiscrimination agency 1946 Republicans control Congress for first time in 14 years 1946-48 Strengthening of civil rights provisions in federal and military employment 1947 All U.S. armed forces administration consolidated in Defense Department; James V. Forrestal is its chief 1947 Truman sets loyalty standards for executive employees 1947 Presidential Succession Act puts House speaker and Senate president *pro tem* next in line after Vice President	1945 Yalta and Potsdam Conferences 1945 Germany dismembered and occupied by the Four Powers 1946 Massive reductions in American armed forces 1946 Termination of Lend-Lease 1946 U.S. proposes international control of atomic weapons and sets up Atomic Energy Commission 1946 United Nations Educational, Scientific and Cultural Organization (UNESCO) 1947 "Truman Doctrine" protects Greece and Turkey from Communism in Europe 1947 Rio Pact for Western Hemisphere defense 1947 Marshall Plan implements European recovery	1945-46 End of wartime rationing and price controls on most items 1946 American Federation of Labor readmits United Mine Workers 1946 Office of Economic Stabilization (OES) re-established 1946 Federal government seizes coal mines during a long strike 1946 onward Great expansion of investment companies 1946 onward Appearance of ranch-style and split-level homes 1947 Taft-Hartley Act on labor organizations 1947 Start of "Operation Bootstrap" for Puerto Rico 1947 End of sugar rationing	1945 Completion and explosion of first atomic bombs 1946 Radar signals bounced off the moon 1946 Atomic bomb tests at Bikini atoll 1946-50 Atomic elements 96 to 98 identified 1946-52 Development of cortisone 1947 Air Force Captain Charles E. Yeager makes first deliberate supersonic flight 1947 Extensive experiments in cloud seeding produce some rain	1945 Richard Wright's *Black Boy* 1945 Aaron Copland wins Pulitzer Prize in Music for *Appalachian Spring* 1946 *The Age of Jackson*, by Arthur Schlesinger Jr., wins Pulitzer Prize 1946 Canonization of Mother Cabrini, first U.S. citizen so honored 1946 Billy Graham begins evangelistic career 1947 Massachusetts ban lifted on *Forever Amber* 1947 Jackie Robinson is first Negro in major league baseball 1947 Peak year of college enrollment by World War II veterans 1947 Premiere of *A Streetcar Named Desire* by Tennessee Williams

1948 Years of Ferment Abroad

WORLD EVENTS	POLITICS	MILITARY and FOREIGN AFFAIRS	ECONOMICS	SCIENCE	CULTURE, RELIGION and SOCIAL EVENTS
1948 Israel gains its independence 1948 Communist coup in Czechoslovakia 1948 Benelux customs union goes into effect 1948 Yugoslavia leaves Stalinist camp 1949 North Atlantic Treaty Organization (NATO) set up 1949 Chinese Reds proclaim People's Republic of China 1949 Russia explodes an A-bomb 1949 Indonesia becomes independent 1949 West Germany set up as a republic 1949 onward Kashmir border disputed by India, Pakistan, Red China 1951 Churchill again becomes Prime Minister 1952 Mau Mau terrorism in Kenya 1953 Stalin dies 1953 East German riots 1953 Mt. Everest conquered 1953 First Red Chinese Five-Year Plan 1954 Partition of Vietnam 1954 onward Chinese Communists bombard offshore islands 1955 Anthony Eden succeeds Churchill as British Prime Minister	1948 Supreme Court rules against racially restrictive covenants 1948 Dixiecrats bolt the Democrats in election campaign 1948 Henry Wallace organizes independent progressive candidacy 1948 Truman re-elected 1948-50 Alger Hiss case ends in his conviction for perjury 1949 Hoover Commission reports on government reorganization 1950-51 Espionage convictions of Harry Gold and the Rosenbergs 1950-51 Kefauver investigates interstate crime 1950-54 Era of McCarthyism 1951 22nd Amendment limits Presidency to two terms 1952 Eisenhower elected President and visits Korea to carry out campaign pledge 1952 Supreme Court bars subversives from teaching in public schools 1953 Puerto Rico given commonwealth status 1953 Department of Health, Education and Welfare established, with Oveta Culp Hobby its secretary 1953 Earl Warren appointed Chief Justice of U.S. 1954 Supreme Court declares "separate but equal" school facilities unconstitutional 1954 Puerto Rican nationalists shoot five Congressmen 1954 Senate condemns McCarthy	1948 Formation of the Organization of American States (OAS) 1948-49 Berlin Airlift 1948-60 U.S. spends $55.2 billion in foreign aid 1949 Point Four plan for economic assistance of underdeveloped nations 1949 U.S. occupation zone of Germany gets civilian high commissioner 1950 Ralph J. Bunche wins Nobel Peace Prize 1950 Truman orders development of hydrogen bomb 1950-51 Formation of SHAPE to coordinate European defenses 1950-51 Peace treaties signed with Japan and West Germany 1950-53 Korean War 1951 Truman removes General MacArthur from command 1951-53 Korean truce talks 1952 Development of the B-52 bomber 1952 Australia-New Zealand-U.S. (ANZUS) Pact 1953 Testing of atomic artillery shells 1953 George C. Marshall wins Nobel Peace Prize 1953-54 U.S. negotiates permission for bases in Spain and Libya 1954 U.S.S. *Nautilus*, first atomic-powered submarine	1948 33⅓ rpm phonograph records first marketed 1948 General Motors signs the first sliding-scale wage contract 1948 Idlewild (later renamed Kennedy) Airport opens – the largest in world 1949 Minimum wage raised from 40 to 75 cents an hour 1949 Walkouts in soft-coal and steel industries 1950 President authorized to stabilize wages and prices 1950 Census shows 150,697,361 inhabitants in continental U.S. 1951 Employment of women reaches a new peak of 19,308,000 1951 American Telephone and Telegraph becomes first corporation to have more than one million stockholders 1951 onward Rapid growth of the paperback book and long-playing record industries 1952 Ultra-High-Frequency (UHF) channels open to television 1952 U.S. stockholders number more than six million 1953 onward Increased use of automation and computers in industry	1948 First artificial production of the meson, one of the fundamental particles of the atom 1948 Invention of the transistor 1948 Mount Palomar Observatory, with 200-inch telescope, opened 1948-50 Aureomycin and Terramycin discovered 1949 Dramamine developed 1949 American Medical Association supports voluntary Medicare plan 1949 Brookhaven Laboratories cosmotron being constructed 1949 First nonstop flight around the world 1951 Completion of microwave relay facilities for first transcontinental television 1952 Presidential commission recommends national health insurance program 1952 12th moon of Jupiter discovered 1952 U.S. announces first successful tests of hydrogen bomb 1952-57 Atomic elements 99 to 102 are produced	1948 Supreme Court declares religious education in public schools unconstitutional 1948 Norman Mailer's *The Naked and the Dead* and Kinsey's *Sexual Behavior in the Human Male* published 1949 Last encampment of the Grand Army of the Republic 1949 Premiere of Arthur Miller's *Death of a Salesman* 1949 William Faulkner wins Nobel Prize in Literature 1950 *The Lonely Crowd*, by David Riesman and others 1950-52 Lever House built in New York with glass-wall architectural technique 1950 onward Trend towards unity in U.S. Protestant churches 1951 Menotti's *Amahl and the Night Visitors*, first opera produced for television 1951 James Jones's *From Here to Eternity* 1952 First appearance of three-dimensional movies 1952 *The Invisible Man*, by Ralph Ellison 1954 Retirement of Arturo Toscanini 1954 Ernest Hemingway wins Nobel Prize in Literature 1954 *Poems 1923-1954*, by e. e. cummings 1954 Inauguration of Newport Jazz Festival 1954 Adoption of codes by comic-book industry

1955 Marian Anderson makes her first Metropolitan Opera appearance
1956 *The Organization Man,* by W. H. Whyte Jr.
1956 Floyd Patterson wins heavyweight boxing title
1956 Avant-garde "beat" literature, Alan Ginsberg's poem, "Howl"
1956 Grace Metalious' *Peyton Place* published

1954 "Fall-out" problem widely debated
1955 Salk polio vaccine developed
1955-56 Discovery of the anti-proton and anti-neutron
1955 onward Tranquilizers come into widespread use

1954 Flexible parity for farm produce established
1954-59 Construction of the St. Lawrence Seaway
1955 American Federation of Labor (AFL) and Congress of Industrial Organizations (CIO) merge
1956 Federal Highway Act provides for vast road-building projects
1956 Soil-Bank Act encourages limited farm-acreage production

1954 U.S. signs mutual defense treaty with Nationalist China
1954 Geneva Conference on Indochina
1954 U.S. leads in Southeast Asia Treaty Organization (SEATO) Pact
1954 Air Force Academy established
1955 "Summit Conference" at Geneva
1955 Peace treaty with Austria
1955 U.S. ends German occupation
1955 U.S. pledges defense of Formosa and the Pescadores

1955 First Presidential press conference filmed for TV
1955-57 Unsuccessful bid for public power on Snake River in the Northwest
1956 Montgomery bus boycott brings Dr. Martin Luther King Jr. to national prominence
1956 Independent gas producers included under utility rate controls
1956 onward Supreme Court limits states' powers of investigation in search for subversives

1955 Warsaw Pact formed as a counter to NATO
1955 Argentine dictator Perón overthrown
1955 onward Terrorism on Cyprus
1956 Revolt in Hungary and unrest in Poland
1956 Egypt nationalizes the Suez Canal
1956 Khrushchev makes anti-Stalin speech
1956 Tunisia, Morocco and Ghana gain independence
1956-59 Cuban civil war

1957 Into the Space Age

1957 Jack Kerouac's *On the Road* published
1957 Premiere of Archibald MacLeish's drama, *J.B.*
1958 National Defense Education Act
1958 Harry Golden's *Only in America* published
1958-60 TV quiz program scandals
1960 Large-scale mergers of book firms
1960 Presidential campaign debates are seen for first time on TV
1961 Supreme Court upholds some state and local censorship of motion pictures
1961 America and Russia sign agreement for exchange of scholars
1961 Harper Lee wins Pulitzer Prize for her novel *To Kill a Mockingbird*
1962 John Steinbeck wins Nobel Prize for Literature
1962-63 Supreme Court outlaws New York school prayer, later rules that no state or locality may require the recitation of the Lord's Prayer or Bible verses in public schools
1963 Samuel Barber wins Pulitzer Prize for Piano Concerto No. 1
1964 National Book Award for Poetry won by John Crowe Ransom
1965 Pope Paul VI visits New York to plead for peace at the UN
1966 Timothy Leary founds religion based on LSD, a psychedelic drug
1967 Stalin's daughter defects to America and publishes *20 Letters to a Friend*
1968 Pope Paul VI reiterates ban on birth control
1968 onward Yale, Princeton, Sarah Lawrence and other colleges become coeducational
1969 More than 250,000 people mass in Washington, D.C., in antiwar demonstration
1969 Norman Mailer wins Pulitzer Prize for *Armies of the Night*
1971 Riots at Attica state prison in New York inspire prison reform
1974 Russian author Solzhenitsyn exiled
1976 United States wins all Nobel Prizes

1957 Asian Flu epidemic
1957 Synthetic manufacture of amino acids
1958 First American artificial satellite is orbited
1959 Development of synthetic penicillin
1960 Tiros weather satellites
1960 First aerial recovery of satellites
1961 Alan B. Shepard Jr., first American in space, rockets 116.5 miles up
1961-62 Exposure of birth-deforming drug thalidomide brings stiffer federal drug act
1962 John H. Glenn Jr. becomes first American to orbit earth
1962 Telstar satellite used for worldwide communication tests
1963 Mariner II relays information about Venus
1964 Federal medical panel calls cigarette smoking health hazard
1964 Ranger VII takes close-ups of moon
1965 First American "walk in space"
1965 Astronauts in Gemini 5 stay aloft a record 8 days
1965 Medicare bill in effect
1967 Fire kills Astronauts Grissom, White and Chaffee
1967 First human heart transplant
1968 Hong Kong flu epidemic
1968 Apollo 8 orbits moon
1969 Neil Armstrong, Michael Collins and Edwin E. Aldrin Jr. complete journey to the moon
1971 U.S. robot spaceship Mariner 9 orbits Mars
1972 First stage of manned space exploration ends with Apollo 17
1973 Skylab placed in orbit
1973 Pioneer 10 spacecraft transmits information about Jupiter
1974 Mariner 10 photographs Venus and Mercury
1976 Viking 1 and 2 land on Mars

1957 Congress investigates labor racketeering
1957 AFL-CIO expel the Teamsters Union for corruption
1957-58 Recession
1959 Rising popularity of American "compact" cars
1959 Four-month-long steel strike
1960 American average per capita income hits a new high of $2,218
1961 Federal budget of $80.9 billion sets peacetime record
1961 Kennedy-backed minimum-wage bill loses in House by one vote
1962 New York Stock Exchange shares lose $20.8 billion in value on May 28; greatest one-day drop since 1929
1962-63 Strikes shut down nine New York City newspapers for 114 days
1963 Kennedy authorizes $250-million wheat sale to Soviet Union
1964 U.S. civilian labor force rises to 72,975,000 while unemployment is above four million
1964 Congress passes tax cuts estimated at $11.5 billion
1964 Severe earthquake damage in Alaska
1964-65 New York World's Fair
1964 War-on-poverty program passes Congress
1965 First commercial satellite launched to relay television signals and telephone calls
1965 Power failure causes blackout in the Northeast
1966 Dow-Jones Industrial Average breaks 1000
1966 Airlines struck for 43 days
1966 Inflation becomes serious problem
1967 U.S. population passes 200 million
1971 Anti-inflation policies freeze wages and prices, add surcharges to imports and devalue the dollar
1973-1974 U.S. sinks into worst recession since 1930s
1975 Recession brings highest unemployment since the Depression

1957 Eisenhower extends "Truman Doctrine" to the Middle East
1959 Eisenhower makes a good-will tour of 11 nations in Europe, Middle East and Asia
1959 Atomic submarines equipped with Polaris missiles
1960 U-2 shot down over Russia
1961 America ends diplomatic relations with Cuba
1961 Kennedy proposes Alliance for Progress to raise Latin American living standards
1961 Anti-Castro invasion of Cuba at Bay of Pigs is crushed
1962 Russia returns U-2 pilot Francis Gary Powers in exchange for spy Rudolf Abel
1962 Russian missiles in Cuba withdrawn after firm American stand
1963 Kennedy gets tumultuous welcome in West Berlin
1963 America, Russia and Britain sign nuclear test ban treaty
1963 Washington and Moscow open "hot line" phone connection to reduce risk of accidental war
1965 Johnson sends first combat troops to South Vietnam
1966 Four H-bombs, lost after B-52 crash over Spain, recovered safely
1967 U.S. troop strength in Vietnam nears 475,000, exceeding maximum deployment of Korean War
1967 Johnson and U.S.S.R. Premier Kosygin meet at Glassboro, New Jersey
1968 Capture of intelligence ship *Pueblo* by North Koreans
1968 Vietnamese peace talks begin in Paris
1971 Vietnamese troops invade Laos
1971 Vietnamization policy lowers U.S. forces to less than 159,000
1972 President Nixon visits Peking and Moscow
1972 Last U.S. ground troops leave Vietnam
1973 Cease-fire agreement between U.S. and Vietnam signed in Paris
1974 President Ford and Soviet leader Leonid Brezhnev meet in Vladivostok

1957 Racial riots in Little Rock
1957 Civil Rights Act provides for federal regulation of voting
1959 Alaska and Hawaii admitted to statehood
1960 John F. Kennedy elected President
1961 Peace Corps established
1962 First Negro is enrolled at U. of Mississippi
1962 Supreme Court issues "one man—one vote" ruling
1963 Supreme Court legalizes peaceful sit-in demonstrations
1963 Racial violence in Birmingham, Alabama
1963 John F. Kennedy assassinated; Lyndon B. Johnson becomes President
1964 New Civil Rights Act passed
1964 Three civil rights workers are murdered in Mississippi; race riots in Harlem and other Northern urban areas
1964 Johnson elected President by biggest popular margin in history
1965 Malcolm X slain at Black Nationalist rally
1965 Federal troops sent to Alabama to protect civil rights marchers
1967 Race riots in Newark, Detroit and other cities
1968 Assassination of Dr. Martin Luther King Jr.; riots in Washington, D.C., and elsewhere
1968 Assassination of Robert F. Kennedy
1968 Nixon elected President
1969 Dwight D. Eisenhower dies
1970 Four Kent State University students killed during demonstration over U.S. involvement in Cambodia
1971 26th Amendment to Constitution lowers voting age to 18
1971 Secret Pentagon papers published by newspapers
1972 Five men are arrested for bugging Democratic National Headquarters
1972 Nixon re-elected President
1972 Harry S. Truman dies
1973 Lyndon B. Johnson dies
1974 Nixon resigns under fire and Gerald R. Ford becomes President
1974 Ford pardons Nixon
1976 Jimmy Carter elected President

1957 Russia launches Sputnik, first satellite
1957 Khrushchev becomes Soviet Premier
1958 Algerian rebellion. De Gaulle returns to power in France
1959 Russian satellite Lunik III orbits moon
1959 Fidel Castro becomes dictator of Cuba
1960 Soviet-Chinese Communist ideological rift begins
1961 Soviet cosmonaut Yuri Gagarin becomes first man to orbit earth
1961 Communists seal off East Berlin with a wall
1962 Communist China attacks India in Himalayas
1963 Pope John XXIII is succeeded by Paul VI
1964 Prime Minister Nehru of India dies
1964 Soviet Premier Khrushchev ousted
1964 First Red Chinese A-bomb test
1965 Churchill dies
1967 Israel defeats Arab states in Six Day War
1968 Russian invasion ends Czech liberal trend
1969 De Gaulle resigns
1969 Civil warfare begins in Northern Ireland
1969 North Vietnam President Ho Chi Minh dies
1969 The U.S. and Soviet Union begin talks on Strategic Arms Limitation Treaty
1970 Egypt's President Gamal Abdel Nasser dies
1970 Charles De Gaulle dies
1971 Nikita S. Khrushchev dies
1971 Communist China admitted to the U.N.
1973 Arabs launch Yom Kippur War against Israel and cut oil shipments to U.S., Europe and Japan to reduce support for Israel. Oil prices jump, with widespread economic effect
1976 Mao Tse-tung dies

FOR FURTHER READING

These books were selected for their interest and authority in the preparation of this volume, and for their usefulness to readers seeking additional information on specific points. An asterisk (*) marks works available in both hard-cover and paperback editions.

GENERAL READING

*Agar, Herbert, *The Price of Power*. University of Chicago Press, 1957.
Chambers, Whittaker, *Witness*. Random House, 1952.
Davids, Jules, *America and the World of Our Time*. Random House, 1960.
Freidel, Frank, *America in the Twentieth Century*. Knopf, 1960.
*Goldman, Eric, *The Crucial Decade*. Random House, 1960.
Graebner, Norman, *The New Isolationism*. Ronald Press, 1956.
Hofstadter, Richard, William Miller and Daniel Aaron, *The American Republic* (Vol. II). Prentice-Hall, 1959.
*Johnson, Walter, *1600 Pennsylvania Avenue*. Little, Brown, 1960.
*Leuchtenburg, William E., *A Troubled Feast*. Little, Brown and Company, 1973.
*Link, Arthur S., and William Catton, *The American Epoch*. Knopf, 1974.
Moos, Malcolm, *The Republicans*. Random House, 1956.
Morison, Samuel E., and Henry S. Commager, *The Growth of the American Republic* (Vol. II). Oxford University Press, 1962.
Roseboom, Eugene, *A History of Presidential Elections*. Macmillan, 1957.
Truman, Harry S., *Memoirs* (2 vols.). Doubleday, 1955-1956.

COLD WAR (CHAPTER 1)

Byrnes, James F., *All in One Lifetime*. Harper & Row, 1958.
Clay, Lucius, *Decision in Germany*. Doubleday, 1950.
Daniels, Jonathan, *A Man of Independence*. Lippincott, 1950.
Davison, W. P., *Berlin Blockade*. Princeton University Press, 1958.
Ferrell, Robert, *American Diplomacy*. W. W. Norton, 1959.
Mann, Martin, *Revolution in Electricity*. Viking, 1962.
Rapport, Samuel, and Helen Wright, *Great Adventures in Medicine*. Dial Press, 1961.
Solomon, Louis, *Telstar*. McGraw-Hill, 1962.
*Spanier, John, *American Foreign Policy since World War II*. Pall Mall Press, 1962.
White, Theodore H., *Fire in the Ashes*. Sloan, 1953.

THE FAIR DEAL (CHAPTER 2)

Abels, Jules, *Out of the Jaws of Victory*. Holt, Rinehart & Winston, 1959.
Carr, Robert, *The House Committee on Un-American Activities*. Cornell University Press, 1952.
Cooke, Alistair, *Generation on Trial*. Knopf, 1950.
*Lubell, Samuel, *Future of American Politics*. Harper & Row, 1952.
McNaughton, Frank, and Walter Hehmeyer, *Harry Truman, President*. Whittlesey House, 1948.
Rogge, O. John, *Our Vanishing Civil Liberties*. Gaer Associates, 1949.
*Rovere, Richard, *Senator Joe McCarthy*. Harcourt, Brace & World, 1959.
*Taylor, Telford, *Grand Inquest*. Simon and Schuster, 1955.

AN ERA OF BAD FEELING (CHAPTER 3)

Berger, Carl, *The Korea Knot*. University of Pennsylvania Press, 1957.
Donovan, Robert, *Eisenhower: The Inside Story*. Harper & Row, 1956.
Duncan, David Douglas, *This Is War*. Harper & Row, 1951.
Esposito, Vincent J. (chief ed.), *The West Point Atlas of American Wars* (Vol. II). Praeger, 1959.
Fehrenbach, T., *This Kind of War*. Macmillan, 1953.
Feis, Herbert, *The China Tangle*. Princeton University Press, 1953.
Higgins, Trumbull, *Korea and the Fall of MacArthur*. Oxford University

Press, 1960.
Jowitt, William Allen, *The Strange Case of Alger Hiss*. Doubleday, 1953.
*Leckie, Robert, *Conflict*. G. P. Putnam, 1962.

"I LIKE IKE" (CHAPTER 4)

Anderson, Jackson, and F. G. Blumenthal, *The Kefauver Story*. Dial Press, 1956.
Angle, Paul, *The American Reader*. Rand, McNally, 1958.
Costello, William, *The Facts about Nixon*. Viking, 1960.
*Goldman, Eric, *Rendezvous with Destiny*. Knopf, 1952.
Lubell, Samuel, *The Revolt of the Moderates*. Harper & Row, 1956.
Mazo, Earl, *Richard Nixon: A Political and Personal Biography*. Harper & Row, 1959.
McCann, Kevin, *The Man from Abilene*. Doubleday, 1952.
Rorty, James, and Moshe Decter, *McCarthy and the Communists*. Beacon Press, 1954.
Rovere, Richard, and Arthur M. Schlesinger Jr., *The General and the President and the Future of American Foreign Policy*. Farrar, Straus and Young, 1951.
White, William S., *The Taft Story*. Harper & Row, 1954.

EISENHOWER ERA, KENNEDY ELECTION (CHAPTERS 5, 6)

Blum, John, and others, *The National Experience*. Harcourt, Brace & World, 1963.
*Burns, James MacGregor, *John Kennedy, a Political Profile*. Harcourt, Brace & World, 1960.
Childs, Marquis, *Eisenhower: Captive Hero*. Harcourt, Brace & World, 1958.
Donovan, Robert, *Eisenhower: The Inside Story*. Harper & Row, 1956.
Fuller, Helen, *Year of Trial*. Harcourt, Brace & World, 1962.
Ginzberg, Eli, and Hyman Berman, *The American Worker in the 20th Century*. Free Press, 1963.
Hughes, Emmet, *The Ordeal of Power*. Atheneum, 1963.
Kelly, Alfred H., and Winfred A. Harbison, *The American Constitution*. W. W. Norton, 1948.
*Lerner, Max, *America as a Civilization* (Vol. II). Simon and Schuster, 1957.
Pusey, Merlo, *Eisenhower, the President*. Macmillan, 1956.
Schlesinger, Arthur M. Jr., *Kennedy or Nixon: Does it Make Any Difference?* Macmillan, 1960.
Sevareid, Eric (ed.), *Candidates*. Basic Books, 1960.
Wechsler, James A., *Reflections of an Angry Middle-Aged Editor*. Random House, 1960.
*White, Theodore H., *The Making of the President, 1960*. Atheneum, 1961.
Wise, David, and Thomas B. Ross, *The U-2 Affair*. Random House, 1962.

JOHNSON AND NIXON (CHAPTERS 7, 8)

*Bernstein, Carl, and Bob Woodward, *All the President's Men*. Warner Books, 1974.
*Congressional Quarterly Service, *Watergate: Chronology of a Crisis*, Vols. I and II, 1973, 1974.
Evans, Rowland, Jr., and Robert D. Novak, *Nixon in the White House*. Random House, 1971.
Goldman, Eric, *The Tragedy of Lyndon Johnson*. Knopf, 1969.
Lukas, J. Anthony, *Nightmare*. Viking, 1976.
*Schell, Jonathan, *The Time of Illusion*. Vintage, Knopf, 1976.
Sidey, Hugh, *A Very Personal Presidency: Lyndon Johnson in the White House*. Atheneum, 1968.
* *The White House Transcripts*, Submission of Recorded Presidential Conversations to the Committee on the Judiciary of the House of Representatives by President Richard Nixon, *The New York Times*. Bantam Books, 1974.
White, Theodore H., * *The Making of the President, 1964*. Atheneum, 1965. * *The Making of the President, 1968*. Atheneum, 1969. * *The Making of the President, 1972*. Atheneum, 1973. * *Breach of Faith*. Dell, 1975.

ACKNOWLEDGMENTS

The editors of this volume are particularly indebted to the following persons and institutions for their assistance in the preparation of this book: James P. Shenton, Associate Professor of History, Columbia University, New York City; the late President Dwight D. Eisenhower, Gettysburg, Pennsylvania; Dr. Marshall Nason, Cleon Capsas and Ed Heath, Peace Corps, University of New Mexico, Albuquerque; Robert L. Tonsing, Martin Company, Denver, Colorado; John F. Stacks, TIME Washington Bureau; Hans H. J. Hoogendoorn, Trans World Airlines, New York City; Robert C. Albrook and Paul Thayer, University of California, Berkeley; Sol Noven, Culver Pictures, Inc., New York City; Carl Stange, Library of Congress, Washington, D.C.; Roberts Jackson, The Bettmann Archive, New York City; Gisela S. Knight, indexer for the entire History series; Melvin Ingber, revision indexer; Judy Higgins and Michael Merrill, Columbia University, New York City.

The author, for his part, wishes to thank his research assistant, Carol Moodie, for her invaluable help, and to acknowledge his debt to Jean Christie and Daniel Leab for aid in research and to Jean McIntire Leuchtenburg for editorial suggestions.

PICTURE CREDITS

The sources for the illustrations in this book are shown below. Credits for pictures from left to right are separated by semicolons, top to bottom by dashes. Sources have been abbreviated as follows: Brown—Brown Brothers; Culver—Culver Pictures; UPI—United Press International

CHAPTER 1: 6—Dmitri Kessel. 8,9—Merritt Ruddick; UPI. 10,11—TIME covers by Boris Chaliapin except top left TIME cover by Ernest Hamlin Baker. 12—Copyright 1945 Bill Mauldin—Matt Greene. 13,14—Culver. 15—"Don't Mind Me—Just Go On Talking"—from *The Herblock Book* (Beacon Press, 1952). 16—Courtesy Public Affairs Press. 17—TIME cover by Boris Chaliapin. 18—TIME cover by Artzybasheff—TIME cover by Ernest Hamlin Baker. 19—Fitzpatrick, *St. Louis Post-Dispatch*. 20,21—UPI. 22,23—UPI—David Douglas Duncan, Thomas D. McAvoy. 24—Fenno Jacobs from Black Star. 25—UPI—Pierre Boulat. 26—James Burke. 27—James Burke—Brian Brake from Rapho Guillumette.

CHAPTER 2: 28—James Whitmore courtesy Grand Lodge A.F. and A.M. of Missouri. 30—"You Folks Hear Any Talk About A Housing Shortage?"—from *The Herblock Book* (Beacon Press, 1952). 31—TIME cover by Artzybasheff. 32—UPI. 33—Wide World Photos. 35—TIME cover by Ernest Hamlin Baker. 36—The New York Public Library—Dan Hardy. 37—Brown. 38—W. Eugene Smith. 39—TIME covers by Ernest Hamlin Baker except top TIME cover by Artzybasheff. 41—TIME cover by Boris Chaliapin. 42—Howard Sochurek. 43—Hank Walker. 44,45—James Whitmore except top center Thomas D. McAvoy. 46—Left UPI; right Hank Walker; Robert W. Kelley—Hank Walker, UPI. 47—Joe Scherschel. 48,49—Hank Walker.

CHAPTER 3: 50—Michael Rougier. 52—"You Mean I'm Supposed to Stand on That?"—from *The Herblock Book* (Beacon Press, 1952). 54—TIME cover by Artzybasheff. 55—UPI except bottom. 56—Mark Kauffman. 57—U.S. Army. 58—"Those Are the Flags of Various Gangster Mobs and Millionaires, Now Shut Up"—from *The Herblock Book* (Beacon Press, 1952). 60—TIME cover by Giro. 62—Wide World Photos—Cornell Capa from Magnum. 63,64—Culver. 65—Culver—Warshaw Collection of Business Americana. 66—UPI. 67—Joe Scherschel. 68,69—David Douglas Duncan—U.S. Air Force. 70—John Dominis—Hank Walker—David Douglas Duncan. 71—David Douglas Duncan. 72,73—Left Jun Miki—Harries Clichy Peterson; right Michael Rougier. 74,75—Michael Rougier.

CHAPTER 4: 76—Authenticolor by Lavelle-Crandall courtesy West Point Museum Collections. 79—TIME covers by Artzybasheff. 80—George Skadding. 81—Frank Jurkoski from UPI. 82—TIME cover by Artzybasheff. 83—Culver—"It Never Existed—And I Killed It"—from *Herblock's Here and Now* (Simon and Schuster, 1955). 84—Brown. 85—UPI—Carl Iwasaki. 86—Culver. 87—TIME cover by Ernest Hamlin Baker. 88—A. C. Barrington Brown, Cambridge. 89—George Silk. 90,91—Michael Rougier, George Leavens for TIME, Stan Wayman. 92,93—J. R. Eyerman; Texas Instruments for FORTUNE. 94,95—Ronald L. McGlothin, courtesy St. Luke's Episcopal. 96—Bill Eppridge. 97—NASA.

CHAPTER 5: 98—John Bryson. 100—Don Uhrbrock. 101—Wide World Photos. 102—Frank Williams in *The Detroit Free Press*. 103—UPI. 104—Gimbels Stamp Collection. 105—Bruce Shanks in *Buffalo Evening News*. 106—Nina Leen—Thomas D. McAvoy. 107—UPI. 108—Paul Schutzer. 109—Culver—Bill Mauldin from the Jan. 14, 1959, *St. Louis Post-Dispatch* copyright 1961 by Bill Mauldin. 110—Hank Walker. 111—Jack Zwillinger for NBC. 112,113—Top Ronald Searle. 114—Howard Sochurek. 115—Hank Walker. 116,117—Bottom Larry Burrows; Michael Rougier. 118,119—Robert Lackenbach—Grey Villet; Hank Walker. 120,121—Loomis Dean; Carl Mydans—Carl Mydans, John Launois from Black Star.

CHAPTER 6: 122—Alfred Eisenstaedt. 124,125—Paul Schutzer. 126—Paul Schutzer—UPI. 127—Wide World Photos. 128—Wide World Photos—Jack Beers copyright *The Dallas Morning News*. 129—UPI. 130—Flip Schulke from Black Star. 131—Cornell Capa from Magnum. 132—Charles Moore from Black Star—Frank Dandridge. 133—Charles Moore from Black Star—Steve Schapiro. 134—J. R. Eyerman; Bud Lee. 135—Co Rentmeester—Lee Balterman. 136,137—Bob Fitch from Black Star; Charles Phillips; Bill Eppridge—Ward Sharrer for the *Sacramento Bee*.

CHAPTER 7: 138—Henri Dauman. 140—Cecil Stoughton. 141—Fred Ward from Black Star—Francis Miller. 142—Bill Ray—Flip Schulke from Black Star. 143—From *The Herblock Gallery* (Simon and Schuster, 1968)—Wide World Photos. 144—UPI—Fred Kaplan from Black Star. 145—Burtin Berinsky for TIME—Lee Balterman—Robert L. Purdy. 146—Larry Burrows. 147—James Pickerell from Black Star. 148,149—Catherine Leroy from Wide World Photos; Horst Fass from Wide World Photos. 150—UPI—Dick Swanson. 151—Rowland Scherman—Wide World Photos. 152—Leonard McCombe—Stan Wayman. 153—UPI.

CHAPTER 8: 154—Don Carl Steffen for TIME. 156—Heinz Kleutmeier. 157—Howard Ruffner—Wide World Photos. 158—Copyright Presseagentur, Sven Simon. 159—Ken Regan from Camera 5—Bill Thompson. 160—Steve Northup for TIME—Fred Ward from Black Star. 161—Harry Benson, TIME-LIFE Picture Agency. 162—Steve Northup, TIME-LIFE Picture Agency. 163—*The Washington Post*—Ricardo Thomas, TIME-LIFE Picture Agency. 164—Steve Northup, TIME-LIFE Picture Agency. 165—Walter Bennett, TIME-LIFE Picture Agency. 166,167—Dirck Halstead, TIME-LIFE Picture Agency.

INDEX FOR VOLUME 12

*This symbol in front of a page number indicates a photograph or painting of the subject mentioned.

LIST OF MAPS FOUND IN THIS VOLUME

All maps by Rafael Palacios

MASTER INDEX

For Volumes 1 through 12

*Each number in italics indicates an individual volume, 1 through 12, while
an asterisk (*) in front of a page number indicates a picture.*

CUMULATIVE LIST OF MAPS FOR VOLUMES 1 THROUGH 12

180